# THE
# MANGO
# TREE

# THE MANGO TREE

*A Memoir of Fruit, Florida, and Felony*

ANNABELLE TOMETICH

LITTLE, BROWN AND COMPANY
New York Boston London

Little, Brown and Company
Hachette Book Group
1290 Avenue of the Americas, New York, NY 10104
littlebrown.com

First Edition: April 2024

Little, Brown and Company is a division of Hachette Book Group, Inc. The Little, Brown name and logo are trademarks of Hachette Book Group, Inc.

The publisher is not responsible for websites (or their content) that are not owned by the publisher.

The Hachette Speakers Bureau provides a wide range of authors for speaking events. To find out more, go to hachettespeakersbureau.com or email hachettespeakers@hbgusa.com.

Little, Brown and Company books may be purchased in bulk for business, educational, or promotional use. For information, please contact your local bookseller or the Hachette Book Group Special Markets Department at special.markets@hbgusa.com.

Book interior design by Marie Mundaca

ISBN 9780316540322
LCCN 2023935645

Printing 1, 2024

LSC-C

Printed in the United States of America

*For Linco and Peeps*

*For all the seedlings fighting for sun*

# CONTENTS

**THE PIT** 1

**PART I: THE SEED** 9

**PART II: THE ROOTS** 99

"When a tree is cut down and reveals its naked death-wound to the sun, one can read its whole history in the luminous, inscribed disk of its trunk: in the rings of its years, its scars, all the struggle, all the suffering, all the sickness, all the happiness and prosperity stand truly written, the narrow years and the luxurious years, the attacks withstood, the storms endured."

—*Hermann Hesse*, Bäume: Betrachtungen und Gedichte


"I shook my family tree and a bunch of nuts fell out."

—*My mom's Facebook feed*

# THE PIT

**R**ows of orange people sit handcuffed in a beige room. One of them is my mother.

I squint at the TV that the bailiff has rolled in on a cart. The people aren't orange, their jumpsuits are. My shoulder presses against my sister's on the hardwood bench we share, our legs shaking in unison as the heels of our stilettos patter urgently against the courtroom's marble floor, a mix of nerves and shivers fueled by the pounding, midsummer air-conditioning. I tilt my head at the screen, trying to figure out which of these neon uniforms contains our mom, trying to confirm this is real.

Mom is on closed-circuit television and not here in person, which blurs that confirmation. She is not Mom. She is TV Mom. Fuzzy and orange like a peach—or the flesh of a mango.

First-appearance hearings aren't like they look on *Law & Order.* There was no perp walk today, no flashing cameras or microphone-pushing reporters as we ducked our faces in shame. It's just me and Amber sitting in a half-empty courtroom with my friend who's our attorney and this blurry flat screen that plays our new reality.

It shows a room speckled with inmates in the jail on the other side of the railroad tracks. These potential criminals are kept separate from us, the law-abiding do-gooders who make up this downtown courtroom. They are not like us. We are not like them.

They sit on rows of metal benches lined up like the pews of a church. They wear white socks, sandals, and coveralls the color of traffic cones. Most stare at the floor beneath their feet. TV Mom stares off in the distance, even as her name is called and mispronounced, *Ho-SEH-fee-nuh Toe-MEHT-ick*, even as the prison guard takes her by the arm and leads her to the microphone so she can speak with the judge in our courtroom.

TV Mom still looks like Mom. Even with the wild hair, the jumpsuit, the shackles binding her wrists and ankles. When the guard nudges her, TV Mom winces like she's been shocked. She shrugs her arm out of the guard's grip, saying something that sounds like "Don't freaking touch me." Each word becomes clearer, louder, as she approaches the mic. I hold my breath and lean into my sister.

"Dude, she doesn't even have her hearing aids in," Amber whispers, her body warm against mine as our legs continue to flutter.

"I know. She can't make out any of this."

The judge starts in about Mom's charge: firing a missile into an occupied dwelling, vehicle, building, or aircraft. Or, as we've come to know it in our family: The 2015 Mango Missile Crisis. Our attorney tells us *missile* is, in this case, a good thing, that even though it makes Mom sound like an assassin, it's better than *firearm*, which would mean a mandatory twenty years in prison.

TV Mom stands behind the thin lectern, staring directly into the camera. The fingers of her cuffed hands interlace under the belly of her orange suit.

Mom has spent the night in the Lee County Stockade, a crude Old Florida prison where, just a few years ago, inmates shared open-air cells swarming with mosquitoes. She really does look like a mango, like an overripe one left to rot in someone else's yard. Her face is gnarled. Her pockmarked cheeks and thick moles stand out in the jail's harsh fluorescent light. Fits of hair jut from her head like threads of wire.

I realize that to the uninitiated she looks unhinged. Amber and I know: This is just Mom.

When I think of my mother, I don't see her, I feel her. She's a stake driven deep into the ground, the kind you see tethering newly planted trees and disaster tarps in place. She has kept our family from toppling sideways while punching a hole clean through our middle.

I have never seen my mother wear a stitch of makeup. Not a swipe of mascara, not a touch of blush. Unlike me, she has nothing to hide. She cuts her own hair with a Flowbee she's kept in the olive-green bathroom for the better part of two decades. Once a month she hacks off her finger-nails while standing over the kitchen sink, picking them from the crevices they fly off to, then squirting them down the drain with the spray nozzle.

The judge talks through bail and discusses Mom's potential flight risk. Our attorney, one of my oldest friends, points to me and Amber. He tells the judge our brother, Arthur—the third and final of Mom's As—has work but wanted to be here. He assures the judge that Mom has a loving family, that we will keep her safe, hold her accountable. I wince when he says "loving," at least in my head. On the outside I smile, no teeth, big eyes, as I've taught myself to.

I am wearing a pencil skirt, silk blouse, and ivory cardigan. The dia-mond earrings Mom gave me when I graduated from the University of Florida thirteen years ago dot my earlobes. My hair has been blow-dried and flat-ironed and finished with sprays that make it as glossy as water. In the hall, before entering the courtroom, I dabbed on another layer of lip gloss, a neutral pinkish beige that wouldn't detract from the subtly smoky eyes I painted on earlier. After taking my seat, I placed the ivory tote that matches my ivory heels squarely in my lap so as not to take up more room than needed.

I don't dress up often for work. When I'm not reviewing a restau-rant or on assignment for my beat as a food writer, I'm usually in a ratty T-shirt and too-short shorts that I tug at self-consciously when the UPS driver knocks, disrupting my work-from-home routine. But I can play the part when the situation demands. Playing the part is the beat of my life, be it the part of loving daughter, model courtroom attendee, concerned citizen, or, today, all three.

The judge seems to mull this over, this loving family of ours. TV Mom threatens to rat us out, to strip us of our lip gloss and cardigans and lay our collective dysfunction bare. She rambles on about her diabetes, her insulin pump, her blood sugar. Her voice gets louder. My smile fades.

"I am going to freaking die in here! And you people don't give a god-damn shit!"

"Ms. *Toe-MEHT-ick*, please," the judge says, voice booming.

If I were a different person, I'd correct him: "It's Tometich, Your Honor. *JOE-suh-fee-nuh TAW-muh-titch*."

Our attorney-friend apologizes on our collective, loving behalf. TV Mom keeps rambling.

I lean away from Amber as tears nip the corners of my eyes, blurring the scene playing out on this television. I blink them back, hold them in. I make myself watch. TV Mom is Mom. This is real.


When Mom called from jail that morning, I didn't freak out. If thirty-five years with my mother has taught me anything, it is not to freak out. I called my sister, my brother, that close friend who's a defense attorney.

I led with: Mom shot a man's car window out.

I followed with: He was messing with her mangoes.

They got it.

I know Mom loves us. In her own Josefina Tometich way. I'm equally certain she loves her mango trees—deeply, fondly, unabashedly. I'd put her banana trees in a close second for her tropical affections, followed by her atis, calamansi, avocado, and tamarind trees. If her pineapples are fruiting, that throws it all off.

The tidy suburban Southwest Florida yard of my childhood has become a tropical menagerie. For Mom it's a numbers game. Plant enough things, and surely one or two—or two hundred—will take root. Plant enough things, and maybe this faraway world she's in will feel a tad more like her Philippines birthplace.

Her yard she can control. Her philandering white husband and all-too-Americanized children she could not, no matter how hard she tried.

As word spread of this Fort Myers grandmother shooting it out over mangoes, possibly the most Florida of *Oh, Florida* stories that month, my phone rang. The name of my newspaper's breaking-news reporter glowed across the screen as it vibrated in my hand. I answered on the third buzz.

"I guess you heard," I said, trying to sound chipper as I sat in my car in the parking lot of the courthouse after Mom's first appearance, wondering if I had enough funds on any of my credit cards to post bail.

I nodded as he spoke, kicking myself for never changing my byline. I'd been married for seven years. Legally I was Annabelle Martin, but I still wrote as Annabelle Tometich. I should've known better by then. Tometiches can never be normal.

I spent my childhood making sure this Tometich faded into the background. I never sat too close to the front or too far in the back of my classes. I was never goth or preppy or hippie. My style was my lack of style: jeans that looked like everyone else's jeans; tanks and tees that could belong to any Amy/Ashley/Angie. I curated this look as carefully as I did my courtroom look, to show the world that there was *nothing to see here!* I thought my fake Keds and 5-7-9 baby-doll dresses made me perfectly normal, perfectly average, as much as a towering half-Filipina girl can be in a county named for Robert E. Lee.

And yet here I was with that one thing all other writers want: name recognition.

Shit.

I could see the headline: "Mother of Restaurant Critic Jailed for Mango Shoot-out." I'd click on that. "Mango" is the kicker. Anyone can get into a shoot-out. This is America. But a mango shoot-out? Get ready to go viral. "Restaurant critic" ensures this bit of clickbait will get bites. It's more tempting than "food writer," which is what I mostly do. Folks will wonder if they know this critic. Their shoulders will slump slightly when they realize they've never, ever heard of me.

That's the one thing I've done right. While I write recipes and chef profiles under my own byline, I write my restaurant reviews under a pseudonym, Jean Le Boeuf. The fake name is meant to sound French and pretentious. It's meant to hide me. I appreciate that now more than ever.

I shook my head and tried to collect my thoughts, reorganize them, layer this new narrative carefully into the structure of my painstakingly curated life.

"That's my kooky mama," I said, trying to keep my tone cheerful, trying to be the same upbeat person I expect myself to be, the girl who can roll with the punches, the one Tometich who never loses her cool. Certainly not over a mango.

"I'm so sorry, Annabelle."

My colleague sounded calm, businesslike. I tried to match his tone but couldn't.

"You *have* to write something, huh?"

The question came out despite my best efforts.

"I mean, of course you have to, but, you know, it's like a thing then, like a sure thing," I stammered. "There will definitely be a story."

Each word was a statement and a question, a certainty rimmed with foolish hope.

There was a half beat of silence, and then I went on, rushing through the rest, because this phone call was just a courtesy. The story would be written. I would not get a say.

"Yeah, of course there will be. I know how it works," I said. "I just, you know, please be fair. I know you'll be fair. So, yeah, thank you. Thank you so much for the call."

"Of course," my colleague said, sounding like every teacher and adult figure from my childhood: patient and levelheaded as they gauged my ability to handle what stood in front of me.

Business over, his tone softened.

"Is your mom OK? Did she really shoot at that guy—over a mango?"

My head nodded. "Of course she did," I wanted to say. "You have no idea what that tree means to her." Instead, I stayed silent. This isn't the kind of thing that can be explained over the phone. I thought about the right way to answer. I kept it short, cool, honest.

"It's complicated," I said. And I meant it.

PART I

# The Seed

## CHAPTER 1

# Fort Myers

Nobody's from Fort Myers.

That's what people say when they learn I was born here, that I still live here, that I write for the newspaper I grew up reading.

Some people achieve nobodiness, stumbling through wholly unexceptional lives, until it engulfs them. Other people, people like me, are born nobodies. Born into bodies that can't be neatly categorized, into skins that aren't quite Black or brown or white, into shapes that aren't Asian, with features that are.

I am a nobody by virtue of birthright and birthplace. A nobody, squared.

Fort Myers is a place without context. A clod of swamp torn from the hands of the Calusa and Seminoles, drained, razed, and carbon-copied from the cities surrounding it. A bit of Tampa. A bit of Miami. We'll name it for Abraham C. Myers, a Jewish Confederate colonel who's never actually been here. We'll call it Fort Myers. It'll be a stop on the *Tamiami* Trail (see what we did there?), a place to rest, not a place to stay.

The people who spend time in Fort Myers, here on Florida's southern Gulf Coast, are from Michigan, Massachusetts, Minnesota. Meaningful places. They fly south each winter to escape their frozen hometowns. They use their pensions to snap up parcels of this copycatted paradise a quarter acre at a time. They build ticky-tacky houses picked from catalogues, three-twos with pools shaped like jelly beans for the one week of spring when the grandkids visit. They landscape their yards with exotic ornamentals from Asia and South America, sprawling invaders that take over the native species, swallowing this land, this sun, as they multiply unchecked.

They call themselves "snowbirds." They arrive in a great migration each fall. Come spring, they flit off to where the grass is greener, unwilling to tolerate the summer's choking heat. Unwilling to endure the season's house-rattling thunderstorms and bloodthirsty mosquitoes. Unable to imagine summer here could be more; as sweet as lychees, as bright as mangoes glistening in the sun. Come spring, they fly back to their real homes up north, where people are Somebodies.

My parents weren't from Fort Myers.

Mom came from Manila, a city two hundred times the size of Fort Myers. I imagine her plane as it landed at our one-strip airport in 1978. I see the old her, the pre-motherhood Mom, stepping onto the sweltering tarmac. A twenty-seven-year-old version of herself, springy and lithe, soaking in the familiar heat in bell-bottoms and big sunglasses, a Filipina Eva Gabor surveying the "Green Acres" of her new home, still unaware of its terrors. Unaware that she was less a pioneer and more a piece of infrastructure, a tool slapped with a MADE IN THE PHILIPPINES label. The Asian model, far less expensive than the MADE IN THE USA one. My mom was a means of keeping these snowbirds in good health. She was an IV pole that could speak, a crutch that could calculate antibiotic dosages.

My mother never wanted to be a nurse. She wanted to be an engineer, to design, create, perfect. As the oldest of seven children living in inner-city Manila, Mom renounced most of her wants before she could get to know them. As soon as she could wipe a butt or boil a pot of rice, she lost herself, absorbed by the needs of others. The only want Mom clung to was escape. In the Philippines, that meant nursing.

In the 1960s, the Manila Educational & Exchange Placement Service ran ads in newspapers and magazines. One showed the Philippine flag as a basket cradling brochures for Canada, Europe, and the USA.

I imagine Mom reading the ad after volleyball practice at the Catholic high school her grandmother paid for, the one where Mom perfected her English so that any hint of a Filipino accent disappeared, after riding a packed bus through roiling city smog, after returning to her two-room home with its roof of corrugated tin to feed and bathe her siblings and tuck them into bed on the two threadbare mattresses they shared head-to-toe-to-head like sardines. I see Mom curled up on a thin mat on the dirt floor in the flickering light of a kerosene lamp, rubbing her youngest sister's back with one hand, holding the pages of newsprint in the other.

*Dear nurse,* the ad began, *If you're not happy wherever you are right now, why not take the easy way out and go someplace else....We can't promise you'll find happiness but we can help you chase it all over the place.*

It listed an address and a five-digit phone number.

I imagine Mom committing them to her photographic memory, tucking them into a file in her mind somewhere near her mom's nilagang recipe and her cousin Nestor's birthday: Nursing. Or maybe a few slots before those, in the H section: Happiness.

Mom has a frightening memory. She never owned a textbook. Her family couldn't afford them. When she borrowed one from a teacher, library, or friend, she memorized it. She took notes on the words and filed the graphs and charts in her snapshot brain. When exam time came, Mom was the person students went to with questions, not the teachers. In a place of so little, this—this was something big.

The United States needed nurses. The Philippines needed the money work-abroad nurses sent home to their families. Manila was being rubbed out by the brutal first decade of Ferdinand Marcos's rule. The US was the land of the free.

It was a no-brainer for my mother: Pick freedom. Chase happiness. Be Somebody.

Or at least try.

My father was an only child.

I'm tempted to stop there.

I knew my dad for only nine years. I often wonder if I'm remembering him or Magnum P.I., whose eight seasons overlapped neatly with Lou Tometich's fatherhood.

My dad's dad, Lou Tometich Sr., was an immigrant who fled war-torn Yugoslavia and escaped to the US, sort of like Mom. Dad's mother was Josephine Tometich, another Jo, a frail and placid-looking woman who'd spit out an embarrassment of profanities if you dared cross her. They raised their son in Woods Hole, Massachusetts, a Meaningful place in the southwest corner of Cape Cod.

I don't know if they wanted more children but couldn't have them or if, as Dad once said, they were so thrilled with him, they saw no point in trying again.

They gave my father everything my mother never had: a bed, new clothes, textbooks. Dad repaid his parents by smoking copious amounts of pot and losing himself in booze. He flunked out of Syracuse University, then followed his mom and dad south to their retirement home in North Fort Myers.

When they didn't blink at his heady lifestyle—*anybody* can be an alcoholic stoner—Dad revolted in a different way. He forsook drinking, drugs, and his mother's WASPiness. He sought enlightenment. A holier kind of rebellion. He joined the Baha'í faith, memorizing prayers from Bahá'u'lláh and the writings of Shoghi Effendi. Gramma accused him of becoming a Muslim, told him he'd *lost his goddamn mind*. And then she wrote him checks for rent and groceries. Money was her tool, the one she used to keep her only child from slipping too far into nobodiness.

My father spent this money on flip-flops and corduroy shorts that showed off his pearly white thighs, a look that said: on permanent vacation. When I was an infant, he had a bushy lumberjack beard. He played tennis in gold Ray-Bans and Reebok low-tops that he polished to a glossy sheen between matches. His too-tight T-shirts read ONE PLANET ONE PEOPLE PLEASE and WORLD CITIZEN.

Dad pursued whichever passion called him at any given time. He snapped pictures of pelicans and egrets and developed the film in a closet-turned-darkroom in the tiny apartment he rented in Lou Sr.'s name. He bought a guitar and performed Bob Dylan covers. His biggest gig was a friend's backyard wedding. They paid him in Swedish meatballs and imitation crab.

Dad never had a plan. He was the kind of Somebody who didn't need one. He moved to Fort Myers to stay close to his true source of income, his parents, no matter how much he rebelled against them. This was, perhaps, my dad's defining struggle: his desire to divorce himself from his WASPy roots without losing the WASPy privileges they entailed.

My dad's Somebodiness was his burden, an anchor from which he couldn't untether. He was born into privilege, molded by it. He needed it. And he hated that.

I sometimes wonder if that is what drew him to my mom, a woman born from nothing. A woman who carved her own path and made her own way. A woman so polarly opposite of him, she left him in awe.

Dad rebelled by quitting school. Mom rebelled by excelling at it.

Dad couldn't bear to leave his parents' sides. Mom couldn't bear to stay.

Dad lived off his parents most of his life. Mom supported hers until the days they died.

When I was old enough to ask about such things, Mom told me Dad made the first move. He asked her out over french fries in the cafeteria of the hospital where they worked, he as an orderly, she as an intensive-care nurse. He invited her to a friend's party, super casual.

I imagine them making small talk over Cheez Whiz and Hawaiian Punch, swapping stories about their backgrounds, realizing it was true: *Nobody's from Fort Myers!* The host of the party was from Indiana. His girlfriend was from Maryland. The guy from radiology was there, too. He was from New York.

My parents didn't kiss that night. Mom said they didn't even hold hands. I believe her. They weren't looking for love, they were looking for context: Dad for his rebellion, Mom for her across-the-globe move.

Mom needed to create her own infrastructure in this new world. She needed her own tool, one made in the USA that would clear her path to a green card and citizenship. I think Dad saw Mom as a tool as well—a crowbar that could finally wrench him free of his parents, one last act of revolt.

I sometimes wonder if my siblings and I are divine accidents. Maybe divine punishments. My parents having sex feels gross, sure, but also impossible.

Can screaming make babies? Can punching a man in the eye get you pregnant? What about kneeing him in the groin for playing computer games instead of mowing the lawn? I'd think that would have the opposite effect.

When I ask Mom what attracted her to Dad, she shrugs. I can't tell if her indifference means the answer is obvious or unknowable. This spoiled-rebel only child had flaws, but he was assuredly a Somebody. My father knew this as well as he knew his tennis-shoe size. He knew it by his white skin, by his penis—the Somebody prerequisites of 1978.

Mom, on the other hand, was taught repeatedly that she was nothing in the US. By her mother-in-law. By the patients who demanded white nurses and refused her care. By the doctors who ignored her perfect score on the board exam, who ignored her in general until a bedpan was full.

When a Somebody weds a nobody, there is tumult. It's hot air slamming against cold, spinning off great thunderstorms and cyclones that destroy all they touch. The snowbirds feared these storms. They winged back to their northern nests when foul weather threatened, boarded up their ticky-tacky houses, and tied down their exotic ornamentals before fleeing, hoping they'd have something to return to.

Those who stayed claimed there was nothing to fear. Batten down the hatches. Ride it out. Those who stayed often didn't have a choice. They'd waded too deep into this swamp. Its muck held them tight.

Along with destruction, these storms brought rain. Rain brought growth; it turned twiggy branches into flowers, and flowers into fruits. These fruits often rotted in the snowbirds' yards, too exotic for their Yankee taste buds. That's if they weren't first gobbled up by tropical natives eager for a bite of home.

Eleven months after my parents' wedding day, I was born in a small rental house east of the railroad tracks. In Fort Myers.

"Wow," I hear you saying, "but nobody's from Fort Myers."

And you're right. Nobody is.

## CHAPTER 2

# Caloosahatchee

D ad's Dakota-beige Volkswagen Rabbit rumbles across the Edison Bridge and over the Caloosahatchee, the back seat piled with the remnants of our rental house and with me, a toddler who should be in a car seat but is instead wedged between a box of books and the Rabbit's rattling back door. Our new home is off Moody Road, near Dad's parents in North Fort Myers. It's on the right side of the railroad tracks but the wrong side of the river.

Below us, the Caloosahatchee's waters flow clear brown like sun tea, stained by native mangrove tannins and the rotting debris from so many exotic plants. It streams from Lake Okeechobee at the center of Florida to the sugar-sand beaches of the Gulf of Mexico, where its dark contents muddy the turquoise waves.

"People who don't know better call it the Caloosahatchee River," Dad tells me as I survey the waters, how they sparkle in the sunny spots, how they're flat and dark in the cloudy ones.

"But in the Calusa language, *hatchee* means river," he says, taking a drag of his Marlboro Red, then leaning his head out the hand-cranked window and exhaling, to keep the smoke out of my hair and Mom's blood-hound nose later.

"They're saying Caloosa River River. That's stupid. We just say Caloosahatchee. That's how you know who the locals are."

I am their anchor. I make us locals.

CHAPTER 3

# Rituals

I wear a white dress trimmed with yellow eyelets. My matching bloomers pinch the tops of my chubby thighs.

This is my first semiclear memory. It's the memory I go to when I flip through the Rolodex of my mind, this inaugural entry that's always reliably there. White doughnut-shaped stickers reinforce the holes punched at the top of this memory, lest it fly loose into oblivion. Its ragged edges are lined by tape smudged with people's fingerprints; Mom's are sharp and clear, Dad's faint, fading. It's my memory, and it's not.

I stand on the wooden deck outside our dining room, cupping my hands over my face as I press it against our sliding glass door. Mom stands in the kitchen in a sundress. Its spaghetti straps are knotted in bows at her shoulders. Their long ends unfurl down her tawny arms.

Mom's not in a muumuu or her nurse's whites. Today is different.

I was inside moments earlier. I sat on the Formica counter patterned with eggshell cracks, next to a bowl lined with paper towels and Mom's just-fried lumpia. I watched her cook, breathing in the steam of chicken stock and sautéed cabbage that I'd already come to associate with celebrations.

Mom pulled a sheaf of rice noodles from the woven sack in the pantry. She eased them into her boiling stock, her pancit almost done, then went back to plucking chicken meat from steaming bones with her flameproof fingers as I watched, bored, my hands too weak to help.

I started by bouncing my legs, swinging my bare feet in the air but stopping them before they banged the doors of the cabinets and got me in trouble. Then, hands halfway under my thighs, I shuffled along the counter, closer and closer to the stove.

"Ay nako, Annabelle Marie, you are going to get burned! Don't you know that!"

I winced, wondering if there would be more. A smack to my calves, a house slipper removed and whipped at my backside. But Mom stopped at ay nako.

Ay nako is not bad. Ay nako means Mom's annoyed, like when Gramma says "Oh, Lordy." Punyeta, that's bad. Pakshet means Mom's had it, start running. But ay nako, I can live with. Mom's in too good a mood to be punyeta mad. It's this new house, this new kitchen. She lowers me to the floor and sends me here to the outside.

In the glass door I see my reflection, an alternate me that is still inside with Mom. I knock. I cup my eyes to shield them from the sun. I look for Mom. She dries a pot and then her hands, smoothing the front of her sundress. I wave. Mom smiles, crooked teeth and crinkled eyes, the real deal. She gives me the A-OK sign.

Today could be the day.

I have a lot of rituals as a kid. Walking these red deck planks—step on a crack, break your mom's back—is the first I remember.

I squint against the thick late-morning sun. I look down at the slats of the deck, where the world seems clearer. I choose the thickest plank.

One sandal in front of the next, I walk the beam like Mary Lou Retton, right hand thrown high in the air, the other flung out to my side for balance. There is no furniture out here yet, just Dad's shiny black kettle grill with its tripod legs, plus a built-in bench that rises from the deck's far end. I've never made it past the grill, not on move-in day, nor on any of the days after, when Dad marched at my side, when he unknowingly imparted to me the vital importance of this balancing act.

"Step on a crack, break your mommy's back," he said, his arms out like airplane wings. "Step on two cracks, break your daddy's back!"

Could it be that easy? Maybe. Our family seems to crack and break all the time, mostly at night, when the air cools and makes space for my parents' hot tempers. I can handle Mom cracking. She is made of steel with flameproof hands. She doesn't play kid games on the patio. If she cracked, she'd weld herself back together, no sweat.

But Dad is softer, more tender—so easily breakable. His pale skin needs hats and long sleeves and thick smears of sunscreen to protect it from the pounding sun. Dad can't handle the heat. I figure that's why he never cooks and rarely mows the lawn, why he hides away at his computer desk in the dark. He's so fragile.

Me, I'm somewhere in between: delicate but capable. In this mixed-up childhood head of mine, I believe avoiding these cracks can stop us from breaking.

I take another step and another. As the grill moves out of view, my breath quickens. I'm so close. I thrust my tongue out in concentration, biting it lightly in place along my right cheek. I have touched only the one plank. If I can make it to the bench, touching just this one strip, I think it may change things. There will be no yelling. No breaking.

Then I see something curling up from between the planks ahead of me, something inky black and slithery. I don't know what it is, only that it scares me. I turn and run back to the slider, stepping on crack after crack. Mom meets me at the door, and I crack open and spill out tears. "It was just a black racer," she tells me. "It won't hurt you." But it's too late. I was close but not close enough.

\* \* \*

Mom works days at the hospital, and Dad works nights, handing off baby me and then toddler me between shifts like a relay baton. One bleary-eyed from work. The other bleary-eyed from parenting. A quick kiss at the moment of transfer. One duty bleeding into the next.

This handoff, those bleary eyes, they afford me freedom; time to flip through the ten touch-button channels on our Zenith, time to explore. When I get hungry, things can get complicated. Dad sleeps like the dead. I push him, sit on him, peel his heavy arms up from the bed by his fingers and then watch them flop back down, lost in the puffy comforter.

Eventually I give up.

I traipse into the kitchen to gather eggs, milk, and butter from the fridge. I climb onto the counter I'm not supposed to climb on and pull the jar of flour from the corner. Crouched on the Formica like a gargoyle, knees to ears, I stir my ingredients into a messy paste with my hands and Mom's favorite wooden spoon. I turn on the stove, pushing the dial right instead of left, all the way to high. I've seen Dad make pancakes every weekend. I get most of it right—except for the bowl and pan parts. I mix everything directly on the counter, then slop it onto the electric burner, watching the dry patches of flour slip like sand between the rings of the heating element. The stove hums steadily as it warms. I see the rings glow red beneath my splotches of batter. The paste crackles and hisses. Tendrils of smoke snake up from between the coils in warning.

The flames start small, little sparks dancing from one dry bit of flour to the next. I wonder for a second if I'm flameproof like Mom. Then a chunk explodes, shooting an orange fireball into the air, singeing my face. Nope, I am not.

I stumble and lose my balance on the counter. I fall forward into the stove. My right hand lands atop the melting, smoking paste. It sinks through to the glowing coils. I try to pull it back and I can't. It sticks, flesh fusing with metal. Piercing shrieks fill my ears.

They're my own.

I come to on the other side of the kitchen, clutching the singed flesh of my right hand with my left, holding my wound close to my heart as I curl my body against the cream linoleum floor. Dad stands at the stove, his legs and feet wet with water. I wonder where he came from, if maybe he, too, has superpowers like Mom.

Dad scoops me up and kisses the top of my head. He takes me to the master bathroom and sets me on the counter as he fills the tub with cool water. He eases me in and inspects my mangled right hand. He grabs the beige portable phone to call Mom.

"I was really hungry," I tell him.

"I can see that."

"Is she going to be mad?"

"Probably just at me."

Mom's back before Dad's finished cleaning my wound. She rushes in, still in her nurse's whites. She grabs me and scans me with her dark eyes without showering first. She always showers first. I think of the germs and dirt that must still be covering her, the ones she warns me about every other night when she comes home from work and tells me not to touch her. I wonder why it's OK for them to get on me now. Maybe Mom forgot. I think of them on me, crawling and growing. I shrug out of her grasp in time for the fighting to start.

Dad thinks we should go to the hospital. Mom thinks he's an idiot. She reminds him we're not made of money, that he just bought a brand-new freaking computer without even freaking asking her. "Punyeta ka!"

She's punyeta mad. I start to cry again. I cry at what's to come, the inevitability of it.

The fighting doesn't start in earnest until after my wound has been properly cleaned and bandaged, till after we've eaten lunch—*Jesus Christ,*

*Louis! It's eleven a.m.! Of course your daughter is starving!*—fried Spam, tomatoes, and rice, my and Mom's favorite. Mom sends me to my room with an orange Popsicle. She tells me to close my door. I suck on my ice pop as it begins, a trickle of unanswerable questions and words I'm not allowed to repeat.

"*How could you? For fuck sake, Louis.*" This trickle becomes steadier, harder. The same questions and bad words but louder, faster.

"*HOWCOULDYOUFORFUCKSAKELOUIS!*"

When people say things louder, that makes them mean more. I know this as well as I know my numbers or the answers to the jokes on my Popsicle sticks. The screaming turns into banging. I hear something shatter. I feel the floor beneath me rattle with one boom and then another.

I pretend it's a storm. Storms are normal. Especially in Southwest Florida. They're so normal, we keep track of the biggest ones on a map taped to the door of the garage.

We get the maps from Publix each spring, Dad and I, with our bags of groceries and glass bottles of Coke. We take down last year's map, carefully stowing the colorful pushpins in Dad's tool chest. We stick up the new map, fresh and clean and free of holes. When the season's first tropical storm appears on the radar, we count out the latitude and longitude points as printed in the newspaper. Dad glides one index finger up from the bottom of the map, the other left to right along the side. Where his fingers meet, I pop in a pushpin. A series of red ones for this storm, dotting its path west and then north, maybe yellow pins for the next storm, maybe blue for the one following.

There are always more storms. They churn in the Atlantic to our right, in the Gulf of Mexico to our left, in the Florida Straits beneath us.

"If we know where they are, we can prepare for them," Dad says, as we press another Hurricane Diana pin into the papery expanse of ocean to our east.

The storms that roll through our house don't afford me such luxuries.

They can be sensed but not tracked: the shifts in air pressure, the gusts of yelling that cause animals and small children to seek shelter.

Still stuck in my shelter as this current storm rages, I set my Popsicle stick on my pillow. I pull my yellow-and-white-checked quilt across my lap and start counting its squares: eight across, twelve down. Each yellow square is printed with nine white polka dots; three rows of three. I run my fingers along them—three up, three down, three diagonal. I count them, again and again, *one two three, one two three, one two three.* I count until the numbers are all I can hear, until I can't keep my eyes open, until this storm passes.

I feel a calloused hand on my forehead. I know it's Mom before I open my eyes. I know it's time for our nightly routine, that which can never be skipped, even with a burned hand and a storm-ravaged house.

"Ay nako, look at you," Mom says.

She seems weathered as she tugs the Popsicle stick from my tangled hair and pulls my bandaged hand from the rainbow belly of my Care Bear. She holds my hand gingerly as she leads me the nine steps—three to the door, three down the hall, three to the sink—from my bed to the bathroom and tosses the stick into the mustard-yellow trash bin.

She grabs a bar of Dial and wets and cleans my good hand. She dries it on a taupe towel printed with mustard-yellow flowers that match our mustard-yellow toilet. She wets a washcloth and cleans the fingers of my burned hand, making sure the bandages are still to her liking. She squirts Aquafresh onto my toothbrush, plops it into my mouth, and checks the second hand on the thin gold watch encircling her wrist.

"Two minutes," she says.

Usually I'd whine. Tonight I do as she says.

As I clumsily scrub my teeth left-handed, Mom runs a hairbrush through my sticky tangles. Twenty strokes on the left side, twenty on the right, twenty more on the back, a bonus ten to work out the orange goo. I count them quietly under my breath, a check to Mom's accuracy, which never fails. Mom doesn't need to count. Each stroke feels programmed into her, part of her wiring. She checks her watch and tells me to spit. She plucks a paper cup from the Snoopy dispenser on the counter, fills it with water, and tells me to drink. When I finish, I place the cup back in the dispenser to Mom's smiling approval. It's a brand-new paper cup. It's got another week of life, easy.

Mom kneels down and scoops my face up with her hands. She inspects my teeth, scratching each one with her long nails to scrape the shaggy bits of plaque from my gumline. She checks behind my ears for crud. She drags the curved nail of her index finger across the folds of my neck. She scrapes out a bit of dirt, burnt flour maybe, and holds it to the fluorescent lights overhead.

"Libag," she tsks, shaking her head.

That means "face dirt" in the language Mom speaks late at night on the phone. It's one of the only other words of hers I know, along with *punyeta* and *pakshet* and *ay nako*. Mom almost never speaks to me in her phone language unless she can't help herself.

"You will take a bath in the morning. You cannot be burnt and dirty."

I nod. Then I wait for the last part of our routine because it's my favorite.

Mom smooths my ebony hair again. She runs her thumb and index finger down the bridge of my nose, coaxing it outward, like pinching Play-Doh into a ridge. She squeezes the bulbous tip, then moves her fingers to my nostrils, pinching them shut. She holds them there as I breathe through my mouth. She checks the gold watch on her wrist again. When enough time has passed, maybe a minute, maybe more, she lets my nostrils go. We look in the mirror to see if my nose is thin and pretty yet. I tilt my head down and from side to side, checking for progress, silently wondering if Mom's nose, which is broad and flat like a mushroom, is the source of her superpowers; if this is an attempt to keep me weak.

But Mom pinches at her own nose, too. If it is the source of her powers, she seems happy to be rid of them. I try to squeeze her nostrils, but my little fingers aren't strong enough. Mom laughs, and I smile.

She really is made of steel.

CHAPTER 4

# Heartbeats

The rhythmic laughter of the live studio audience fills our living room. Gramma sits in Dad's overstuffed armchair, sucking the chocolate from a bowl of Raisinets nestled in her lap. I watch her as she watches the practical-jokes show, laughing along with Dick Clark and Ed McMahon. I see her clack her dentures and scratch at her wig. I think *she's* hilarious, with her pretend teeth and pretend hair. I wonder why Mom hates her.

Mom and Dad return smack in the middle of prime-time TV. Gramma looks annoyed when she hears the Volkswagen pull in. She tells me to turn up the volume. I run to the TV and happily obey.

I'm still watching Gramma watch the Zenith when the door opens, my knees tucked into the oversize T-shirt she's put on me as a nightgown. Mom sinks down next to me on the couch. I sense her warmth, the Ivory soap smell of her skin. I hear Dad's camera clicking, capturing the moment from behind his lens.

"This is your sister," Mom says as I look up from my Gramma trance to see a wriggling bundle of blankets. "This is Amber."

Am-ber. I break the word into its syllables as Mom's taught me to. I roll them around in my head. They feel unfair. Amber's such a better name than Annabelle. It's easy and uncomplicated. It's like Abby, the blond girl from down the street. Or Carrie, Abby's blue-eyed sister. I look at this swaddled, jumbo egg roll, and my head goes cloudy with jealousy. *Why couldn't I have been an Amber?*

Dad named me after Edgar Allan Poe's final poem, a ballad of loss and eternal love. A poem I hear him whispering under his breath sometimes, always the first verse and only the first verse; saying it to himself the way one might hum a show tune.

*It was many and many a year ago, In a kingdom by the sea, That a maiden there lived whom you may know, By the name of Annabel Lee; And this maiden she lived with no other thought, Than to love and be loved by me.*

Mom got to name Amber.

"I just liked the name Amber," Mom will tell the well-wishers who stop by with bouquets of flowers and sacks of diapers. "There was no sad poem or whatever." She drags the word *poem* into po-em, giving it two syllables, too.

Mom hands me the wiggly blankets. I look at this baby with her deep, curious eyes. I'm thankful they're as dark and brown as my own, that we at least have that much in common. This bundle we call Amber peers back at me. She studies me as I study her, sizing each other up.

*Who is this stranger? Why is Mom fussing over her? Why is Dad taking her picture?*

*I was here first,* I think.

Amber starts to wail.

"I'm here now," her cries seem to answer.


Amber's skin is fair, almost pearly. Mom's Filipino friends ooh and ahh over it, calling her mestiza and tisoy, words they've never used with me.

Words that I assume mean "beautiful." They run their fingers up her lily arms and snowy legs. I look at mine, earthy and brown like my mother's.

Mom says we're exactly alike, Amber and me. She says it's my job to look out for Amber, and her job to look out for both of us.

"What's Daddy's job?"

"God only knows."

Mom gets our ears pierced when Amber's six months old and I'm four and a half. She buys us tiny matching studs of diamond and gold, knowing we'll lose them, but wanting our jewelry to be real.

"I don't want their ears turning green and rotting off their heads," she tells Dad to justify the expense—in her mind, not his.

These sparkly additions tack on another five minutes to our nighttime neck-scraping and nose-pinching regimen. Amber joins this routine when she turns two, as soon as she has enough teeth and can reach the bathroom sink from our shared step stool. After the two minutes of teeth brushing, the twenty-twenty-twenty strokes of hair brushing, the everything else, Mom takes out our earrings. She cleans them with an alcohol swab pilfered from her hospital, then runs it over and behind our earlobes; a satiny chill that makes me shiver and giggle. She squeezes the studs back into place. When there's time, I convince her to listen to our hearts, too.

"Get your black thing out, Mommy," I say. "Tell me what my heart's saying."

"OK, if you hurry and bring it to me."

I sprint to her nursing bag and grab the shiny black tubing of her stethoscope, careful to hold it by its metal headset the way Mom taught me. I run it back to her. She places the rubber-tipped ends in her ears and holds Amber in her lap. She rests the bell on Amber's back and listens to her breathe. She brings it around to Amber's chest and holds it for a few seconds as Amber squirms, grunts, and wriggles free.

"What'd it say, Mommy?" I wonder, eyes wide.

"It said: *Get-me-outta-here-get-me-outta-here!* It said: *Your sister is getting too big for her britches!*"

I laugh at Mom's hilarity.

"My turn! Do me!"

I pull up my nightshirt and press myself into Mom's lap. I bend over so she can listen to my lungs through my back. I breathe the way Mom's taught me, slow, slow, slow in—then slow, slow, slow out.

She brings her arm around to my front and moves the bell to my chest. I feel cool metal circled by the warmth of Mom's hand. I am frozen in silence, until I can no longer contain myself.

"What's it saying, Mommy? Huh?"

Mom holds the bell in place, keeps it still. Her face looks concerned. She scrunches her lips and raises both eyebrows.

"Wow."

"Wow?"

She flicks the bottom of the bell with a finger, then returns it to my chest.

"Mommy?"

"Yeah, it's still saying the same thing."

"What? What, Mommy?"

"It's saying *woompa-woompa-woompa, whump-whump-whump.*"

"But…what does that mean?"

Mom shakes her head, solemn and grim. I can't stand it anymore. I grab her pockmarked cheeks in my little hands and make her look me in the eyes.

"What does it mean, Mommy!"

"Well, it means *Mommy-loves-you-Mommy-loves-you! Go-to-bed-go-to-bed! Get-some-sleep-get-some-sleep! Hurry! Before she makes you clean the bathroom!*"

I leap off her lap, laughing myself silly. I run into my bedroom and burrow under the covers. I look up at Mom and wait for her to say my favorite twelve words, the ones that end all my days. She tucks Amber into the bottom bunk, then reaches up to find me at the top.

She pulls up my covers and begins our mantra.

"Good night. I love you. Sleep tight. Don't let the bedbugs bite."

I look at her silhouette in the dark. I repeat the twelve words back, but louder and faster because that makes them mean more.


Mom is on hands and knees, crawling around the perimeter of the kitchen with a toothbrush and a bucket of bleach, scouring the crevices where the linoleum meets the cupboards.

Dad is playing computer games.

Mom is in a deep squat, waddling around the mustard-yellow toilet, scrubbing it with a Brillo pad from top to bottom, back to front.

Dad is playing computer games.

Mom is high on a stepladder, wiping dust from the blades of my ceiling fan with a wet cloth.

Dad is playing computer games.

Mom is behind the stove, sweeping shards of glass, a vase toppled by a recent storm, into a dustpan.

Dad is playing computer games.

Mom is standing in the dining room, spackling a wall with plaster to fix a hole created by a hurled saucepan, more storm damage.

Dad is playing computer games.

Mom is in the backyard, her skin slicked in sweat as she shoves the twirling blades of our cheap manual lawn mower through the too-thick grass. Mom is standing at the glass door in a pair of old nursing shoes plastered with lawn clippings.

"Where the hell is your father?" she yells through the dining room, her words bouncing into the living room, where Amber and I are absorbed by cartoons.

"I don't know," I lie, annoyed at the interruption.

Mom takes my lie and runs with it. "Go find him, then," she says, her voice rising, as if he could be anywhere among the vast grounds of the Tometich Estate. "Find him and tell him I need his freaking help!"

I look longingly at *The Wuzzles*, at Amber sucking her thumb from the comfort of Dad's armchair. I look toward my parents' bedroom, see the glow of Dad's Commodore 64. I count out my eleven steps—six to their hallway, five to their bedroom door—slowly and methodically. I stand at the edge of the doorway for a beat, nervous to go in, not wanting to be the one to deliver this message. I turn back to the family room, thinking I should leave things alone. I feel hands grab my shoulders. They swing me around, pick me up, and hold me in the air.

Dad pulls my face to his. He smells like stale tobacco and lingering Old Spice. I can see each stubbly pore on his chin and cheeks.

"Tell your mommy this is my day off," he yells, not at me but through me and past me. "Tell her I told her I would mow the lawn tomorrow, and she can *STOP BEING A BITCH ABOUT IT.*"

I realize, with a flood of relief, that she can hear him. I don't actually have to tell her these things. I'm like the beige portable phone that charges in the kitchen. I'm the conduit.

Dad puts me down and brushes off my shoulders. I turn to walk away, thinking I can make it back to the couch in ten steps if I make each one a little bit larger.

"Come in here."

Dad's words freeze me in place. He's never invited me into his inner sanctum. I turn, as slowly as the earth on its axis. I look past the big bed my parents sleep in, though rarely together. I see Dad's computer desk with the funky ergonomic chair and its cushioned shin rest. The one that makes Dad look like he's praying at the Commodore's glowing altar. On the screen I see pixels that form a gray Statue of Liberty standing in front of two matching high-rise towers.

"You wanna play?" Dad asks.

I'd never considered the question. I'd never thought it was one that could be asked. I run to Dad's side. He scoops me up and places me in his lap.

"This game is called Where in the World Is Carmen Sandiego?"

I nod.

"We are detectives, and our job is to capture Carmen, an elusive criminal mastermind."

He sounds like a voice from a TV commercial.

I nod again, eager to buy whatever my father's selling. I watch Dad type commands and click keys. I lean my head against his chest. I can feel his heartbeat, steady and calm. I hear the Weedwacker whir to life in the backyard. Through the slatted blinds of the window I see Mom wielding it against the chain-link fence, hacking down the blades of grass to keep them in order, to stop them from getting too big for their britches.

I feel like a traitor. I'm certain the next time Mom listens to my heart, it will rat me out. But for now I don't care. I don't want to be tough like Mom. I want to be fragile like Dad with his white skin that always needs to be protected. I want to lounge in the cool dark, playing computer games. This is our day off.

CHAPTER 5

# Orange Grove Boulevard

I sink my hands into the brown fibers of the carpet, running them left to make them darker, then right to turn them light again. I kneel outside Gramma's bedroom, watching her through the sliver of space between the door and its jamb. We are always here at Gramma's little condo, me and Dad. She always has a chore she needs done. She always requires help. Dad, her only child, is the one person left on earth willing to oblige.

My grandfather, Dad's dad, died shortly after we moved into our new house. His lung cancer went undiagnosed for years, till it had riddled his body and stolen his breath.

I quiet my own breath, knowing full well, even at five, I shouldn't be doing what I'm doing. I watch, eyes like saucers, as Gramma pulls off her hair to expose the few patches of snow-white fuzz left on her head. She takes her bushy wig, the one that makes her look like Bea Arthur in *Maude*, and sets it on the birch veneer of her dresser. Her teeth come out next, bottoms, then tops. They clink into a glass on her end table.

She peels off her housedress and unhooks her bra from the front, sending her pancake breasts cascading away from her midline toward her armpits and the soft rolls of her belly. What little is left of Gramma shrugs into a sherbet-orange nightgown tufted like upholstery across the chest.

She walks by the door and reaches for her cane. I crouch on the other side, frozen in silent wonder, hoping she won't come do the same to me: scalp me, de-tooth me, shrivel my skin to match hers. I hear cackling. I leap up and run, my ruby-red house slippers fighting for purchase in the shag.

"I'll get you, my pretty," Gramma says as she flings open her door. "And your little dog, too!"

She stabs at me with the prongs of her cane, twisting her hands into claws like the Wicked Witch of the West. I scream and giggle, crashing into Dad's legs and a tangle of cables as he finishes installing Gramma's new VCR. Gramma hobbles down the hall, bent in half with laughter, her empty, gummy mouth covered by one wrinkled hand while the other clutches her cane. She pats me on the head.

"Don't you ever smoke."

It's the one piece of advice on which Mom and Gramma can agree.

With my grandfather's death and Amber's birth, my place in the world has shifted. Dad is consumed by the former and seems happy to avoid the duties of the latter. My dad became his dad, doing all the things to help frail Gramma with her crinkly skin, which is even more lily-white than Amber's. At home, he escapes to his computer desk and his garage workbench to play games, to read and reread the same George Orwell and Shirley Jackson books.

Mom works and cleans and tends to Amber. I watch more and more television, my glowing friend, the one thing in the house that does not yell or cry, that won't use me to send messages to others.

The only living thing that seems to want my company is Gramma. I spend almost every weekend, and often a night or two each week, at Gramma's tiny condo. It's three turns from our ticky-tacky North Fort Myers house. Go left, go right, go left, and here we are on Orange Grove Boulevard.

Gramma's condo is an actual Candy Land, home to colorful dishes brimming with butterscotches and those foil-wrapped strawberry candies with the jammy centers. Her cabinets are laden with Chips Ahoy!s and Oreos, with elf-shaped cookies filled with fudge, with popcorn and Frosted Flakes and blue canisters of Planters Cheez Balls—all the junk food Mom forbids.

After shrinking out of her day skin and chasing me into the living room, Gramma grabs her Canada Dry from the kitchen, her coffee, and her bowl of Raisinets, too. She sets her menagerie of snacks on a TV tray, then settles painstakingly into her recliner, the plug-in one that Dad bought her off TV. She pushes its button, and it lurches slowly and surely upward, till Gramma can lean against its puffy brown cushions, move her silver cane to the side, then hit the button and ease her way back down to earth.

"Put the movie on, Lou. I'm exhausted. And I'll be up all night with that one."

I cackle from my spot on the couch, amid bags of chips and boxes of candy, my hands cool and slick around a tub of ice cream, my ruby-red house slippers kicked off under the coffee table—primed and ready for another of our sleepovers.

Dad puts the VHS tape into the player. The screen turns blue with FBI warnings, then sepia and black as the MGM lion roars and Judy Garland and her little-dog-too take the screen. *The Wizard of Oz* is our thing, Gramma's and mine. We watch it nonstop; enough to wear out her old VCR, necessitating another visit from Dad, who takes me with him as his shield, a five-year-old set of armor used to deflect Gramma's blows—about his lacking job, his failure to finish college, his brown-skinned nobody wife.

As Dorothy starts to sing, Dad gets up to go, kissing Gramma quickly on the head, then doing the same to me. Lost in a fugue of Cheez Balls and Farm Stores ice cream, I don't budge. He leaves and slides the dead bolt, returning to Mom and my baby sister in our little house three turns east of Gramma's. Go right, go left, go right to get home.

When the lock clicks and Dad's Volkswagen rumbles to life, when its headlights paint the living room in long stripes that grow thicker and then fade, I run to the VCR and smash fast forward, blurring the boring sepia reel as quickly as it will go, until the Kansas house spins down, down, down, and Dorothy steps out into a dazzling new world of Technicolor.


Before the condo that took three turns, but after her husband died, Gramma lived with us for a bit. She resided in the room next to mine and Amber's, making us, for the briefest of times, a family of five.

I can't control the storms or the bad words they rain down, but I can control numbers. I've never liked the number 5. By itself, it's uneven, irregular. I prefer numbers that make sense. Two 5s is much better. Two 5s is 10, which is also five 2s. Ten gives me options. Five does not. The thirteen steps from the Zenith to the beige portable phone can become twelve if I make each step a tad longer, or fourteen if I take a tiny baby step at the end, which is kind of cheating. I can brush my top teeth for twenty-two strokes and my bottom for twenty-two more, then add two more to the top and two more to the bottom if the two-minute timer on Mom's watch is still ticking.

I love the number 9. I was born in the ninth month of the year at 9:49 in the morning, Mom tells me. Nine is three 3s. It's 3 three times. I know that from counting the dots on my yellow quilt: three up, three down, three diagonal. It's how I still pass the time when storms roll through the house. And with Gramma, with our family of five, the storms multiply.

I'm not sure if Gramma is our guest or our prisoner. She locks herself in her room and in our bathroom, rarely venturing beyond the small alcove we share. On the rare occasions when she leaves, to go grocery shopping with Dad for her Raisinets and ginger ale—things she doesn't trust Mom to buy for her—that's when Mom and I go on our scavenger hunts. We scour Gramma's drawers for packs of cigarettes and pick the pockets of her housecoats for loosies. Mom digs through the bathroom garbage can, through yellowed Q-tips and phlegmy wads of tissue, to find the half-smoked butts Gramma throws in there, the ones she'll relight and smoke again if we don't do this job properly.

We take our plunder to the big brown garbage can on the side of the house. We drop it in triumphantly, every pack and stump, and then Mom tops it with the wet, gooey garbage from the kitchen to try to deter Gramma from rooting through it in the middle of the night.

"I swear to Christ, she's trying to kill herself, punyeta ka na," Mom says as a slop of coffee grounds and day-old chicken bones falls into place, replacing the menthol-tobacco smell with one of rot.

Mom is stomping and huffing now, as if a part of her is in the garbage can, too. She slams its lid shut and flings open the door. I don't like this mom. I want to slink back to my bedroom and count the dots on my comforter, but the decision isn't mine to make.

"Get in here, we have to clean you up," she says as I dawdle in the garage. "Hurry!"

She leads me to the kitchen sink, jams the faucet to hot, then pulls me up so my belly is pushed between her and the counter. My chest and arms tip into the basin, steam envelops my face as hot water swirls down the steel drain. I focus on the swirling, like the hurricanes all around us. I listen to the gurgles and the steady white noise of the gushing faucet. I count the seconds till Mom deems the water to be scalding enough to clean me. I get to five, then she starts.

Mom grabs the steel wool she uses on her stewpots and takes it to my hands. She pulls it between the webs of each finger and grates it against the undersides of my nails. I cry. Even though crying never changes things. I've touched the cigarettes. Cigarettes are disgusting. I must be cleansed.

I wriggle against Mom's weight, bracing for the worst of it: the soap that will sting my raw flesh; the hot water that will turn my hands red, then purple, as Mom uses her superhero strength to force me into the steaming water, holding my hands there for exactly eleven seconds, till every bubble of soap has swirled down the drain, along with the tears silently pouring from my eyes.

"Good girl," Mom tells me, easing me back to the floor and handing me a dish towel. "Good job."

I cradle my hands in the towel. When I pull it away, my skin is pink and tender, born anew.

In our bedroom, Amber's still napping when Gramma and Dad come home. He unloads her groceries in the kitchen. She rushes to her room and our bathroom. Something clangs. There is more banging. Then the screaming starts, first Gramma, then Mom, then Dad joins the mix.

I look at my quilt, at the yellow squares with polka dots, three three three, and the white squares with little girls carrying baskets of flowers. I count all the little girls. There are forty-eight of them. I count all the girls' flowers, till I get to one hundred, then two hundred, then three hundred. I slink down from the bed to the soft pile of my carpet. I look at Amber in the bottom bunk and wonder how she's still sleeping. I crawl to my door and peek into the alcove. I see Dad stomp into the garage, escaping to the seclusion of his red workbench. I see Gramma still raging. I see Mom stone-faced and square-shouldered, standing inches from Gramma's fury, letting it wash over her—baptism by ire.

"Are you going to punch me again?" Mom says, frozen in place, her face snarled to match that of her mother-in-law's.

"I'd rather not touch you," Gramma spits out.

"I don't want to send you to some goddamn nursing home, Jo," Mom says, the younger Jo rebuking the older. "I want you to stay here. I want you to see your grandchildren grow up. Don't you want to see your granddaughters graduate? Don't you want to see them walk down the aisle on their wedding days? You cannot smoke like this. This is *my house*. I won't allow it."

I can see Gramma shaking, the whole of her frail body rattling back and forth, side to side, like a bomb about to explode.

"My son could have done better than some Chink bitch."

Gramma is the one crying now, whiny sobs that make her sound broken. "I don't know why he did this to me! How could he hate me this much? How could my son hate his own mother?"

Gramma moves out a few days later. Dad finds her the little condo three turns west of us on Orange Grove Boulevard. The condo that transforms Dad into a gopher.

"I have to gofer half-and-half, I'm taking Annabelle, be back soon."

"I have to gofer a plunger, bringing Annabelle, we'll call you."

"I have to gofer her VCR, it's on the fritz, I'll take Annabelle, maybe she can spend the night."

In Gramma's war against Mom, this proves to be her most useful weapon. Dad comes whenever Gramma calls, be it lunchtime or three in the morning.

I see it as no coincidence that Gramma's name is Josephine and my mom's is Josefina; that they both go by Jo. My mom and her mother-in-law are as exactly the same as they are different. They both stand around five foot three. They both love Dad and drive him crazy. They both tolerate his streaks of laziness and apathy—to a point. But where Mom's rounded muscles stretch her cocoa skin taut, Gramma's ivory skin hangs like crinkled gauze over frail bones. Gramma looks weak and powerless.

But Gramma is white.


My grandmother rarely makes it to the Emerald City. By the time Dorothy and the Scarecrow find the Tin Man, she's usually fast asleep. When the movie ends, I pick through her candy dishes and drink the last warm, fizz-less sips of her Canada Dry. I look around at my wonderful world of Oz and its endless possibilities.

I eat fistfuls of Frosted Flakes chased with Oreos. I ride her walking cane like a broom. Some nights I grab her wig off her dresser and pull it down over my bowl cut, inhaling the old-lady funk that sticks to everything Gramma touches, yeasty and stale like shoving your face into a moldy bag of Wonder Bread. I gently tug her oversize glasses from her face, then climb onto the shaky vanity in her condo's lone bathroom, leaning into the trifold mirror/medicine cabinet to admire my bulging eyes and choppy gray locks. I pinch my nose shut, making it thin and beautiful.

"Fuck off, you Chink bitch!" I tell my mirror self.

I take off the glasses and wig, unpinch my nose.

"This is my house! You fuck off!" the new me answers back.

When Gramma eventually wakes, she herds me to her bedroom and the pallet she's made for me on the floor.

"You're too wild to sleep in my bed," she says, "way too much of a monkey."

As I stare up at the swirls of plaster on her ceiling, I ask Gramma to tell me a bedtime story, the same bedtime story I always ask her to tell, about the little boy who didn't listen, the little boy who's just like me. Gramma never hesitates. She loves the story as much as I do.

"Should I start from the beginning? I dunno, it's pretty late," Gramma says, teasing me, knowing the story must start from the beginning, that there's no other way.

"Yes, Gramma! You have to!"

"OK, OK, all right. Once upon a time, in a town not far from here, just on the other side of the state, there was a cute little boy who played baseball and loved his grandmother so, so much. One day, the little boy went to the mall. His mommy was looking at lamps and grown-up things, and the little boy wanted to play video games and look at toys."

I pull my covers over my head, playing her words like a film in my mind. I tell the little boy in the movie to stay with his mommy. I yell at him in my head not to leave her. He never listens.

Gramma pauses. I hear her cough up something greasy and wet. I hear her flick a tissue from the box on her end table. I hear her spit and then toss the tissue into the trash bin near my head, then hear the quiet ticking of Gramma's windup alarm clock.

"Tell the rest, Gramma, tell the whole thing," I say, prodding for the gory details, even if Gramma makes a few up as she goes.

"Well, he was exactly your age and exactly your size with big brown eyes just like yours. He even had your haircut, those silly bangs and all.

"At the mall, a strange man came over to the little boy. The man offered him candy and toys if the little boy would come to his van. And the little boy followed him. His poor daddy and mommy and gramma never saw him again. It killed his grandmother, you know that? She couldn't handle losing her grandbaby. It made her heart so sick, she died."

"And then what?"

"Let's see, a couple weeks later, the police officers found the little boy's head in a drainage ditch along the Florida turnpike, right over on the other side of the Caloosahatchee and Lake O. Just his head. They never found his body."

"Never?"

"Nope, never."

"Did the boy die because the man chopped his head off?"

It's a logical question, and Gramma treats it as such.

"No, sirree. The man strangled the little boy. He choked him, so he couldn't breathe anymore."

"And then the man chopped off his head?"

"Yep, the man decapitated the poor little boy."

I break the word into its syllables: de-cap-i-ta-ted. Five. That's a lot. That's more than Ann-a-belle or To-me-tich. It's more syllables than syl-la-bles and way more than Gram-ma or mon-key. De-cap-i-ta-ted. Getting your head chopped off. One, two, three, four, and an uneven five. I don't think I've ever known a word with that many syllables.

"Did he use an axe?" I ask, bringing myself back to the story.

The question of how Adam Walsh's head left his body-just-like-mine gnaws at me with every retelling. Heads seem hard to remove. I have trouble cutting through Dad's steaks. How would you cut through the flesh and bones of a neck? Usually, Gramma has had enough of me by this point. Usually, she tells me I ask too many questions, that it's way too late for such nonsense. Usually, she clicks on her radio, and I listen to Delilah soothe the broken hearts of callers. But this night, Gramma keeps going.

"The man used a machete."

Muh-sheh-tee, three syllables.

"Like the one Mommy has? For the yard?"

"Just like the one your mommy has. All crazy people have machetes, I guess."

I stare back into the plastered abyss of the ceiling as Gramma's snores fill the room. I picture Mom lopping off Gramma's head with her machete. De-cap-i-ta-ted. One, two, three, four, five. I picture it popping off cleanly and bloodlessly like the head of a Barbie doll. I picture Mom smiling for a second, then going back to her yard work.

Dad comes back in the morning and finds me feral on sugar and too little sleep.

"This is why Jo doesn't want her here," he says to Gramma as I snarl and body-slam the Robo Chair, mashing its arrow-up button till the seat tilts at a precariously vertical angle. I cling to the side, teeth bared like one of the Wicked Witch's flying monkeys.

"If you people raised those kids with manners, they wouldn't act like this! They're wild mongrels. Where do you suppose *that* comes from?"

Gramma introduces me to lots of fun words. *Mongoloid* might be the most benign, probably because she says it so frequently, as if it were *sweetie* or *dear*, just on the other end of the love-hate spectrum.

"How's that *Mongoloid* you married?"

"Is that *Mongoloid* still around?"

"It's a good thing these kids didn't get her *Mongoloid* eyes, too. Their lives are going to be so difficult as it is. My God, those noses."

When Gramma gets testy, her words do, too. *Tramp, whore,* and *bitch* are the natural escalation of things. Mom starts out as the *T* word, graduates to what I thought for a long time was the *H* word, then winds up as the *B* word. Often in the span of a single breath.

That night, as Mom brushes my hair and I brush my teeth, I ask her what a mongrel is. She asks me where I heard that. I lie and tell her it was on the radio.

"A mongrel is like your friend Abby's little doggy with the curly hair," Mom says. "It's a puppy from two different breeds of parents."

I like dogs. I want a dog. This strikes me as positive news. I smile and continue brushing, adding two strokes to the top and two more to the bottom, keeping things even, waiting for Mom's gold wristwatch to tell me to stop.

"Next time you are at your grandmother's," Mom says, pausing to collect her thoughts, "tell her to stop being such a Wicked Witch, OK?"

I laugh as I spit out my toothpaste. I laugh because Mom's funny, and her request is impossible.

# CHAPTER 6

# Pine Island

**M**ango rumors travel fast among a certain sect of the Florida population.

A Jamaican friend of a Puerto Rican friend of another Filipina nurse on Mom's floor tells her about a mango orchard where you can buy bushels of the honey-sweet fruits for next to nothing if you pick them yourself on Pine Island, a long, narrow strip of mangroves and farmland thirty minutes west of Fort Myers. Each summer, right when school lets out and the weather turns from hot to insufferably blazing, we stockpile cans of Off!, load into our copper Toyota Van, and drive west, through the razed plains of Cape Coral and the colorful fishing shacks of Matlacha, down a two-lane road into the Old Florida wilds of Pine Island.

A mango farm isn't like the apple orchards up north, or even the citrus groves that speckle the Sunshine State's inland areas. Mango trees need room to breathe. They require space. If you plant them too close together, the humid air gets caught in their overlapping branches and the trees go soggy with rot. Too close together and their growth will be stunted, the trees will never reach their full potential.

In summer, Pine Island's mango farms look like sparsely filled fields.

Leafy trees heavy with clusters of yellow-red fruits stand at random distances from one another, like the crowd at a concert when the opening act starts playing. Mom's favorite mango farm sits to the right of the island's main intersection. We park, then drench ourselves in mosquito spray, tiptoeing over the sandy hills of fire ants that dot the weedy parking area like land mines.

The only building on the property is a pole barn. It shelters a Coke machine, an ice-cream freezer, crates of already picked mangoes, and a man in a baseball cap. He leans over the counter, chin in hands, listening to the far-off crackle of an Atlanta Braves game from his radio. Mom nods at the man, so we do, too. Mom bypasses these more expensive mangoes. The fruits we seek are still on the trees. Mom gives us each a plastic Publix bag, a pair of pruning shears, and specific instructions.

"Choose fruits with a little red to them. And *do not pull them*," she says, waving her shears in front of our little faces. "Cut them at the stem and put them *gently* into the bag."

Mom is all business. She takes off, guided by some unseen force to a faraway tree that pings her mango radar. Dad sticks by Amber and me, hoisting us onto his shoulders, one after the other, so we can hack at the lowest mango stems with our dull shears, eventually yanking the sticky bastards off with all our little-kid might, breaking all of Mom's rules.

Dad wants to be here about as much as we do. It's fun for five minutes, and then it's just hot and itchy. With a bagful of twisted and gnarled mangoes, Dad nods and turns back to the pole barn.

"Where you going?" I ask, still holding Amber's hand.

"Crazy. You wanna come?"

I laugh as my sister and I run to him. He scoops us up, one under each arm, and carries us and our bags of mangoes to the shade.

Dad buys us each an icy bottle of Coke and tilts a box fan in our direction. Its roaring hum fills our ears, sends our dark hair flying, so it clings to the dewy sides of our sodas. Dad walks closer to the man in the baseball cap, listening in to the Braves game, talking sports and his beloved Red Sox to pass the time.

Mom is trying to grow her own mango trees. She's gotten a few seeds to sapling stage before they wither in the backyard or are cut down by Dad with the mower. She says our yard isn't big enough, that the citrus and ficus trees need to go if we want to make room for her mangoes. Dad says we need a bigger house all around, and so, while they house hunt, we continue our summer tradition of mango picking. To the three of us, the ones I think of as the white folks of the family, this is another chore. To our brown Mongoloid mom, it's the happiest day of the year.

When Mom hits a mango hot streak, Dad appeases us with a second Coke, maybe a Good Humor Bar from the freezer. When we burn through those, we make him sing his silly songs.

"'Hello, Muddah,'" Dad starts, rapping our empty soda bottles against the sandy ground for percussion, *tap-tap-tap*, "'Hello, Fadduh,'" *tap-tap-tap*, "'Here I am at,'" *tap-tap-tap*, "'Camp Granada!'"

But my favorite is the one about the hearse going by. Mom says it's too morbid (mor-bid, two syllables), so Dad sings it only when she's not around to hear.

"'The worms crawl in, the worms crawl out; The worms play pinochle on your snout; They eat your eyes, they eat your nose; They eat the jelly between your toes.'"

"That is why I want to be cremated!" Mom calls out.

She's back, smiling, arms loaded with bags of mangoes. She leans into the breeze of our box fan and wipes the sweat from her face, neck, and arms with a rag slung around her neck.

"Never," Dad says, faking a yawn. "Find me the biggest, comfiest coffin. I'll be taking the world's longest nap."

Mom hoists the new bags onto the scale, then helps Dad get them into the back of the van. She settles up with the man at the cash register, haggling him down in price for a couple of mangoes she claims she salvaged from the ground.

"OK," she says. "Let's go."

Mom cuts into the first mango before we've left the gravelly parking lot. She passes slippery slivers back to us. Despite the Cokes and ice cream, Amber and I fight for them, cupping the wobbly bits in our hands like we do the baby lizards we catch in the backyard, pressing our skinny fingers tightly together so nothing can escape.

No part of these mangoes goes to waste. Mom saves the skins in a bowl that hums with clouds of fruit flies on the counter. When the bowl overflows, I run it to the scraggly citrus trees in our yard and spread the scraps at their bases, an offering to the fruit-tree gods.

The mango pits, though, are gold.

Mom sifts through to find the ones that look most promising. She runs a paring knife down their sides to shave as much fruity flesh off as possible, then cracks open the shell to reveal the seed within. She sets some seeds in jars of water. She swathes others in wet paper towels and places them in sandwich baggies in the kitchen window so they can bask in the warm sun in their shiny mango-seed saunas. We check them each morning for sprouts.

"Here's one," Mom says, cradling the itty-bitty seedling in her upturned palm. She shovels a trowel of potting soil from the bag she keeps under the sink into an old yogurt container, then eases in the prize. If it takes root, she transfers it to the yard, where, inevitably, Dad will run it down with the mower, mulching it into oblivion before it has a chance. This will cause another fight, create another opportunity for Mom to remind Dad he can't freaking do anything right, another chance for them to ruin our house with one of their thunderstorms.

But, for this one summer night as we face down bags of just-picked mangoes, we can hope this cycle may not repeat. On this one night, mangoes are all that matter.

Amber and I strip down to our undies. Dad lines the dining room table in newspaper and more plastic Publix bags. Mom slices the mangoes lengthwise down either side of the pit, handing us the oblong halves so she can gnaw on the flat seeds before tucking them into a Tupperware bowl for safekeeping. We eat mangoes as Mom taught us to, skin-side down in our hands, digging our spoons into the sunny flesh till they hit the rind, which doubles as a flimsy bowl. When our spoons have gotten all they can, we turn the rinds inside out, chewing away any last scraps. No bite left behind.

Rivulets of sticky juice trace pale-yellow paths down our arms and necks, like water spreading in veins across parched earth. This mango liquor stains our nail beds and makes the skin around our lips look jaundiced. We eat mangoes at breakfast, lunch, and dinner for a week straight. Mom will freeze some and dry others into candy-sweet mango jerky. If she does it right, we'll be in mangoes through winter.

I eat until my stomach bulges. I eat until Mom scoops me up and hauls me to the bathtub to join Amber. Mom peels pages of newsprint from my chest and twiggy arms. She pats my belly tenderly. It's fat, sticky, and sweet. Just like a mango.

## CHAPTER 7

# McGregor

A slick of sweat glues the skin of my thighs to the hot leather as I ride in the back seat with Mom and Amber. I feel the car turn and turn again. I see pastel houses and then the gray-brown trunks of palm trees. I listen to Dad talking to the yellow-haired woman in the driver's seat.

"This is the very best neighborhood in Fort Myers, perfect for a young family like yours, Mr. Toe-meh-tick," the woman says.

I wait for Dad to correct her. It doesn't take long.

"Taw-muh-titch," the woman says, repeating after him, careful to get it right this time. "That's right, sir. I apologize."

We've just left a house with a yard that's too small, and another that's too far from Mom and Dad's hospital. We have been house hunting for what feels like forever, for two of my eight years on this earth, a quarter of my young life.

There have been respites. We lived in a house on a canal for a little while, a two-story ranch with an eat-in kitchen, a pool shaped like a kidney bean, and a family of coral snakes that lived under the front porch. The side yard had something Mom called "the alligator *sex* place," the emphasis on *sex* her own; an expressly forbidden area just beyond a tangle of mangroves. We lasted there six months, until a girl the same age as Amber was eaten by an alligator two towns north of ours, and Mom made us move.

We've spent the past year living in the Sunsets, a low-rent apartment complex that sits behind Fort Myers's best elementary school. I pass women in smeared lipstick and torn stockings on my morning walks to second grade. In the Sunsets apartment, it isn't snakes or alligators that threaten us, it's Dad's ineptitude as a father. He is, at Mom's insistence, going to nursing school at night, which she works overtime to finance while also saving for another down payment after "losing our asses" on the alligator *sex* house. With Dad out at night, though, it means even when he is home, he's sleeping more than parenting.

One evening Mom finds Amber playing on the rickety balcony, one skinny arm and one skinny leg pushed through the bars of the railing three stories above the asphalt parking lot. Another night, she comes home to two hungry children, one of whom, Amber again, took matters into her own hands by eating an entire bottle of children's Tylenol, thinking it was candy.

There is screaming and ipecac syrup and a foamy splat of pink vomit that puddles atop the apartment's threadbare carpeting. Dad sleeps in the van that night. The next morning he wakes us with bacon and eggs, wrapping plates of leftovers in plastic and setting them on the lowest shelf of the fridge. He moves all the snacks to within reach and teaches me how to work the toaster.

Our weekend house hunts speckle these misadventures. Dad wants a pool. Mom wants us to stay in this school zone. Dad wants his-and-hers sinks and an office for his Commodore 64. Mom wants to be away from horny, hungry alligators. Dad wants a walk-in closet and a waterbed. Mom wants a place that won't kill us.

They tell this to the lady with the yellow hair. She listens to Dad, rapt and nodding.

"Yes, Mr. Taw-muh-titch, a pool is an absolute necessity in Southwest Florida," she agrees.

When Mom speaks, she keeps staring at Dad.

We look at a clapboard crackerbox house with creaky floors and a huge backyard that costs less than our van. Mom loves it. Dad hates it. So I hate it, too. We look at a Spanish-style house not far from the Caloosahatchee with four bedrooms, an upstairs master suite, and a star-fruit tree. Dad loves it. I love it. Mom says he'd have to drop out of nursing school and get through medical school to afford it. We look at newly constructed model homes in gated communities and fixer-uppers on stately streets, at a home with an indoor pool we all agree is weird, at one with skylights and a glass-encased palm tree–filled atrium we all agree is overkill.

After a series of break-ins at the Sunsets, our never-ending house hunt comes to an end. The woman with the yellow hair turns her sedan onto a quiet street guarded with more royal palms. She parks in front of a beige house with brown trim. It's right off McGregor Boulevard, the street where Thomas Edison and Henry Ford lived, along with most of the kids in my new second-grade class. It's got a yard filled with citrus trees and room for more. It's got a pool, a two-car garage, and his-and-hers closets in the master.

The yellow-haired lady leads us to the front door, which is caged in by screens and a gate made of wrought-iron bars. She points to the matching bars covering the windows.

"You can easily take those down," she says, eyes locked on my father. "They're hideous, I know."

"We'd keep them," Mom says.

The woman glances at her, head cocked to one side in confusion, like the words came from my mouth or Amber's. She turns back to Dad. "It's up to you," she says.

She shows us the kitchen, the patio, the glistening pool. The bedroom Amber and I would share is next to a bathroom with olive-green fixtures.

There's a family room with a nook for a breakfast table, and a formal sitting area off the dining room, which is crowned with a chandelier dripping in crystals. It's the nicest thing I've ever seen at eight years old, like something from the Ewing mansion on *Dallas* or Cinderella's castle in Disney World.

We're standing around the chandelier, looking out at the spacious backyard, when Mom decides. Its tear-drop crystals cast shards of rainbows on my Kmart Keds. The yellow-haired lady is telling Dad about insulation and attic space. Mom interrupts her.

"We'll take it," Mom says.

The woman turns. She looks Mom in the face for the first time. She locks eyes with her, raises an eyebrow, and nods, as if realizing she's been barking up the wrong tree all this time.

"That sounds great, Mrs. Taw-muh-titch," she says. "An excellent decision. Your family will be very happy here."

Mom and Dad pack up our things at the Sunsets apartment. From the flimsy balcony, I see a woman steal the ironing board Dad left next to the van. I sing the *Jeffersons* theme song in my head as I watch her. I know what she's doing is wrong. I don't know what to do about it. And anyway, we're movin' on up, not to a deluxe apartment in the sky, but to our fairy-tale house with its crystal chandelier. To the house off fancy McGregor Boulevard. To the house that's close enough to school that I can ride the ten-speed bike Dad promises to buy me. To the house where we can get a dog and drink orange juice squeezed from our very own fruit trees.

To the house where we're going to live happily ever after.

On move-in day, the neighbors are quick to greet us, this young new family. Dr. Johnson lives in the imposingly impressive white house next door. Mrs. Philpot, a lady with crinkly skin like Gramma's and sparkly rings on all her fingers, lives in the bungalow mid-street. She waves to us from her driveway as her assistant, a Trinidadian woman in white scrubs, walks over a tin of biscotti.

The Allards—he an anesthesiologist, she an attorney—live in the river-front estate at the end of the road, their driveway hidden by a wall of Clusia shrubs with leathery, paddle-shaped leaves. He and Mom work in the same hospital. Mom knows this. Dr. Allard does not. He and his wife bring a tray of cookies and a bottle of wine. They don't know we're Baha'ís. They don't know Baha'ís don't drink wine.

"This is the perfect little starter house for a family like yours," Mrs. Allard tells Mom.

I wait for Mom to correct her, to tell her we've had other houses, that we're not *starting*. Mom sets the bottle of wine on the kitchen counter and smiles, a smile that spreads slowly from her lips and never branches to her eyes.

Our road is bookended by McGregor on one side, its royal palm trees famously planted by Mr. Edison himself, and by the Caloosahatchee on the other. We are on the "river side" of McGregor, as people on this side of McGregor like to boast.

But just barely.

Our house is the street's sentinel. It's the first house on the road, the one that absorbs the noise of McGregor traffic so it doesn't foul the pool-front patios of the doctors and lawyers who are our neighbors. It's a modest three-bed-two-bath, a humble thing compared to the surrounding estates, which get grander and more splendid as you approach the river.

Our house is the welcome mat on which the other houses wipe their feet. The black bars covering our windows are pounded into curling scrolls that make them look ornate yet imposing, that make this already different house that much more so. Dad hates the bars. I hate them, too.

"Which box has my drill?" he says, tugging at the set covering the front window. "I can get these down before the end of the day."

Mom hauls another crate through the gated front door. She looks at Dad and shakes her head.

"I told you, we're leaving them."

"No way, Jo, they're a fire hazard."

"We are right on a busy street," she says. "Too many crazy people in this world. Leave them. They'll keep us safe."

I'm with Dad. I think they make us look weird, different. Nobody else has bars on their windows, and they all seem to be doing fine.

"Your mom worries too much," Dad says. He rolls his eyes, so I roll mine, too. He heads to his workbench to grab his Marlboros.

As Mom hauls boxes and Dad smokes, I wander around the front yard, curling my toes in the weedy grass, hopping onto the low wall that surrounds the pebble-filled front porch and walking along it like it's a balance beam, like the red-plank deck of our first house—step on a crack, break your mom's back—only now my steps are surer, and, in my slightly more grown-up head, the stakes aren't as high.

Arms flung to either side, tongue bitten into place along my cheek in concentration, I sense someone watching me. Across the street, I see a girl in a yellow jumper with a pineapple crocheted across the chest. She walks to the edge of her driveway and waves. I wave back, lose my balance and hop down.

"You wanna play?" she calls over to me.

Mom's still going back and forth with boxes. Dad's in the side yard, holding a Marlboro Red at his hip as he plots a place for a doghouse. I catch Dad's eye. He sees the girl and smiles, gives me the A-OK.

I look both ways and cross the street to her driveway. Each step I take feels more intimidating. I've never made a friend on my own. My friends are the children of my parents' friends. The girl in the pineapple jumper is taller and older than me. She has big blond hair and boobs the size of Mom's. I know I should say something, but I don't know what.

The girl saves me.

"I'm Cathy," she says. "You live there now?"

I nod, suddenly feeling self-conscious about my ratty tank top and bare feet. This girl named Cathy grabs me and hugs me. She smells like green-apple hair spray. I still haven't said anything. Cathy goes on, "Cool. We can be friends."

And so we are.

Cathy is royalty as far as second-grade me is concerned. She carries herself with an effortless ease that I cannot understand but will come to realize is the byproduct of wealth. She has no chips on her shoulders, not yet. She is a young, doted-upon, all-American child. I love her. I want to be her.

Cathy's grandfather, her mom's dad, they call him Papa, owns the local Budweiser distributorship. Every Christmas, Papa gives each of his grandchildren two $500 bills—the only times in my life I've seen one. He calls me over to his easy chair one day, runs his gnarled fingers through my dark hair and hands me $20. I like him, too.

Cathy lives across the street and on another planet.

Her house is lined in plush white carpeting and has beige overstuffed furniture that pulls you in like a warm hug. Tubes of lipstick and compacts of blush tumble across her mom's makeup vanity, which is trimmed in bright bulbs like those of movie stars. Cathy has multiple shampoos and conditioners in her bathroom; fancy bottles printed with hard-to-say words that make them extra fancy: Système Biolage, Fabergé, L'Oréal. They make her thick waves of permed blond hair smell like jasmine and cucumbers and sunshine. My hair smells like Pert, which Mom buys from Phar-Mor along with generic crackers and bottles of Drano.

Cathy's walk-in closet overflows with clothes from the Gap and the full-priced racks at Burdines. She has rows of real Keds and polo shirts with horses and alligators stitched to the breasts. She has an endless supply of scrunchy socks and a drawer just for hair bows and headbands. She's two years older than me and light years cooler.

Early on, I go to her house to play. We slink from her room to the door of her older sister, Jenna, then snort with laughter as we listen to Jenna gush to her boyfriend on a phone shaped like red kissy lips. Cathy has her own phone, too, a clear one that shows the colorful inner workings, and she has her own TV, where I can watch the Disney Channel or *Fraggle Rock* on HBO. When we get bored with that, we run across the street to my house, where the move-in process has been replaced by major construction.

Mom and Dad are turning this humble three-two into what I think will be a stately five-three, just like Cathy's house and Dr. Johnson's. When finished, our house will be an L. My parents' bedroom will be at the top of the L, my new bedroom will be the end of the L's arm. When I look out my finished sliding glass door, I will see the pool and, beyond it, the sliders that open onto our dining room and, at the end, those that open onto my parents' room. Amber will get her own room, plus we'll have a playroom and a guest bedroom. The configuration of the addition means we'll have back-to-back bathrooms. The house's original one is that drab olive-green. The new one, next to my new bedroom, is bright peach, sunny and fresh.

A wall of tarps marks the end of the old house and the start of the new one. On the other side, saws whir and hammers whack.

"You do not go on the construction side," Mom tells me, her face stern and honest.

I will heed her words. She knows it as well as I do. And then Cathy comes along. She wanders into the construction zone without blinking. My heart races as I follow her, not saying a thing.

"It's so cool back here," she says, running her hands along dusty boxes of tiles and sheets of drywall. "I can't believe you get to build your own bedroom. That's, like, a dream."

My house is cool. Cathy thinks it's cool.

This is it. This is home.

CHAPTER 8

# The Commode

I get my first up-close taste of death in third grade. I start to learn its contours, its smells.

Gramma moves back in on a hot late-summer day. Mom and Gramma, the two Jos, must have reached a truce. Gramma's health is failing. She has emphysema and can barely make it from the door of her condo to Dad's car. Dad wants to put her in a nursing home. Mom, of all people, won't allow it. That's not what Filipinos do.

"You want our kids to send us away when we're old, to be taken care of by orderlies? By high-school dropouts making minimum wage?" Mom says, knowing full well Dad was an orderly when they met.

"If I'm old and batshit crazy, what do I care?" Dad argues. "You don't even like her—and she hates you."

Mom sits on the couch next to a pile of laundry, folding and refolding the same frayed washcloth as I watch from the end of the hall.

"Why did we add those two bedrooms and that bathroom? For our family," Mom says. "You don't leave your family to strangers. I wouldn't wish that on my worst enemy, and that woman might be my worst enemy."

Dad shakes his head and rolls his eyes. He stares at the ground as he leaves Mom to her pile of laundry, as he paces to the garage and the quiet of his workbench with a piece of Nicorette gum and a Stephen King paperback. He is defeated, overruled.

He rents a hospital bed and hauls it piece by piece into the new room next to mine. He plugs it in, and it breathes its first breath, mechanical and slow, a *whoosh—whoosh—whoosh*, like an elephant's heartbeat. He brings in a walker with tennis balls for feet and a wheelchair and a bedside commode with rubber-wrapped arms and a removable opaque bucket. Gramma's Robo Chair, the one Dad bought off TV, that comes, too.

I am excited. I love that Robo Chair. I imagine the candy dishes Gramma will bring, the two-liter bottles of orange soda. She'll need a TV and a VCR for our late-night *Wizard of Oz* watch parties.

But this Gramma isn't that Gramma. This Gramma is shrunken and surly, like the Wicked Witch of the West halfway through being melted, all the same evil but concentrated.

She comes in silently on a wheelchair that barely fits through our hallway. Dad has to push it by its gray vinyl back so as not to scrape his knuckles. Gramma slinks to her right. Her head bounces with each of Dad's steps, the way a baby's will if you aren't holding it properly. I watch from my bedroom door as Dad wheels her into the room next to mine. I listen as he switches on the bed, as it starts breathing again. I wonder if it will breathe for Gramma.

"Here we are, Jo," Dad says as he tucks his mom under one of my mom's crocheted quilts.

He always calls his mom Jo, not mommy or mom or momma. He calls our mom Jo, too. For a while I thought all moms were called Jo. Jos all around.

Gramma doesn't answer, just flicks her wrist toward the door, the universal leave-me-alone signal. There will be no jam-filled candies with this Gramma, no Raisinets. Not in Mom's house. Not under the other Jo's roof. This Gramma cannot ply me with Cheez Balls. She cannot coax me to get her lighter or another Virginia Slim from the baggie hidden at the bottom of her purse. She can barely get out of that big rented hospital bed that hums as though it's alive.

Still, she scares me. The whole situation scares me. Nothing about it feels natural, least of all that slow *whoosh—whoosh—whoosh* of her bed.

"It inflates and deflates, that's all the humming is," Mom says as we change Gramma's sheets one day, "so your Gramma doesn't get bedsores on her heinie, since she never, ever moves."

Mom's voice rises on those final words. She makes them louder, clearer, to make sure everyone in the room can hear.

Gramma sits in her wheelchair in the corner, staring at the fuzzy ankle socks covering her cockeyed feet. Her powder-blue housedress is hiked up to her thighs, showing the web of purple veins speckled by age spots along her calves.

"What a goddamn waste," Gramma mumbles. "I was fine without you."

Mom ignores her. She loads the sheets into her arms and heads to the washing machine in the garage. She scoops up a stained pair of Gramma's saggy undies with her big toe on the way out the door, flicking her leg deftly behind her like a flamingo so she can add the panties to the load of wash. She looks at Gramma in the corner.

"Make sure she doesn't go anywhere."

It takes me a second to realize Mom is talking to me. I lean against the bed's vinyl mattress, wondering what I will do if Gramma makes a run for it. I look at Gramma for a half second, then at my feet, happy to sit in silence till Mom returns and the cleaning resumes. When the door to the garage bangs shut, Gramma peers up from her lap.

"Sweetheart," she says, her voice soft as corn syrup, "does your daddy still have any of his Marlboros?"

I shift my weight, sinking into a different part of the mattress. I gnaw my lip. I don't dare look up. Gramma knows Dad doesn't smoke anymore.

I think maybe I could grab her a piece of the nicotine gum Dad keeps in his tool drawer. I can maybe get her a whole packet, even. I want to help.

Gramma pounds her gnarled fists against the arms of her wheelchair.

"Is there anything to fucking smoke in this house, Annabelle Marie Tometich?

"I am talking to you!

"I know you can hear me! Listen to me! And find me a fucking cigarette, you fucking mongrel!"

I shrink into the mattress, pushing my body into it and away from Gramma.

She screams until she coughs, until she gasps for air and clings to the sides of her chair. I grab the box of tissues from her end table and jab them in her direction. I push them at her as I move farther away.

"No!"

The word bursts out between wet spurts. It is a *No!* to the tissues and a *No!* to me leaving her. Gramma hacks again, still gripping her wheelchair. She looks me in the eyes, her face hard and insistent. I freeze and stare back, too afraid to do anything else. Gramma sucks hard from deep in her throat. A sick, damp, rasping sound escapes her, loud as thunder. She keeps her eyes locked on mine as she works her tongue around something greasy and slimy in her mouth. She spits a wad of gray-green phlegm onto the floor between us. It hits the newly installed carpet with a dull splat. Spittle covers her chin. It hangs in wet threads that dribble onto her powder-blue lap.

She keeps her eyes on me, gauging my reaction. I stare back blankly.

"Get the fuck out of this room."

I scoot to the edge of the bed, then hurry to the door, trying to reach it in three steps but tripping and taking five. Gramma has never been mean to me. She's been mean around me, but she's never directed the full force of her wickedness at me. I sit in the hallway in the nook between Gramma's door and my own till Mom comes back with a pile of clean sheets.

"What'd she do?"

I hesitate, shifting my knees from my chest to the floor and back again. Then, quietly: "I think she wants a cigarette."

Mom sucks her teeth as she takes a deep, slow breath.

"She wants to kill herself. That is what she wants."

Gramma starts fights at every turn. Dad brings her the wrong kind of eggs one morning and she launches them across the room. The sound of the plate shattering against our shared wall wakes me. Some loud noise or another is what wakes me most days.

Usually it's an argument over having to bathe or go number two, neither of which Gramma enjoys. Dad sneaks Metamucil into Gramma's morning coffee to try to keep her regular. Mom fills Gramma's candy dishes with individually wrapped prunes.

Gramma's bowel movements are something we track with diligence, like the hurricanes on the map in the garage, only stinkier.

"Did she go yesterday?"

"Not in the commode. Did you take her to the bathroom at some point?"

"No, she wouldn't let me. It's been five days."

Gramma's bedside toilet fascinates me. I've never seen anything like it. The idea that you can take a dump, lay a turd, drop a deuce, IN YOUR OWN BEDROOM is equal parts horrifying and engrossing.

I am happy to join the Poop Patrol. I am even happier to enlist Amber's involuntary help. One morning, as our parents wheel Gramma, cursing and spitting, to an equally involuntary sponge bath, I remind Amber how important it is to see if Gramma has done her business.

"You have to open the lid and put your face in to see if she went number one or number two," I tell my five-year-old sister.

"Gross. I don't want to."

"You have to. We have to make sure Gramma is healthy so she doesn't die."

I shove Amber into the room with my orange plastic flashlight to protect her. Across the hall, Mom and Dad help Gramma into the peach bathroom's tub. Unrepeatable words hurl out through wisps of steamy fog.

"Jesus Christ, get your Chink hands off of me!" Gramma shouts at Mom.

"Louis, control your goddamn mother," Mom growls in response.

"Jesus Christ, Jo, just calm down!" Dad says, though I'm not sure to whom.

Amber comes running out of the bedroom, her mullet bowl cut bouncing wildly atop her twisted face, her eyes as wide as the commode seat.

"THERE IS A POOP!"

"Really? Did you see it? Was it like a log or like soup? What color was it?"

"I CAN SMELL IT!" she screams. "I don't have to see it! It stinks!"

"Get back in there." I grab her by her shirt and push her over the threshold. "You have to look. You have to see the actual turds and tell me what they look like. Gramma's life depends on it!"

I push Amber one more time, then freeze in place as I hear the bathroom's pocket door slide open behind me.

"Leave your sister alone."

I feel my dad's hand on my head and instinctively apologize.

"*You* can clean the commode this morning," he says. "Flush whatever is in there down the toilet in the green bathroom, then leave the bucket outside."

I sink to the floor, rolling from my side to my back. "Daddy, no. That's disgusting."

He pulls me up and walks me to the bedside toilet. Amber is right. It stinks. He lifts off the plastic gray seat and sets it to the side. He grabs the opaque bucket, its contents sloshing unevenly as it moves. He hands it to me.

I hold the edges with the cells of skin at the fringe of my fingertips. Dad places his giant hands over mine, forcing them into a firmer grip.

"Don't you dare drop it," he says.

Breathing only through my mouth, eyes fixed firmly ahead of me, I make it to the green bathroom and dump the contents down the toilet as Dad watches from the doorway. I take the bucket to the patio and watch him slosh it with bleach, then rinse it with the hose we use to bathe Bo, the new dog.

"This is your job now," he says. "Every morning, you will help clean Gramma's commode."

And every morning thereafter, I do.

When Gramma can't make it to the commode and starts soiling herself, Mom relents and lets Dad admit her to a nursing home. The humming hospital bed goes back to the rental company. The wheelchair gets stowed in a closet. The commode gets folded up behind it. Dad gives the Robo Chair to a woman named Henrietta who wears big fake-pearl clip-on earrings. She's Gramma's only friend.

The day Gramma leaves, Mom scrubs the room from baseboards to ceiling fan with bleach. Slowly, our toys filter into it: a blue Playskool easel, bins of stuffed animals, a low table we use for sculpting Play-Doh. It finally becomes the playroom it was meant to be.

These are the happiest days of that room's life.

CHAPTER 9

# The Seedling

The yelling has stopped and the house is still. I sit on my parents'
waterbed, watching cartoons with Amber, thankful to escape to these
made-up worlds.

The thunderstorms that started all those houses ago have followed us
to this one, infiltrating this happily-ever-after home like sideways rain.

I hear Dad's car, the sensible gray four-door Mercury Sable that Mom
pushed for after the Rabbit died, start up and roll down the driveway.
I sneak through to the kitchen, looking for food, and see Mom on the
couch, turning a white stick between her hands, her face wet with tears.

"Come here," she says.

I'm still in a nightgown, even though it's almost lunchtime. My breakfast has been a banana from the fruit bowl on the dining room table, a
demilitarized zone buffering the fight in the family room from our
master-bedroom bunker. I snuck a banana for Amber, too. But that was
hours ago. I feel my stomach rumble, part hunger, part nerves, as I clear
the neutral zone and go to my mother.

"What's wrong, Mommy?"

"We're having a baby," she says, tears still slicking her eyes.

The words don't register. Their tone is wrong. Babies aren't sad, they're joyous, at least on TV, like the Keatons were on *Family Ties* when they welcomed baby Andy. Mom opens her arms and draws me in, hugging me tight as she sniffles.

Is this joy?

I pull away and look at her face. She smiles and dabs the back of one hand across her cheeks.

I guess it is. We're having a baby.

A few months earlier, my parents had a different fight. Dad said he wanted a boy, an heir to the Tometich name. Mom told Dad she couldn't handle a fourth child, implicating him as her third. She called him a selfish-arrogant-son-of-a-bitch, the nine syllables hooked together like the cars of a bullet train.

"I should have given them my maiden name for all you've ever done for those girls," Mom said, rabid with anger, spitting the words into Dad's face on her tiptoes.

He slapped her hard across the cheek. She charged at him and pushed him into the garage, shrieking like she'd gone mad. Our bikes clattered to the cement floor under the weight of Dad's falling body. He landed with a "Jesus fucking Christ, you crazy fucking cunt." I closed my door and pulled the covers over my head.

It was the first time I can remember the neighbors calling the police on us. I heard the sirens as they got closer, as they turned from long wails to short, quick gasps. I saw fragments of red and blue lights as they pierced the slats of the fence into the backyard. Mom came into my room with a bruise shaped like Dad's palm on her cheek. For a man who could barely hold a Weedwacker, he had a surprisingly strong hand.

"Your daddy will be home later," she said.

The police took him on suspicion of battery, but Mom declined to press charges. They released him in the morning. From behind my bowl of Frosted Flakes at the breakfast table, I watched him walk in. I saw his two blackened eyes and the swollen bridge of his nose. He threw some things into a duffel bag, then slipped out without a word. He was gone for a month.

It was a good month, filled with trips to the park and swims in the pool, Mom all in with wet hair and plunging cannonballs. She stood at the stove one night and fried tuyo for her dinner, little dried fish that smell like the Caloosahatchee at low tide, which was against Dad's rules. Tuyo wasn't allowed to be cooked in the house, only on the patio. But here Mom was, stinking up the kitchen as Amber and I laughed and ran circles around her, pinching our flat, hand-me-down noses shut to keep out the fishy stench. For us, she picked up fried chicken with steamy yeast rolls and thick gravy from Grandy's, a fast-food joint Dad called trashy.

The next day, Mom paced the yard, checking on the mango seedlings Dad was always mowing down with the Snapper. She found an especially promising one in the middle of our freeze-tag field, smack-dab in the center of the front lawn. She circled it with white rings made of concrete and shell, little barriers to keep it safe from Dad's ambivalence.

She took my hand and showed it to me one morning.

"Do not touch this, Annabelle Marie. Don't let your sister touch it. Don't let Cathy touch it," she said. "I need this to grow."

When Mom went to work, she dropped Amber and me at her Baha'í friend Liz's house. Liz and her husband, Rik, lived a few blocks over from us with their four children. They lived on the other side of McGregor, the non-river side, as fancy river-side people like me tend to point out. Their street is one of the most famous in Fort Myers. It's marked by the GOD IS LOVE sign, the nine letters written in neon that glows soft green at night.

Everyone had a "God Is Love" origin story back then.

The story Liz's kids told me involved an elderly couple who had never been able to have children, but who loved each other so much, it didn't matter. One day, the wife got sick. Cancer. She died soon after the diagnosis. The husband, grief-stricken, stayed in bed for weeks. He couldn't go on without her; he'd never again know a love like hers. Late one night, something woke him. Soft light filled his windows from the yard. It was his wife. She glowed like an angel. She stood in front of the house with a sign that read GOD IS LOVE, and for the first time since losing her, the man felt whole.

He erected the sign the next day. And there it stayed, to fill the hearts of all who passed.

Or so their story went.

At the end of the "God Is Love" street, Liz ran an in-home day care and charged Mom next to nothing, Mom's favorite price, for watching us. Mom's nursing shifts ran seven a.m. to seven p.m. Amber and I were the first kids to get to Liz's those days and the last to leave.

Mom picked us up after *Wheel of Fortune*, still in her nurse's whites, still smelling of antiseptic and iodine. Mom didn't touch us at Liz's or on the two-minute car ride home. She'd push us into her bathroom, start a shower, and pile all three of us into it. I washed Amber as Mom washed me. Mom brushed our hair, twenty strokes on each side. She clocked our teeth brushing at two minutes, scraped our necks, and pinched our noses. She tucked us into our beds, leaving us with her same twelve parting words: *Good night. I love you. Sleep tight. Don't let the bedbugs bite.*

People always say how children thrive with routine, and for that month we thrived. No screaming. No storms. No *Punyeta ka, it's your goddamn turn to take the girls to school, Louis!* I knew what to expect each morning, each afternoon, each night. I didn't have to count my steps or the dots on my comforter. I could count on my mom.

As our just-the-three-of-us routine takes shape, Dad returns.

He slips back into the house as quietly as he left. I wake up one morning, and there he is, standing at the kitchen counter, sipping his Folgers from one of Mom's hospital mugs. And there Mom is, cooking eggs at the stove, as if nothing had ever been wrong.

I walk back to my room, turn around, and try the morning again.

Dad is still there, so I play along with their game and sit at the breakfast-nook table like it's just another Saturday. Dad finishes his coffee and meets Mom at the stove. He flips the strips of bacon sizzling in the frying pan. He loops his free arm around Mom's waist.

I will learn, decades later, that Dad came home the night before. He crawled back to Mom. He told her he'd realized the error of his ways, that he could not live without her. He said he'd gotten a vasectomy and spent the last few weeks recuperating at a motel on Fort Myers Beach. He was sorry for what he'd done, for how he'd raised a hand to her. He couldn't face Mom until he'd made it right, until he'd done as she asked.

Snip, snip.

Mom took him back. A month later she was pregnant.

CHAPTER 10

# The Skunk Ape and the Mountain

"Señora, por favor, qué hora es?" a woman with a long, dark ponytail asks Mom as she pushes her own daughter in the swing next to mine and Amber's at Lions Park.

It's the first time I remember someone speaking Spanish to Mom.

"Lo siento," Mom says. "Mi español no es muy bueno, pero…" she trails off, then moves one arm away from the swings and tilts it near the woman's face so she can see Mom's gold wristwatch.

"Muchas gracias, thank you," the woman says, smiling.

I watch her gather up her daughter and walk to the minivan parked next to ours.

"What was that about, Mommy?"

"She wanted to know what time it is."

"How did you know what she was saying?"

"You know how I say your Gramma is crazy?"

I nod reflexively—*sure, of course*—then kick my legs to keep my swing going.

"Well, *my grandmother* would only let us speak English or Spanish in her house, so I know a little bit of Spanish."

In this moment, I take "Spanish" to mean any language that's not English. Just as all moms are Jos, all non-English languages are Spanish. When Mom's on her late-night phone calls with her family in the Philippines, I assume that's Spanish they're speaking. When Mom presses the phone to my ear and some faraway aunt or cousin shouts, "Kamusta, Annabella!"—that's Spanish in my head.

When Mom's parents move in with us, I switch Dad's new big-screen-projection TV to Univision, thinking that will make them feel more at home. When they look confused, I click over to *The Cosby Show*, because my grandparents have even darker skin than mine, so maybe they'll identify with the Huxtables.

"Aye, Beel Coessbee! Faht Albeart!" Grandpa says, laughing. "*Hey hey hey!*"

My eyes light up. I knew I'd figure them out, eventually.

Mom's parents are here to help Mom through the pregnancy and take care of the new baby when it comes. Mom hopes they'll stay. I don't share that hope. Life is just starting to normalize for me, and then these two brown people came in and ruined the balance. Mom introduces her parents as Lola and Lolo, but I won't have it. Cathy doesn't have a lola and lolo, she has a nena and a papa. On TV they just have grandmas and grandpas. I never use "Lola" or "Lolo." I hear Mom calling her mom "Nay" (like "the end is *nigh*"), so I follow suit, as does Amber. And "Lolo"? Uh-uh. He's just Grandpa. I've never really had a grandpa.

Nay and Grandpa don't speak much English, and Mom's never taught us Spanish (or Tagalog). Mom thinks Tagalog is useless, the same way her grandmother saw it. It's something Mom can turn on and off like the garden hose, spraying words like "punyeta ka na" at us when she's mad, then slipping into her perfectly unaccented English as she gets back on the phone with her charge nurse. Tagalog will only get you by in the Philippines, and even there, just barely.

Her parents, however, have clung fiercely to their homeland ways. I see them as two oddballs cramping my movin'-on-up Jeffersons' house on the good side of town, threatening to expose my foreign roots, my un-Americanness, my non-whiteness. I don't want Cathy seeing them, so I tell her we're renovating again and move our playdates to her side of the street. I cry when Mom asks them to come to my third-grade recital, where I am one of the "seven mosquitoes biting" in our Florida rendition of "The Twelve Days of Christmas." When they don't show, I breathe a sigh of relief from under my cardboard proboscis.

Nay and Grandpa prefer to hide in the guest room. I prefer that for them, too.

Grandpa scares me. He's more apparition than man in my memory. If I am, as Gramma claims, a monkey, then Grandpa is the skunk ape, the mythical creature cloistered in the Everglades, except Grandpa skulks through our yard in tube socks and plastic jandals.

I catch glimpses of him in his bamboo hat passing by my bedroom window as he checks on the yogurt tubs of seedlings that Mom keeps in the old brick barbecue pit. I watch him crouch next to the grapefruit tree for what feels like hours, squatting deep on his haunches in the cool shade, his scrawny behind grazing the prickly tops of the St. Augustine grass.

Of Grandpa's limited English, his best is "I will cook that dog!" He wields the words against Bo, the black cocker spaniel Dad got us as part of our happily-ever-after dream-home package, along with my ten-speed bike, my parents' waterbed, and his prized big-screen television. Bo lives in the fenced-off portion of our backyard. He's become a yapping menace, barking at everything—lizards, birds, Grandpa.

"I will cook you, dog," Grandpa says, grabbing Bo by his collar one day as I scream in protest. Grandpa looks at me and smiles, showing the gleaming, too-big dentures Mom bought him. He pats Bo gently on his curly black head, then shoves him into the doghouse. I feel a moment of relief. And then dread.

Brandon Darby called me a dog-eater once. He said his family didn't eat Chinese food because everyone knows they cook the dead dogs from the shelter. I tried to explain how the Philippines is an archipelago of seven thousand islands in the Pacific Ocean, how it's not China.

"It's all the same," Brandon Darby said mid-recess. "You're all dog-eaters. You're all gross."

At the time, I rolled my eyes, to look cool and carefree while also pushing back my tears. Now, as this skunk-ape ancestor of mine strolls back into the house, I wonder: *How did Brandon Darby know?*

After dinner, Grandpa scrapes together bits of chicken gristle and two-day-old rice. He takes my hand and walks me and the food to Bo's doghouse. He sits the plate in front of him, and we watch as the dog laps it up.

"I will make it big and fat," Grandpa says, winking at me, rubbing a big fake belly with his outstretched arms, "and then—I cook it!"

I laugh, hesitantly at first, and then Grandpa doubles over and slaps his hands to his knees, cackling so hard, he has to hold his hand to his mouth to stop his dentures from tumbling out. I laugh harder, too, marveling at this odd old man, wondering what Bo would taste like. Probably chicken. Everything tastes like chicken. Even Chinese food.

If Grandpa is a tiny wisecracking yard squatter, my grandmother is his opposite.

Nay is a mountain. She looms large and silent in the background, so still that I forget she's there till she scolds me for a stinky fart or a burp that rattles the glass sliders. If she needs something, she makes *kiss-kiss* sounds to call me over, the way you'd beckon a cat. She points to the box of Teddy Grahams in my lap or my bottle of Coke. She winks and I run over to share, quietly, lest we alert Mom, who wants Nay to eat steamed fish and saltless vegetables all day.

Nay wears tentlike muumuus printed with dainty flowers. She keeps her waist-length, gray-white hair pulled tight into a bun at the nape of her neck. She is short and broad, a square of a woman. She hobbles along with one bum leg, the meat near her left shin scraped to the bone in an accident no one in Mom's family seems to know anything about. The scarred skin over the wound has gone purple. Nay lets me run my fingers over it when I share my snacks with her. It feels smooth, like shiny leather that's been pulled too tight and could at any moment crack.

Nay speaks as much English as I speak Spanish—or Tagalog. I talk to her the way I talk to the baby growing in Mom's belly. "HELLOOO THERE! HOW? ARE? YOU?" She does the same to me. It works for us. I know when she's mad and when she needs more ice for the giant travel mug of Diet Coke that she keeps at her side. She knows when I'm in trouble and yells at Mom on my behalf, telling her to leave me alone.

More often, though, Nay keeps to herself. She locks herself in the front bedroom, which gets musky with her old-lady funk after a few days. Mom drags her out, forces her to shower and change her clothes. Then Nay goes back into hibernation.

Nay loves us, I think, but she hates life in the US. Back in Manila, people needed her. In America she can hide in a room for a week and the world keeps going.

Mom's parents stay till the baby is born. A few weeks later, they hop on a plane back to their real home. In Manila they have children who depend on them to cook and make runs to the market. They have family who rely on them and a small business to run. In the US they have two mongrel grandchildren who think they speak Spanish and an asshole cocker spaniel they aren't allowed to cook.

CHAPTER 11

# The Backyard

When we find out the baby will be a boy, everything changes.

Dad shows up with flowers and a card and a gold necklace with a heart-shaped pendant outlined in diamonds. Mom loves diamonds. He cleans our rooms. He does our laundry. He moves his new Laser 128 computer out of the office-turned-nursery and into my new room, the one at the far end of the house that I get all to myself, the one that makes me cool in Cathy's eyes, even cooler now that I have a computer and a small monitor that doubles as a TV.

Dad even starts cooking again, grilling thick steaks and serving them with big, fluffy baked potatoes dripping with butter, churning out heaping stacks of pancakes in the mornings and gooey grilled-cheese sandwiches with a buttery crunch for lunch.

Mom cooks to feed people. Dad cooks because he loves food. On Fridays, he grabs the newspaper out of the driveway, hands me the comics, then flips to the restaurant review on the last page of the features section. Once he finds it, I set *Garfield* and *Peanuts* aside and give Dad my full attention. He clears his throat and snaps the pages of newsprint so they're stiff in his hands.

"Let's see where Jean Le Boeuf is taking us this week," he tells me before launching into a review of a new Italian restaurant downtown or a high-end seafood place in Old Naples. I love these Friday mornings with Monsieur Le Boeuf, as Dad calls the local critic. I don't yet understand that Jean Le Boeuf is a pen name. I think he's a fancy French guy with fancy-French-guy tastes. Like I do with our computer games, I hang on every word my father reads. Not because I care about sun-dried-tomato ravioli, but because for these few Friday minutes I have my dad's attention.

Dad always wanted a boy. He dressed me in dungarees and bought me a black-and-red BMX bike for my fifth birthday. He tried to do the same to Amber, but she didn't tolerate it like I did. When they found out this accidental third pregnancy would have a penis, it's like Dad was born anew. One of the only memories I have of my parents being affectionate is of Dad standing behind Mom in the kitchen when she was nine months pregnant, his arms wrapped around her beach-ball belly as he kissed her cheek. Amber and I gagged from the breakfast nook, then went back to our bowls of Cheerios.

Dad named me, Mom named Amber, so I beg for naming rights on this new baby. I want Andrew. It sounds preppy and all-American, like a quarterback with a freckled nose and pearly white teeth. The Keatons on *Family Ties* had an Andrew, why can't we?

Amber likes Andrew. Mom likes Andrew. Dad seems aloof on the subject. Then they disappear one night, leaving Amber and me with Nay and Grandpa.

Dad reappears later the next day to grab a few things to take back to the hospital. He breaks the news. We have a new baby.

Arthur.

"*Arthur?!*"

I can't hide my disgust.

"It was my turn to choose," Dad says, grabbing Mom's favorite pillow and a handful of her underwear as he hurries through the house.

"But Arthur?"

He stops in the small alcove outside the olive-green bathroom. He places a hand on the hallway wall and leans down to lock eyes with me.

"There are a million Andrews. Anyone can be an Andrew. Your brother is an Arthur."

He turns and grabs his keys off the kitchen counter. He nods at the door and his waiting car, where Amber has already buckled herself into the back seat. "Going crazy, wanna come?"

Mom has had gestational diabetes with Arthur, a precursor of things to come for her. He is a massive baby, close to ten pounds. The first time I lay eyes on him, he's in an incubator bathed in blue light. A wee sleep mask is strapped to his tiny head to protect his eyes. He is jaundiced, which has turned the plump rolls of his wiggly thighs and arms a sickly yellow like they've been stained with sweet mango juice.

In the hospital, we take turns feeding him bottles of sugar water to keep his glucose levels up. Amber and I fight over who goes first. Dad tolerates each of us for a few seconds, then grabs the hefty bundle of blankets back into his arms, where Arthur looks most comfortable.

The baby comes home a few days later. I've never seen our dad be more of a dad. He changes diapers, swipes on Desitin, and makes bottles that he tests on the skin of his inner arm. He is the best swaddler in the house, placing a thin blanket across the soft brown carpet of our family-room floor, folding down the top corner, then *whip-whop-whoop*, transforming Arthur from crying baby to sleepy burrito like magic. Dad falls asleep in Arthur's room most nights, rocking the swaddled baby in his hairy arms as I watch crouched in the doorway, seething with jealousy.


"When's the last time you fed the dog?"

Mom smells like sweat and sun as she pulls off her work gloves and pours more ice and water into the travel mug Nay left behind. I'm watching my cartoons on the big screen in an old *Rainbow Brite* nightshirt. Amber is on her seventy-third viewing of *The Land Before Time* in Nay and Grandpa's old bedroom, where Dad wired a VCR to the walnut-encased Zenith. Arthur's down for his midmorning nap.

Dad's been gone for a few days. Another late-night fight, another wordless departure. I haven't thought much about Bo. Since Nay and Grandpa went back to the Philippines, he's gone back to being Dad's dog. Dad feeds him and plays with him. I watch him from my sliding glass door. He sometimes sneaks a cigarette in the process, flinging his Marlboro butts over the fence into Dr. Johnson's bushes, where Mom won't find them.

Bo doesn't bark much anymore. The dog finally yapped at the wrong guy. A foreman building our new pool cage clunked Bo on his curly black head with a hammer, knocking the dog out cold. Dad wanted to sue. Mom said the dog had it coming. Bo lived, but he's not quite the same. He sits in his doghouse and growls at nothing. He lies in the grass in the dappled shade of our grapefruit tree for hours on end, soaking up shards of sun.

"Feed the dog, Annabelle Marie," Mom says. "That poor thing doesn't even know where it is anymore."

I wait for a commercial break, then slip into Grandpa's old jandals and wander through Mom's tomato trellises to get to the far screen door of the pool cage. I click it open and survey the backyard. I see Bo in his usual spot, splayed out under the grapefruit tree. The sky's cloudy and the air is thick as butter, the kind of swampy heat that makes seconds feel like minutes and hours. We keep Bo's food in a container near the pool pump. Walking toward it, I feel bites on my ankles. I assume they're mosquitoes. I slap at them, but the burning continues. I look down and my calves are covered in fleas.

I stumble backward, away from the dog food and the pool pump and closer to Bo. I swipe at my legs with my hands. The fleas migrate to my arms. I feel them on my chest and down my nightshirt. I keep stumbling until my foot catches on something furry and stiff. I fall backward across the body of our dead dog. My screams feel like they're trapped in the soggy air. Flies join the fleas all around me. Their buzzing fills my ears, blunting the sound of my own shrieks. I slip out of one jandal as I run back to the screen door, one shoe on, one shoe off, like Cinderella. I leap in the pool, hoping it will dislodge the fleas, hoping it will stop the buzzing, hoping it will cleanse me. I sit under water for several seconds, looking up at the wave-blurred sun and bright sky overhead, thinking that when I emerge, Mom or Dad will be there to grab me up and whisk me to safety.

I come up for air, and I'm all alone.

Dad comes back that evening. I don't know how Mom found him. I just know he's here. Amber and I watch him from the family room as he picks Bo up from the grass under the grapefruit tree. His body leaves a dog-shaped imprint in the blades. I wonder how long it will stay there. I wonder how long Bo's been dead.

Amber cries when she learns what happened. Arthur rolls around on his play mat, unfazed. As my shock wears off, I cry, too. I've failed Bo. I've forgotten about him. He is dead because of me.

Dad digs a hole in the far corner of the backyard. He eases Bo's body into it. He comes back in and scoops up Amber in one arm and Arthur in the other. He tells me to come along. He walks us to the grave, asks if we want to say anything, to pay our "final respects." Arthur giggles and plays with Dad's graying hair. Amber buries her head in Dad's shoulder, refusing to look anywhere near the burial plot. I scratch mindlessly at the fleabites covering my arms and chest. Dad looks at me.

"Annabelle Marie, you got anything to say?"

This feels like a trial. I cry again. I'm guilty.

"I love you, Bo," I manage through wet sniffles. I lean against Dad's leg to bolster myself.

"Anything else?" he says, his voice cool and even.

"I'm...I'm sorry is all."

\* \* \*

81

Mom rubs pink calamine across my legs and arms. She waits for it to dry before pulling my covers up and tucking me into bed. She kisses my forehead and clicks on my starfish night-light. I click it back off when she leaves, so I can have a better view.

Out my sliding glass door, I see Dad in the last of the day's twilight, shoveling dirt into Bo's grave. I hear him pat the ground back into place, a hollow thud that reverberates all the way to my bedroom, then watch him light a cigarette as the final wisps of dusk fade to black.

I see its red-orange ember glow bright and then fade, glow bright and then fade, like a firefly speaking in bug code. Dad flicks the butt over Dr. Johnson's fence. The yard goes dark. Once again, I feel alone.

CHAPTER 12

# Unleashed

It's just us now. Tometich, party of five. In the grand scheme of my life, this five-of-us moment is a blink. It is a heartbeat—*whump whump*—the last somewhat healthy one to pound in my chest for years.

When it's just the five of us, there is no buffer. Mom's burgeoning front-yard mango sapling, which is now as tall as I am, has those white rings made of concrete and shells to shield it.

We have nothing.

With our houseguests gone, with even the dog gone, Mom and Dad's fights have space to grow. It's like a dam has burst and all the energy that went into caring for others now comes spilling forth, raw, angry, and unfiltered, drenching everything.

"Why don't you go live with her, then? Your little whore!"

It's late at night, as it always is. Amber and Arthur are asleep. I listen to my parents' back-and-forth while staring out my sliding glass door to the pool and the alligator-free yard of this happily-ever-after house. The *whore* word, which I still think of as the *H* word, catches my attention. It's what Gramma called Mom. I've never heard Mom use it.

"You told me you were getting a freaking vasectomy! When really you were living with that woman, having her suck your dick every night, I'm sure. That does not count as a goddamn vasectomy, you asshole!"

I look at Bo's doghouse and wish he were still in it.

"I'm here now, aren't I?" I hear my father say. "I'm trying now. I really am."

"Oh. You are *trying*?" Mom's voice has a maniacal tone. I can imagine her huffing, scanning the room for something she can weaponize.

"THIS IS *TRYING*, LOUIS? No. This is the bare freaking minimum. This is being a goddamn father. This isn't trying."

She mocks him, drawing the last word out for several seconds. I hear Dad get up. I hear his footsteps on the brown kitchen tiles. I hear Mom tackle him. I hear knees and arms pound to the floor. I hear their words turn to grunts, slaps, and punches; the surprisingly sharp sounds of flesh beating flesh.

Then a crash. I hear the dinette table in the breakfast nook flip over. I hear plates shatter across the floor. I can smell our dinner again, chicken and soy sauce and that faintly sweet scent of steamed rice.

"Stop it, goddamn it," Dad grunts, his breaths heavy like when he used to play tennis.

I hear their bodies slam against the wall of Amber's room. I wonder if it wakes my sister up. I wonder if she's listening like I'm listening. I want to go in there and crawl into bed with her, to tell her a story so we can pretend everything's fine, the way I used to when we shared a room. But it's too risky. I can barely stand listening to this. I don't want to see it with my eyes.

The brawling shifts to the dining room, where I hear more plates crash as Dad screams in futile protest. These shatters are finer than the previous. They're the sound of my parents' wedding china being hurled across the kitchen and smashing against the walls.

"Jesus Christ, Jo, just fucking stop!"

I crawl to my slider door and lean my head against its cool tempered glass. I catch a glimpse of something in the dining room, some enraged version of my mother—a Hulk, a Mr. Hyde. I watch from across the pool as this Mom fishes each teacup from the china cabinet, each saucer, each butter dish and gravy boat. I see them fly. I hear their shards and slivers splatter across the kitchen tiles like rain.

When Mom gets tired of throwing things at Dad, she resorts to simply smashing them against the dining room table, leaving dull dings in its glossy top. Then comes a series of long whining crashes, as Mom sweeps an arm along each shelf of the china cabinet, knocking loose any figurines and photo frames left behind. The bottle of wine the Allards gave us as a housewarming gift becomes an inky splotch on the brown carpet.

I hear the garage door rumble open. I hear Dad's Sable back out. I hear Mom grab the broom and dustpan from the pantry as she turns back into Bruce Banner.

I close my blinds and climb back into bed, hopeful this storm has passed.


In Mrs. Clark's fourth-grade class, I'm one of five girls and the only student whose skin color is darker than a Crayola apricot.

Dad's been gone a couple days now, but no longer than he's been gone before. It's early October, almost exactly a month after my ninth birthday. Nine, my favorite number. We have a social studies project due. I have memorized Abraham Lincoln's Gettysburg Address. Mom made me a top hat from black felt. I plan to draw on a beard with washable marker. The night before, Mom lays Dad's lone sport coat along the dining room table. It covers the dents and scars she made a few days earlier.

I wake up, nervous for my speech. *Fourscore and seven years ago.* I mutter the words to myself in the mirror. *We are met on a great battle-field of war. We have come to dedicate a portion of that field, as a final resting place for those who gave their lives that this nation might live.*

I struggle through the middle, confusing the *whos* and *heres* and *theys*, but getting the gist of it.

*…that from these honored dead we take increased devotion to that cause for which they gave the last full measure of devotion…*

"Annabelle Marie, go get your sister up and ready," Mom says, peeking her head through my door. "I'm making breakfast."

Mom's not working today. She's wearing one of Nay's muumuus. Her fingers are wrapped in tape and Band-Aids. Splotchy bruises still mottle her arms.

On my way down the hall, I see Arthur in his high chair, watching the morning news on the big screen. I walk into Amber's room and jump on her bed. I hear the phone ring, two times, then three. Nobody calls at this hour. Mom picks up just before the answering machine clicks.

"Hello?"

I tune her out and straddle Amber. I shake my sister awake and yell at her to get dressed.

"Mom's making breakfast, come on, you've got to go soon."

Amber's in kindergarten. Like me, she also missed the cutoff date for Lee County public schools, so Mom enrolled her in the same Baptist private school I once attended. Most mornings, Mom carts Amber across town as I ride my ten-speed to fourth grade. Cathy's in middle school now, so I usually ride with Ally Thatcher, who lives in the house behind ours. We sometimes catch up with Dylan Larson. His mom lets him bike to school only on sunny days, when no storms are forecast. Today's sunny. I wonder if we'll see him.

Amber has barely moved. I go to her drawers to trawl for some shorts and a half-decent T-shirt. I hear the cars passing outside her window along McGregor, just beyond our orange trees and Thomas Edison's royal palms, people off to work and school like any other Wednesday. I tug the pull-down shade on the window, so it snaps back into its roll, so the soft light of morning spills in through the wrought-iron bars that keep us safe.

Mom's still on the phone. She's oddly quiet. I smell toast burning in the kitchen. I leave the dresser to listen at Amber's door, pressing my body as close to its opening as possible, not wanting Mom to see me watching her, although I'm not sure why.

"Yes, I told the other man, this is Josefina Tometich."

Mom sounds like she's disputing a charge on her credit card. Her voice is professional and businesslike. Whoever's on the line isn't a friend or family.

"Louis is my husband, yes. He is not here right now. Who is this?"

Amber stirs and wakes, launching from zero to sixty as only five-year-olds can. She runs circles over and around the bed, ignoring the clothes I've set out for her, running up, then down, then around, then over again.

"Stop it!" I whisper-scream the words, grabbing her by her arms and holding her in place. My words come out mean. Usually she ignores me. Today she, too, can tell something's different.

"No, you're mistaken. No one is dead," Mom says.

Her voice falters on that last word. As it cracks, I freeze.

"No no no no no no no."

Mom sounds broken.

"He cannot be DEAD. He was just here."

Amber stops, her arms still gripped by my hands, as Mom shatters into slivers of porcelain that splatter to the family room floor.

Amber looks at me. She grabs the clothes I've set out and starts getting dressed, like if she does as she was told, maybe that will fix whatever this is. I see fear in her eyes. I imagine if I look in the mirror, mine will be the same.

My body goes hot and numb. I slide down the wall onto the carpet, hugging my knees to my chest like a cannonball. Arthur's wails join Mom's, just as sharp, yet just as distant. It's like I'm back in the pool after finding Bo's stiff dog body in the yard, like I'm listening to this from deep under water, watching it through blurred waves. All I can feel is the hollow thudding of my heart. I hope for someone to find me, to pull my head up so I can breathe again.

I feel the door push open and see Mom's bare feet cross the threshold. She holds Arthur in her arms as she joins me on the carpet. Amber is there, too, all of us at the bottom of this pool, all of us breathless, fighting for air.

We sit for hours or maybe seconds, caught in this moment where sadness is all that exists. Days or maybe minutes later, our four cries become three. Mom kneels and then stands. She brushes herself off and pulls each of us up.

## CHAPTER 13

# Wite-Out

The bottles of Wite-Out sit at the top of our tallest bookcase. Next to Mom's good scissors and Dad's Bic lighters. On a lower shelf sits our typewriter. When Mom has to type things—Dad's résumés, her requests for nursing promotions that go unheeded—she pulls a bottle from the box and places it on the breakfast table next to our Smith Corona Courier with its ivory body and brown keys.

Mom types slowly. Every few clacks, she cusses at herself under her breath in Tagalog, "Punyeta ka, Jo," twists open a bottle of Wite-Out, and fixes whatever error she's made.

When she's done and lifts her paper to the light, I can see the shadows of her mistakes, the dabs of correction fluid hiding the $a$'s that should have been $s$'s, and the $r$'s that should have been $e$'s.

Mom folds her letters into white envelopes, recaps the Wite-Out bottle, and returns it to the top of the bookcase.

I think the bottles are simply white paint. In December 1988, ten months before that call from the sheriff's office, I build a step stool of boxes atop a dinette chair and scale it to get to the Wite-Out. I take a bottle and use it to dabble snow on the branches of a construction-paper Christmas tree. When Mom catches me, she grabs the Wite-Out from my hands and smacks the tops of my legs with her house shoe.

"This is not a toy," she says. "This is only for adults. Do you under-stand me, Annabelle Marie?"

I don't. But I nod like I do. I take my punishment to mean Wite-Out isn't for painting. It's only for mistakes. Only for erasing things.

The days leading up to my father's funeral are a blur. I spend many of them at Cathy's house, where her mom and stepdad speak to me in whis-pers—*"Honey, if you need anything, anything at all"*—as we retreat to the privacy of her bedroom. Cathy treats me like I'm normal. She doesn't ask how Dad died or what happened or how I feel about it. She knows. Her mom told her. And my mom told her.

Mom is not the kind to keep secrets. Unlike her typos, she feels no need to hide this.

When Mom tells us the details of Dad's death, Amber and I are sitting at the dinette table in the breakfast nook, and nine-month-old Arthur is in his high chair, caring mostly about his Cheerios. Mom's face is puffy, tight, red. That's how it always is now.

The four of us have slept together in Mom's bedroom each night for the past week since the phone call. She ferries us in there after she's done sort-ing funeral-home brochures and packing up the casseroles her Baha'í and nursing friends bring to feed us. She carries Arthur in first, then Amber. She wakes me up and leads me in by my hand. I follow half asleep, then burrow into the soft waves of the waterbed as Mom stands over us, rubbing our backs, one by one, then running her fingers through our dark heads of hair.

I wake up when she starts crying, which she always does. She sits in Arthur's rocking chair and lets herself go each night, soft cries at first, then sobs that rack her body. If I move, she stops. She comes back to the bed and rubs my back till she thinks I'm asleep again. Then she breaks down even harder and crumples into the rocker. I learn not to move, not to shift, to be utterly still, to listen till Mom's cries are replaced by the rhythmic breathing of sleep.

To say Mom sleeps is generous. She nods off now and then but mostly keeps a hawklike watch over us to make sure we're still breathing, still alive.

Her puffy-red face is just her face now. But today, as we sit around the breakfast table, it looks different. Serious. Nervous. Mom sits, too. She pours more cereal for Arthur, mutes *Muppet Babies* on TV, then turns her attention to us girls.

"I want you to know how your daddy died."

She sounds like a schoolteacher about to tell us where babies come from. I want to run, but I worry that will make things worse, harder somehow. In my head Dad died in an accident. That's what everyone's been saying, how it was "such a tragic accident." I assume it was a car accident. Lots of people die in car accidents.

That's normal.

"Your father did not like drinking, because he was a Baha'í, and you know Baha'ís don't drink alcohol," Mom starts, tapping her right foot against the brown carpet in rapid thuds, somehow syncing them with the rapid thuds of the heart beating inside my brown chest.

I nod, slowly, no idea where this could be going.

"Well, your father used to, he would sometimes get high, or get drunk, in other ways."

I look at Amber, who's fidgeting with her yogurt lid. She doesn't seem to understand either.

"Your daddy, he was very sad that night. He thought we were going to get divorced, and he thought he would never see you guys again."

He was right on the second part, I think, as Mom's cheeks go bright red, as her stream of tears becomes a deluge, leaving her puffy-red face wet and shiny, too.

"He wanted to get drunk, I think. He wanted to be numb."

I think about my limbs and lips, my face and entire body and how they went numb listening to that call before the school day that never came. Before my mind can drift any further, Mom pulls me back.

"Your daddy painted a plastic baggie with Wite-Out," Mom says, pushing the words out quickly before she loses her courage. "He was trying to get high because he didn't want to drink alcohol, and so he placed the baggie over his head, but he fell asleep and he suffocated. He couldn't get enough oxygen, enough air. The bag prevented him from breathing."

She looks at Arthur, at Amber, at me.

"And he died."

I stare off past the muted big-screen TV. I think of sandwich bags and grocery bags and the bags that wrap new shoes. I think about the warnings—*Keep away from small children; danger of suffocation* (suff-oh-cay-shun, four syllables). I remember how Mom called Dad a child, said he never grew up. I wonder why she never warned him about the dangers of plastic bags, or if she did and he didn't listen. We kids never listen.

I wonder if she warned him about Wite-Out. I think of my Christmas tree with its Wite-Out snow. How Wite-Out isn't for painting, it's for erasing mistakes. I think of all the times Mom said Dad couldn't do anything right. The time Amber ate all the Tylenol and vomited pink across the floor. The time I seared my hand on the stove. The time we found Amber at the bottom of the pool because Dad was flipping burgers on the grill and not paying enough attention to his goddamn children. The time Mom said she didn't want any more kids. The time she showed me the pregnancy test and told me we were having a baby, her face almost as wet and red as it is now.

Things start clicking in my head. If one parent had to be erased, of course it should be Dad. Everything he did was a mistake.

I think I should be sad at this development, this knowledge of precisely how our father left the earth. I wait for tears, but none come. Instead, I feel something else, something new, something I've seen but never felt.

My body goes hot; my hands and head and ears first, then my face, chest, belly. I'm burning. Every cell is ablaze. I want to flip the breakfast table. I want to smash things. I want to yell all the words I've heard and never repeated—*asshole, son of a bitch, punyeta ka na!*—at the top of my lungs.

Why can't anything we do *just be normal?*

*We can't look normal. We can't church normal. We don't eat normal foods or have normal fights. And now. Now we can't even die normal.* I say none of this. Instead, I shove away from the brown table, march down the brown hall, and slam my brown door.

When the house goes quiet, I tiptoe to the kitchen. I slip open the freezer and scoop a handful of M&Ms from Dad's stash, then a second, realizing he will no longer care if I eat them. I lean against the counter, feeling the colorful shells crackle between my teeth and melt into brown on my tongue.

There are papers spread out next to the cutting board, stamped and signed papers. They list the date and location of Dad's death: October 4, 1989; a Holiday Inn motel room on Fort Myers Beach. The cause of death is at the bottom: asphyxiation. As-fix-ee-ay-shun, five syllables. I've always hated the number 5.

Beneath "asphyxiation," the certificate reads: "Inhalation of toxic chemicals ('LIQUID PAPER') and occlusion of nose and mouth by plastic bag." A few spots down, in a box titled "Probable Manner of Death" it says "undetermined," a diagnosis that still haunts us.

My sister, the Amber of today, thinks our father committed suicide, that he strapped that baggie over his face with the intent of drifting off into an otherworldly abyss where Mom's rage and three needy kids could never again find him.

My brother and I side with Mom. We think it was an accident. We think he was trying to get high and went too far.

The three of us agree on one thing: Our father was trying to erase his mistakes. He thought the Wite-Out would cover them, but when you hold the pages of his life up to the light, they're still there. The *a*'s that should have been *s*'s, the nights with whomever that should have been spent at home. I've come to accept these mistakes. I've learned to see them for what they are: typos, errors that can't be erased but could have been survived.

The me of October 1989 cannot see this future, cannot fathom such blithe acceptance of something so incredibly weird.

The me of October 1989 takes the bag of M&Ms from the freezer to my bedroom, flips on Dad's computer and pushes the floppy disc for Carmen Sandiego into the slot on the side. As I hunt international criminals, I decide I will create my own normal. I will not tell anyone this ridiculous Wite-Out-plastic-baggie nonsense. My family does not cook dogs, and it does not get high on correction fluid and then suffocate to death in a shithole motel on Fort Myers Beach. I will stick with the accident story. Could happen to anyone. Totally normal.

Dad wasn't perfect, but he was undeniably cool. He wore the cool Magnum P.I. clothes and had the cool computer with the cool games. Dad bought the big-screen TV and my ten-speed bike and Bo, our short-lived dog. Dad had the vinyl collection. Dad played the guitar. Dad was white.

Now what did we have?

Mom. A brown woman—what did Gramma always call her? *a Chink-Mongoloid bitch*—whom people always spoke to in Spanish, who fried her stinky fish till the house smelled like a bait bucket, whose idea of fun was scrubbing baseboards and pulling weeds in the yard.

If I think about this for too long, I freak out. Our one all-American parent is dead. Our only white family member is gone, whited out.

We're all brown now.

\* \* \*

In the nights between Dad's death and the funeral, Mom lights candles and leaves them by the slider window atop the kitchen sink overlooking the pool. She calls this a novena, no-vee-nuh, three syllables.

"The candles will guide your daddy's spirit," she says, "to somewhere he can find peace."

When Mom walks away, I blow out the candles, hoping to keep some part of my father. I close the slider and lock it tight.

"I wonder if you'll get to ride in a limo," Cathy says as she helps me into the navy-striped dress Mom and I have decided is just mournful enough for this occasion.

I perk up for a second. "That would be cool," I say.

"That would be cool," she answers.

It's a shockingly beautiful day, bright with sun, the air faintly crisp as it can start to be in mid-October. Amber's in a purple dress with her favorite cowboy boots, the ones that match—that *matched*—Dad's. Arthur sports a baby-size white button-down and poofy plaid shorts, like he's bound for infant prep school. Mom clips a bib around his neck, hoping to spare the outfit from his relentless drool. She wears a silky forest-green top with a long matching skirt. The diamond-heart pendant Dad gave her when he learned the baby would be a boy catches and scatters the sunlight from its spot around her neck. She has on her wedding ring, something I've not seen her wear in ages.

It's not a limo we ride in but a black four-door Buick. I wonder if that's normal. I convince myself it's not, that Mom wouldn't pay the extra money for the limo like everyone else does. Arthur rides on Mom's lap. That's illegal, I think, but I guess they bend the rules in situations like ours. Amber sits in the middle. I sit on the far passenger side, resting my head against the tinted window, watching the usual McGregor Boulevard sights creep past as our processional makes its way to the cemetery: the Tanglewood wall, the Argyle's entrance, the neon GOD IS LOVE sign at the end of Liz's street. I turn my head to study it. The neon is dark and lifeless at this late-morning hour. I think about the glowing angelic wife. I think about Dad.

It's a closed-casket funeral. Mom says that was Dad's wish. I never see his body. I don't remember anyone asking if I wanted to, though Mom says she did. She says I adamantly opposed the offer. Graveside, Mom sits front and center with us girls at her sides. Arthur bounces from Mom's lap over Amber and into Liz's as things proceed, his bib and prep-school top soaked through with slobber. I see Gramma being pushed in a wheelchair to a spot near our side. I try to look at her, but I can't see her face, only the silver footrests of her chair filled with her white-leather orthotic shoes. I give up and stare straight ahead at the unopened coffin, at the way the light glides across a spray of white carnations covering its lid.

The eulogies are short. Rik, Liz's husband, reads some Baha'i prayers. A man in a black suit coat whom I've never met says a few words: a life cut short, a loving father, a dedicated husband, a man of faith. I wonder if this is normal, strangers telling lies about your life as your body starts to decay in a giant piece of Tupperware.

I remember the song Dad and I loved to sing, the one Mom called mor-bid, two syllables, about the worms crawling in and the worms crawling out.

*Don't ever laugh as a hearse goes by; For you may be the next to die; They wrap you up in a big white sheet; From your head down to your feet; They put you in a big black box; And cover you up with dirt and rocks.*

I remember what Dad said that day picking mangoes, how he wanted to be buried in a big cushy coffin. I wonder what it's like in there, if it really is just one long, lovely nap.

The stranger's words sweep over and around me like currents in the Caloosahatchee. I feel them wash past. They do not move me.

I stare at the crack in the middle of the casket, at the flowers in the late-morning sun. I imagine rising from my chair unnoticed, wading against the tide of words. I imagine peeling up the casket's lid, as these people keep speaking and sniffling and staring at the grass under their feet. I hear the coffin's seal break, like the quick hiss of Mom's leftover containers. I crawl in next to Dad. It's cool, dark. He wraps an arm around me and kisses the top of my head, his eyes still closed and sleepy. He whispers, says it's quiet where we're going, that I can nap, too. I've always fought napping, but now it sounds wonderful. I'm so tired. I close my eyes and wrap my arms around my father. I listen to the dirt and rocks as they tumble down, tucking us in.

# PART II

# The Roots

CHAPTER 14

# Elementary

It's one of the first brisk mornings of the fall, cold enough for Mom to make me wear a sweater to school, the South Florida equivalent of a snow parka. I whine as I shrug into it, as it suffocates my usually bare arms, clinging in all the wrong places.

"I'm not even riding my bike, Mom. I'm not going to get cold in the car."

Dad's been dead for two and a half weeks, long enough, I guess, for life to return to normal. At least for me. Today is my first day back at school, and Mom's driving. She has un-enrolled Amber from the Baptist kindergarten across the river. She's on sabbatical from the hospital. She has plenty of time to chauffeur me to school in person.

She buckles Arthur into his car seat, careful not to pinch his slobbery belly in the process. She straps Amber into a booster and lets me sit in the front, in her old spot. We're in Dad's gray Mercury Sable. Mom sold the Toyota Van to a Baha'í friend. We're a family of four now. Families of four don't need vans.

"Just keep it on until you get to your classroom, Annabelle Marie, please."

I roll my eyes. My one tiny act of defiance. I know I'll wear the sweater. I know I'll do as Mom says.

As we inch ever closer to my school, my heart rate picks up. We merge with the traffic in the parent drop-off line, and I can't feel my face. If Arthur is crying or Amber is singing, I do not sense it. I see nothing but the happy, smiling teachers and students going about their Mondays as usual. I hear and feel nothing but the rapid-fire explosions of my heart as it bursts, then somehow re-forms, twenty times each second behind the ribs of my chest.

"Annabelle, Annabelle Marie, are you listening?"

Mom's voice registers from somewhere far away, like she's locked in a room down the hall, whispering important instructions through a heavy door.

"If you can't do it, just go to the principal's office. They know to call me. I will come get you."

I nod, vaguely remembering our plan. The Sable crawls closer to the covered part of the sidewalk, the front entry. A teacher's hand reaches out. It latches onto the handle on the other side of my door in slow motion. I feel the seal break. I feel the brisk morning air rush in. I swing my legs out, wondering if they'll hold me up. When they do, I huff a sigh of relief. I jam my hands into the pockets of my sweater, thankful for its warmth, realizing Mom was right. I look back to thank her, to wave goodbye, but the teacher has already flung the door shut. Our car's still there, but from my vantage point, I can't see into it. My heart explodes again. I hope for numbness but instead get hot tears pouring down my cheeks.

"Oh, sweetheart."

I feel an arm around me, soft and delicate. It's my third-grade teacher from last year, Mrs. Brunick. She pulls me to her and wraps me in a velvety hug, pressing one hand on the spot on my head that Dad used to always kiss. I think she's magic. I imagine her glowing like that old man's angel wife. "God Is Love." She holds me for what feels like infinity, as my tears continue to pour, as I try my nine-year-old best to silence them, to keep my body upright and unmelted. We stand outside the school's automatic sliders for what feels like the entirety of the school day. I become convinced, when I let her go, that the cars will have lined up again and gaggles of kids will swarm us, ready to go home.

When I finally ease away, the drop-off area is empty, but the morning bell hasn't yet rung. Mrs. Brunick takes my face in her hands. She uses her gray cardigan to blot the last of this set of tears. She holds it over my nose and tells me to blow.

I giggle. "Ewwww."

She laughs, too. "You're right. I'll find you a tissue."

Mrs. Brunick ducks into the main office, returning with a box of Kleenex. I flick a few tissues from the opening and tuck them in my sweater pockets.

"Take the whole thing," she says in a sweet Southern twang, pushing the box gently into my arms.

"You know, honey, I lost my daddy not that long ago. It still feels like yesterday. I need a box of tissues sometimes, too."

The rest of my first day back is a blur, save for these twenty minutes. This new morning drop-off routine will repeat itself the next day and the one after: Mrs. Brunick meeting me at the Sable, wrapping me in the warmest hug imaginable, sending me off to class. By the third or fourth week, we'll be down to a quick touch-and-go hug. Then a high five. Then a knowing look, a wink, a nod.

Eventually I'll ride my bike again, at least for a little while.

Eventually I'll see Mrs. Brunick again, eight-some years from now, when she welcomes me into her home one night for dinner with her family. A decade after that, she'll clutch a tissue in her hand and dry tears from her cheeks, happy ones, as she watches me walk down the aisle to marry her son.

CHAPTER 15

# Kendall

H ave you seen the aller-gators yet? What if we run over one? What if they bite us?"

The questions pour from Amber's mouth, one after another, all of them gator-related. They mix with Mom's favorite easy-listening channel, which we are quickly losing with each passing mile. The dulcet tones of Air Supply crackle and break, giving way to brassy mariachi trumpets and ranchera guitars.

"Do aller-gators eat kids? Do aller-gators eat birds? Can the aller-gators bite our tires and pop them?"

"Amberee," Mom says, "why don't you do your coloring for your Tita Perla?"

I pass Amber the crayon box, but she's not interested. She turns away to suck her thumb and look out the window, our five-year-old aller-gator patrol.

To get from Fort Myers to Miami in late fall 1989, you took the Tamiami Trail, the original Alligator Alley, a two-lane sliver of highway that stretches like a taut thread across the vast expanse of the Everglades.

In a four-door Mercury with three kids under ten, it's a heck of a ride.

I'm Mom's right hand. I pass out snacks and find stray toys and tamp down Arthur's waves of saliva with the ramshackle collection of napkins Mom stores in the glove compartment, gleaned from the hospital cafeteria and every fast-food restaurant we've ever visited. A cooler sits at Arthur's feet, filled with cans of soda and bags of frozen mangoes, the latter a welcome-to-America present for our Tita Perla, Mom's little sister. The icy golden-orange slivers are left over from our summer trip to the orchard on Pine Island, the last one we ever made with Dad. Mom's tree is not bearing fruit yet. It's too young, she says. It's a kid still, like us.

I wonder what Miami will be like. Our road trips prior to this one have always ventured north—to Tampa, Orlando, Cape Canaveral, and the many KOAs of the eastern seaboard until we hit Dad's birthplace on Cape Cod. All I know of Miami is from watching *Miami Vice* with Dad; detectives Crockett and Tubbs racing between beachfront high-rises in Ferraris. I imagine emerging from Alligator Alley into a turquoise sea of speedboats, men in white blazers, women in tube tops and roller skates, flamboyances of flamingos crossing the roads.

My idea of Tita Perla is even less clear. It's hard to believe Mom has a little sister, that she has siblings who exist beyond the wires of our telephone. I imagine some poor skin-and-bones woman wearing tattered, thrift-store hand-me-downs, like the emaciated kids on the UNICEF commercials. I imagine her with Grandpa's same plastic jandals on her feet, with odd, unknown injuries about her body, like the purple gash on Nay's leg. I doubt she'll speak English. I wonder if we'll watch *The Cosby Show* later tonight. I wonder if she'll like it as much as they did.

Tita Perla is the second youngest of Mom's six siblings. She's only fourteen years older than me. In spring 1989, she graduated from Pamantasan ng Lungsod ng Maynila, or PLM, the Philippines' only government-funded university, where high-achieving students get to attend for free. PLM is Mom's alma mater. Like Mom, Tita Perla also studied nursing and also followed the health-care pipeline to the US.

Tita Perla tried to get a job at Mom's hospital in Fort Myers. But the closest opening she could find for a critical-care nurse was in Miami, in Kendall, technically, a town south of the Ferraris and flamingos of Miami Beach. Her plane landed a couple weeks after Dad died. Tita Perla will tell me this is a coincidence. Mom calls it divine intervention.

Mom has spent the last few weekends getting Tita Perla settled, leaving Amber and Arthur with Liz, and me with Cathy, so she can help our aunt find an apartment, get her driver's license, and buy a car and a fifty-pound sack of rice. The kinds of things big sisters do, I guess. Mom comes home and tells us Tita Perla stories over Sunday dinners of sinigang that no child but Arthur enjoys.

*Your Tita Perla picked the most expensive apartment with the pool! She does not need a freaking pool. She needs to work. Already she thinks she's an American.*

*Your Tita Perla almost ran over some poor old man! Ay nako, she is a horrible driver!*

*Your Tita Perla can't even cook rice! I had to buy her a rice cooker. What kind of Filipino needs a rice cooker, talaga naman!*

We've heard the Tita Perla stories. We've seen how they've changed our mother from a walking pool of tears to this new person, this new branch of Mom that's growing before our very eyes. But we have not met the Tita Perla person.

Until today.

As we merge off the Alley and into the spaghetti-loop overpasses that make up Miami, I lean into Amber for a better look. I wait for the high-rises, the speedboats; instead, I see factories and strip malls and stucco houses with iron bars over their windows, like the ones covering ours.

We meet Tita Perla at the Miami MetroZoo. She's standing at the entrance as we approach, in puffy paper-bag shorts and a Disney World T-shirt. A neon-pink visor circles her dark, bobbed hair, its flimsy brim held in place by purple corkscrew lacing that reminds me of Cathy's phone cord. She wears a black leather fanny pack, red lipstick, and peach blush on her cheeks. When she pulls down her Jackie O sunglasses to greet us, I see emerald-green eyeshadow shading her lids.

"Ate! Ate! Ate!" she screams, running in high step toward Mom with outstretched arms, the words coming out, "Ah-tay! Ah-tay! Ah-tay!" louder and louder.

*I knew she didn't speak English.*

Their hug is brief, yet still stupefying. Mom does not hug. Not like this. Hugs are for saying sorry. Hugs are for when she loses her temper and smacks me too hard. They're for when she and Dad have torn the house apart in some fight or another and Mom needs my shoulder for a second. Hugs aren't greetings. What has Miami done to my mother?

They speak in high-speed Tagalog, which I still think is Spanish, as the three of us kids hide in the bars of shade cast by a row of palm trees. I push Arthur's stroller back and forth, in and out of the shaded lines, as Amber plays balance beam along a garden curb. Tita Perla grabs Mom's arm and looks in our direction. Her voice gets soft, gooey like honey. It's the same way Mom and Dad talked about Gramma when she lived with us and shit in her bedroom; like we kids are damaged goods.

Tita Perla walks over to our bars of shade. She slips in with no resistance. She reaches into her fanny pack and hands Amber and Arthur Tootsie Pops. I roll my eyes. *Little kids are so easily bought.* She turns to me and digs deeper into this wonder satchel. She pulls out a CoverGirl compact in green plastic made to look like jade. She slides it into my hand, blocking Mom's view of it with her body. I cradle it gingerly, like it might shatter or burst forth a genie.

"Go ahead," my aunt says.

I pull a tab and up pops the clamshell lid, revealing a mirror and a disc of shimmery face powder topped by a velvety pouf. I am silent, reverent.

This. This is makeup.

"Don't tell your mommy," Tita Perla whispers, leaning down just slightly to see me face-to-face. "Ay nako, you are so beautiful, Anna-bella! And so tall!"

She places a red-polished fingernail under my chin, and my smile grows till it kisses my ears. I didn't know what to expect from this *Tita Perla* person Mom's been going on about, but I didn't expect this. Someone who already knows me so well. Someone who makes me think about normal preteen things, and who can stop me from fixating on asphyxiation, Wite-Out, death. Someone with the power to change not just Mom but our whole family. My heart beats fast in my chest—not with anxiety or worry, but with happiness.

"I know, your mommy *hates* makeup. This is our secret."

Utterly enchanted—by her English, her Z. Cavaricci shorts, her sheer brilliance—I offer little more than a slack-jawed nod. I see Mom in the distance, pushing Arthur's stroller to the ticket window as Amber follows. Tita Perla takes the compact and slips it back into the safety of her fanny pack.

"Come on," she says, taking my hand in hers. "I'll show you how to do makeup when we get back to my apartment."

My body shivers with excitement. I squeeze her hand tightly and skip along beside her. I've never been more thrilled to go to the zoo.

I stand near the door with Tita Perla, antsy for our first shopping trip together, my face shimmering with powder from the jade compact I've tucked into the acid-washed jean purse Cathy gave me as a hand-me-down.

The zoo is fun and all, but have you ever gone to an outlet mall with your fresh-off-the-boat, fresh-to-death tita who's got two American paychecks burning holes in her pockets?

Mom doesn't love this idea, but she's allowed it. She ticks through her list of worries, pretending they're factual warnings grounded in reality.

Don't lose sight of her.

Do not take her for a manicure or pedicure. All those germs, it's disgusting, and they never sanitize those tools—did you ever see an autoclave at a nail parlor, Perla? Exactly. It's a staph infection waiting to happen. That's how Cristina almost lost her toe!

Do not buy makeup with dyes from China, and since all the dyes are from China, just do not buy makeup.

No more sugary candies, Perla, look at your skin! And you're getting fat like me already!

Keep your purse across your body and hold your bags in your hands. If someone attacks you in the mall, hit them in the face with the bags, hit them in the eyes, hard as you can. Throw the bags if you have to. And scream, scream like your life depends on it, *because it does.*

Be sure to hold hands in the parking lot. Perla, keep your pepper spray in your free hand at all times out there. Have it ready.

Mom pauses. She looks at the tiny stalactites on the popcorn ceiling of my aunt's apartment, mentally making sure every box has been checked. She looks back to us, to Tita Perla specifically. She sets her hands square on her sister's shoulders.

"Do not lose sight of her," she says. "*Do you hear me?*"

"Yes, Ate, we know."

Tita Perla drives a used Lexus the color of ivory. It's the low-frills model that looks like a Toyota Camry, save for that all-important *L* on the grille. The car is the first thing she bought stateside. She's only the second person in her family to own a vehicle, after Mom.

The next thing Tita Perla bought: a fluffy white stuffed cat named

Whitney that perches in the Lexus's rear window in her very own cat bed. That's right. Whitney, a fake cat *who lives in a car window,* has her own cat bed. Because, AMERICA.

The third thing she bought: a plush Garfield doll with clear suction cups sewn to its limbs, so it can cling to the Lexus's automatic windows and smile its sleepy orange grin at lucky passersby.

If I've not made it clear: I LOVE TITA PERLA.

We ride to Sawgrass Mills to shop for more things, just us two girls in the Lex. A different Whitney, Her Royal Majesty, Queen Whitney Houston, the fluffy Whitney's namesake, plays from the built-in CD player that comes standard in even the low-frills Lexus models. Tita Perla and I sing along, loud and off-key, about waking from dreaming, asking Her Majesty to tell us if this is really love.

Our first stop: mani-pedis.

Tita Perla opts for a salmony pink polish on her fingers and a bold red for her toes. She speaks to the women at the salon in English, even though I assume they speak her language, since we all look more or less the same. The woman at the front calls to two more ladies in the back. They ready side-by-side stations for us, filling basins with water and laying out an array of lotions and tools.

"Can you understand her?" I ask as Tita Perla shakes her bright-red bottle of polish, its little mixing ball clinking and pinging against the glass.

"Who? That lady?" Tita Perla laughs. "Of course not! She's Korean! Look at her! She is tiny and her skin is so beautiful and fair. See how her eyes are flat on the bottom and round on top? And see how her nose is so skinny and pretty, not like ours. And her hair, it's so straight. That's how you know they are Koreans. Korean people don't speak Tagalog, Annabella."

I take mental notes. *Tuh-gah-log, three syllables—that's what Mom speaks? I wonder what Koreans speak. Maybe Spanish.*

I'm not allowed to get color or even clear polish. "Your mommy will see! Too shiny!" Tita Perla says, while I nod. But I am allowed to soak my nails and have them trimmed, to have my hands massaged, and moisturized, and to have my virgin cuticles pushed back with these surely unsanitary tools.

"How would my toe fall off?" I ask as one of the women takes my already-giant Slavic feet into her tiny hands and rubs my soles with lotion that smells like watermelon.

"Your mommy's crazy. That only happens in the Philippines. This is America."

My greased-up feet seep through my socks and into my knockoff Converse as we venture deeper into the cool air-conditioning of Sawgrass Mills. Mom begrudgingly OK'd the powder compact but has forbidden lipstick or anything that would go anywhere near my eyes and render me blind. We skirt Mom's rules with a baby-pink blush that's powdery light.

"This one can't have *too much* dyes," Tita Perla says, scanning the package. "Ay nako."

She finds a little yellow MADE IN CHINA sticker on the back. She carefully scratches it off with one manicured nail, licking her fingertip to rub away any traces of glue before taking it to the register.

We eat bourbon chicken for lunch in the food court. My aunt scrapes every last grain of fried rice from her plate and then mine. "Rice is life!" she says, sounding reinvigorated. At the candy store, Tita Perla scoops together a bag of all-green M&Ms to go with the giant jawbreakers I get for me, Arthur, and Amber.

"These are for good luck," she tells me as she tucks the M&Ms into the bottom of her black Coach backpack. "Don't tell your mommy!"

I wouldn't dare. This has been the greatest day of my post-Dad life. The greatest day, I think, of my life, period.

As we prepare to walk to the car, we slide our bags up our arms. Tita Perla positions her keys between her knuckles and presses her pepper-spray key fob into her palm. She takes my hand into her free one, and we march into the lot, two soldiers in a row. It's still light out. A minivan filled with three generations of family trails us to see if we have a good parking spot. Women in hijabs and flowing, jewel-studded saris stroll by, swimming downstream as we march up. We have nothing to worry about, but this is the one rule of Mom's we heed.

We tuck our purchases into the Lexus's trunk, watchful for lurking predators. A gust of wind lifts a receipt from a bag of banana hair clips. Tita Perla chases after it. She ducks behind a nearby SUV. I lose sight of her and feel my head go fuzzy. The whole parking lot seems to be bobbing up and down like waves in the depths of the Atlantic. I grip the edge of the Lexus's trunk. I try to hold on.

I think of Mom's rules, of what happened to Dad when he didn't listen, about what happens to children and little sisters who get too big for their britches. *Don't lose sight of her.*

I feel my heart pounding yet again in my chest, big and heavy, each beat filled with worry and joy and fear and happiness, all rolled together like Mom's lumpia, threatening to split me open, to burst out and spill all over the parking lot's faded asphalt, which still seems to be rolling in thick swells.

I think of Adam Walsh and Gramma's stories, about his de-cap-i-ta-shun, five syllables. I wonder if this is the same mall. I scan the parking lot for vans without windows. I think of his bodiless head in the drainage ditch. I think of how he should have stayed closer to his mother.

When Tita Perla comes back, eight seconds later, she finds me sobbing, hunched over in her trunk, gasping for air.

"Annabella, what happened?" she asks, wrapping an arm around my shoulders.

"I just want to go home," I say.

And then I start crying harder. I no longer know what home means.

## CHAPTER 16

# Cape Coral

eath seems to be following us, clinging to us like mold.

D Mom and I drive across the Caloosahatchee into the treeless expanse of Cape Coral, turning from one half-empty street onto another. Dad's been dead for less than a year. Mom pulls his Sable into the parking lot of a low and sprawling building with flat brown eaves like mushroom caps. Amber and Arthur are with Liz. I envy them. I look at Mom, hoping this might go any other way than how it's going.

"You're coming with me, right?"

Mom shakes her head. "I can't. But you have to."

I want to dig in my heels. I want to shove the key back in the ignition and force Mom to leave. But I know she's right. I have to. For all of Gramma's wickedness, I love her. I think. And I didn't get to say goodbye to Dad.

We walk together, Mom and I, to the front desk of the nursing home where Gramma has lived for the last two years, since moving out of the room next to mine. We snake through a series of hallways lit by humming fluorescents. The squeak of my sneakers and click of Mom's mules intertwine, one of her steps matched to two of mine.

"I hate these places," Mom says to no one in particular.

I get it. This looks and smells like her hospital. But it feels different. Hollow. Mom and her nurses move quickly and purposefully as they work. The people here look like they're treading water, like they're wading against a tide that never turns.

Gramma's door is closed. Mom takes a seat in the hall; she's gone as far as she can. She locks eyes with me and pushes me onward by pointing her pursed lips at the door.

I press its paddle handle and lean my weight into it. The door doesn't budge. I look back at Mom, thinking maybe it's locked, that this has all been a silly misunderstanding, that we can go home. Then the seal breaks, the vault gives way, and I glide slowly, hesitantly inside.

The smell of antiseptic burns my nostrils. It smells the way my elementary school bathroom smells if I'm the first kid who has to pee in the morning, when the toilet seats are still standing upright. Thick vinyl curtains mute the sun, spreading a dusky gray sheet over everything, including Gramma. She doesn't move. A tangle of tubes and wires connects her to the beeping machines and IV bags keeping her alive. Her head is wigless, crisscrossed by silky white threads. A machine breathes mechanically, heaving and whirring every few seconds as Gramma's chest rises and falls to its beat—*click-suck-whoosh*. First Robo Chair, then Robo Bed, now Robo Gramma.

The little toy she and I sometimes played with at her condo sits on an end table. A spirometer, it's called. It has a mouthpiece and an accordioned bit of plastic attached to a stand with three balls in it, each the size of the big shooters that come in a bag of marbles. One of my last memories at Gramma's condo was of this toy. I blew in, making the red, yellow, and green balls wobble in midair. Gramma clapped me on my back with her gnarled arthritic hands.

"That's my girl! Look at those lungs."

When I asked Gramma to try, she cackled at me in her Wicked Witch way. She smacked her square of Nicorette between her dentures as she took the spirometer and placed it on the end table.

"I don't play with that toy anymore," she said, turning the volume up on *The Golden Girls* and taking another sip of Canada Dry. "Don't you ever smoke."

I grab the spirometer from the side of the nursing home's Robo Bed and tuck it under my arm, the same way I borrow headbands and scrunchies from Cathy's house, certain no one will notice them missing. Gramma's feet stick out from the bottom of her knit blankets. She wears powder-blue socks with grippy rubber treads on the soles. I tap her big toe lightly, thinking maybe she'll laugh and lunge at me. She doesn't move. The ventilator clicks and sucks and whooshes. Her chest rises and falls.

I haven't been in the room for long, but I want to go. I wonder if enough time has passed, or if Mom will send me back in to pay more respects. I keep staring at Gramma's foot, at the knobby bunions she made Dad rub with Vaseline, thinking how her feet were the only things I saw when she was wheeled up to Dad's funeral. I pull the sheet down to cover them.

I cry.

The tears feel different from the ones I cried for Dad. The tears for Dad came rushing out, hot and angry. These trickle like a faucet that wasn't closed all the way. I realize I can stop them if I want. I do for a second. I sniffle and blink. *Click-suck-whoosh.* I am still here. *Click-suck-whoosh.* I am not numb. *Click-suck-whoosh.* I let the tears come again.

Gramma taught me, from as early as I can remember, that I am different, that Mom is less-than, and so are us kids. And yet, she is the one person left on earth who can prove I am partly white, that maybe I do belong here among the Cathys and Carries and Abbys of Robert E. Lee County.

I cry harder.

I hear the seal crack on the beige door. A piercing wedge of fluorescent light sweeps across the room, then narrows back to darkness. A nurse enters, her movements slow, languid. I stop my tears, wipe my face, and tuck the spirometer under the side of my shirt, squeezing it between my arm and my rib cage.

"You must be Jo's granddaughter," the nurse says in that ever-jovial way all nurses seem to have with their patients, if not always their children.

I shake my head, thinking she means Jo-my-mother, forgetting for a second that Gramma's name is also Jo. I shake my head harder, to correct the first gesture, and then start nodding and crying more. These are nervous tears. I don't belong here. I don't love Gramma the way a granddaughter should, I didn't even remember her name. The nurse can see that, of this I am sure.

"Your grandmother talked about you and your sister and the baby all the time when she first got here. Man, she sure loves you guys."

I want to ask her more. I want to ask if Gramma ever called us mongrels or if she called our Mom "a Chink bitch." I want to know if Gramma told stories about Dad. If she talked about what he was like as a baby. If she still blames Mom for Dad going off and doing what he did. But I am out of time. I know that. I press the spirometer hard against my skin and look once more at Gramma's feet and the little tent they've made of the sheet. I try to look at her face, but I stop at the tangle of tubes across her chest. I pull open the vaulted door and step into the light of the hall.

I get home and tuck the spirometer high in my closet, next to Dad's old computer and cases of his floppy discs. A week later, Gramma is dead.

This feels nothing like our last funeral, our first funeral.

Gramma's casket is open, so everyone can see her frail, sunken body, her putty cheeks swiped with too much blush. I think of the dyes from China. I think it won't matter at this point if they make her blind. The limp skin of her face pulls away from her wig; it's pinched at weird angles by her glasses. Gramma looks like she's been deflated, like someone slipped a pin into her side, and all her hot, angry air seeped out.

Dad's service wasn't massive. In my head it was small, a few rows of chairs under a tent, a few stragglers standing to the sides and behind them. Gramma's service pales in comparison. It's Mom, Amber, Arthur, me, and Liz. Gramma's one friend, Henrietta, sits with us for a bit, cooing at Arthur as he runs up and down the center aisle of the funeral home, letting him play with one of the big fake-pearl earrings she unclips from her ear. Some of Mom's Baha'í friends trickle in and out. We're there for an hour before Mom pulls the plug. It feels like an errand we've ticked off the family to-do list.

We order pizza that night. No one brings casseroles for this funeral. There is one spray of flowers sent by Mom's work and a bag of butterscotches left by Henrietta that Amber and I fight over after pizza. I light the novena candles that still sit by the kitchen's slider windows. Two minutes later, Mom snuffs them out and moves them to a high shelf in her closet.

Nobody talks much of Gramma that night. Or ever again.

CHAPTER 17

# How to Clean a Room

The nursing-school pipeline Mom has built to ferry her family to Florida is practically gushing. Another sibling is coming, Mom's little brother, Tito Gary.

I wonder if we'll go Lexus-shopping together, how he feels about Whitney Houston, if he has any Z. Cavariccis. I think if one of Mom's siblings has been this good to us, then two will be even better.

Tito Gary gets luckier than Tita Perla. He secures a position at Mom's hospital, in a unit one floor down from her ICU.

"He's going to live here, with us," Mom tells us kids one night at dinner. "He will take the room next to yours, Annabelle Marie."

"Gramma's room?" I ask, pushing around my sayote with my fork.

"The playroom," Mom says, unwilling to go two uses back to its original tenant and her commode.

We spend the weekend cleaning it, sorting Care Bear figurines and troll dolls and Happy Meal toys into piles per Mom's orders. Crayons and markers are packaged with the blue Playskool easel and sent to Amber's bedroom. Paints, brushes, and pastels go to my bedroom along with a set of canvases Dad bought me after I told him I wanted to be an artist, when

Mom laughed and asked if I wanted to live with them for the rest of my life.

"That is a hobby," she said, "not a job."

A mountain of stuffed animals is divvied up via auction. Amber gets a pink Popple, a Pound Puppy, my tattered Rainbow Brite. I snag a Shamu doll Cathy gave me and the teddy bear in the yellow Butterfinger T-shirt I got for Christmas, when Mom's hospital unit sponsored presents for our poor fatherless family, when Mom tried to turn her coworkers away but we cried till she let them in.

Arthur gets...whatever's left.

Cathy comes over, her blond hair bopping in a high ponytail as she lets herself in through the kitchen door. She calls out from the kitchen, "Can Annabelle play?" It's like she's asking the house or the universe.

"Not until this room is clean!" Mom answers, yelling her reply with a smile—she loves Cathy—as she sifts through more broken crayons, more scraps of dried-out Play-Doh to be saved and reconstituted in wet dishcloths.

Cathy walks back to the playroom and offers to help.

"Great," Mom says, hopping up. "You guys finish this. I've got yard work."

Cathy helps by sitting on a pile of clothes and watching me yell at Amber to move faster. It's slow going.

"Why don't you just take all the things you don't want anymore and put them in trash bags and, like, give them away?" Cathy says. "Or you could have, like, a garage sale and sell them for money. I mean, you don't need any of this stuff anymore."

She picks up a handful of broken holiday pencils and mismatched doll clothes and tosses them in a trash bag, clearing out a corner Mom spent thirty minutes carefully sifting through.

Why didn't Mom think of this? Why is Cathy such a genius?

I grab armfuls of clothes and heaps of broken or unclaimed toys.

Cathy holds open the garbage bags as I load them with books we no longer read, cassette tapes we no longer listen to, clothes and shoes Amber and I no longer wear. In minutes, the room is empty. We drag the bags to the garage and head out to play.

"Is the room clean?" Mom yells from the side yard when she sees me in the street.

"Yep!" Cathy and I say in unison.

"OK, Annabelle Marie. Be home in one hour!"

Cathy looks at me and rolls her eyes. "Your mom's insane. My mom never wants me to come home from your house."

"I know," I say. "At least it's more than twenty minutes."

After Dad's funeral, when life started to resume, Mom would only let me out in twenty-minute increments. If I left for Cathy's house at 10:12 one morning, I had to be back to check in at 10:32. The digital clock on the Magnavox VCR above Dad's big screen served as the master clock. Mom matched it to the time on the scrolling TV Guide channel, her hand hovering over the Magnavox's clock set button, so she could sync it precisely when the minute on the TV changed. This master clock was the clock by which all judgments of timeliness would be made for the next decade. In a pinch, I could call to check in. But if Mom didn't answer, I had to leave a message on the machine and then run over as fast as my bamboo-pole legs would take me.

"If you're late and there's no message," Mom said, "you're grounded for one week."

"Grounded" meant I didn't get to see Cathy. She was the extent of my young life. I could still watch TV or play on the computer or go swimming with my sister. I could still be dragged to Liz's house, even though I thought I was way too old to be babysat. I could still play with her kids. Just not Cathy. She was all that mattered to me, and Mom knew it.

Mom's strict time constraints add to my number obsession. I stare at Cathy's glowing alarm clock as we play Barbies. I watch its digital lights flicker from 12:33 to 12:34, the second-best time of the day: 1, 2, 3, 4. The best time is obviously 9:49, the time I was born, the two 2s safely surrounded by two sets of three 3s. If there's a boring show on television, the nightly news or one of Mom's soaps, I'll watch the VCR clock instead: 3:35 feels stressful, but at 3:36 I can breathe easy: $3 + 3 = 6$. I'll run off to my room or Amber's before it turns to 3:37 so I don't have to worry or be stuck there till 3:39 ($3 \times 3 = 9$) or 3:47, a time that adds up.

I come back this day, after cleaning the playroom, with minutes to spare. The clock says 12:23. I stare until it turns to 12:24 ($1 \times 2 + 2 = 4$), then go off to look for Mom. I find her crouched on the floor of the garage, picking through the contents of the bags Cathy and I had filled with playroom leftovers.

"You're six minutes early," Mom says, checking her watch as she works to reattach a wheel to an old train car I hadn't touched since I was a baby.

"Cathy had to go to her dad's."

"Good. You can help me, then."

I look around the garage. Little piles of things have sprung up like hills of fire ants: pieces of toys in one, scraps of paper in another, broken baby rattles and teething rings, those crayons and markers and doll clothes.

"Cathy said we could donate this stuff, since we don't use it anymore, give it to people who really need it."

"Ohhh, 'Cathy said.'"

Mom sounds disgusted, the way she sounded with Dad when he mowed over one of her seedlings or spent only twenty minutes cleaning a bathroom.

"Just go inside," she says, her focus never leaving that train and its wheel. "I don't even want your help. I'll do this on my own, like everything else in this world."

My feet shuffle to the kitchen door before my mind has time to think any of this through.

An hour passes. Arthur wakes up from his nap, and I feed him banana slices and Cheerios. When Amber emerges from her room, asking about dinner, I peek my head into the garage. I see more piles: our too-small clothes neatly folded and stacked; the naked, broken crayons stuffed into old baby-food jars arranged by color on Dad's workbench. I think about saying something, but the same force that shuffled my feet to the door earlier tells me to keep my mouth shut and figure out dinner on my own.

I heat yesterday's rice from the fridge, sprinkling it with water as Mom taught me before popping it in the microwave. I microwave hot dogs next, setting a paper towel atop the plate to trap the grease spatter. I send Amber to get tomatoes from Mom's patio trellises, and I cut them into wedges with a steak knife as our hot dogs cool. I leave Amber's hot dog whole. I slice Arthur's into coins, then cut each coin into a half-moon. I hear Mom in my head: *Sliced hot dogs are the number one choking hazard for toddlers!*

We watch the nightly news and *Wheel of Fortune* and *Jeopardy!* before I hear the handle on the kitchen door turn. Mom comes in, pours a glass of water from the tap, and heads back to the garage without a word. I carry sleeping Arthur from the couch to his bedroom. I tell Amber to put on her pajamas. I tell her I'll go to her room with her, that we can watch Nickelodeon on the old Zenith.

When I wake up the next morning, the Zenith is dark, and we have been tucked into Amber's bed. I smell bacon. I hear Mom in the kitchen, scrambling eggs. I wonder if maybe the night before was just an odd long dream.

After breakfast, Mom hands me the bowl of compost scraps and asks me to scatter them under the mango tree. I walk through the garage and see every discarded pencil, game, and toy neatly organized by size, function, and color. The dolls' faces have been cleaned, the clothes rematched, the Barbies re-dressed. It's like walking through a toy store.

Mom stays out there all day, packaging the toys into boxes bound for the Philippines. She calls them "balikbayans"—bah-luck-by-uns, four syllables. She takes the least-filled balikbayan box and sets it next to the garbage can and blue recycling bin in the kitchen. She calls me over, holding my arm tight as she explains herself.

"If it's not recycling and not garbage, it goes in the balikbayan box," Mom says.

I roll my eyes. Mom squeezes my arm tighter.

"Listen to me, Annabelle Marie. You are not Cathy. Do you hear me? You don't get to throw perfectly good toys in the garbage when you have cousins who can't afford shoes."

I wonder what toys have to do with shoes? Instead of asking, I just nod and repeat those four syllables in my head: ba-lik-bay-an.

Mom stays up that night, too, cleaning the room next to mine from baseboards to ceiling fan, moving in a bed, a dresser, two nightstands. When I wake up the next morning to Mom scrubbing the hallway, the room next to mine looks brand-new, ready for another life.

I watch from my doorway as she continues to clean, head down, oblivious to my gawking. Part of me fears this side of my mother. The other part is in awe of her. This is yet another of her superpowers. Instead of bending spoons with her mind, she's unbending broken dolls and crooked toy-train wheels by sheer force of will.

CHAPTER 18

# The Bike Ride

A dark figure with stooped shoulders comes down my hallway, their steps heavy yet hesitant. It's Tito Gary, fresh off his flight from Manila. He looks tired, which makes sense. It's late. Amber and Arthur are asleep. Our babysitter has just left.

I stand by my bedroom door at the far end of the hall, wondering if he might rush me and hug me as Tita Perla did, if he might have a fanny pack full of wonders. Tito Gary doesn't look up. I don't think he sees me as he paces the hall in silence. He lugs a blue hard-sided suitcase. He turns into the bedroom next to mine and disappears, closing the door behind him.

I tiptoe to the kitchen, looking for Mom, but she's disappeared, too. I go back into my room, close my door, slip into bed, and stare at the blades of my ceiling fan for what feels like an eternity. I look out my slider and across the pool to the opposite end of the L that is our house. Mom's TV is on. She leaves it on all night now. I push off my covers and head to her room. She doesn't move as I enter. The TV is muted. An old-time Western flashes across its screen. I sneak to the far side of the waterbed. Amber's in the middle. Arthur's closest to Mom. I ease myself in, trying not to make waves. I watch the TV in the reflection of Mom's slider, men in cowboy hats shooting men with feathers in their hair as they ride horseback across some faraway desert. I don't move. The end titles play and a commercial kicks on, and I hear Mom crying. I fall asleep to her tears.


I can't get Tito Gary to watch TV with us, not *The Cosby Show*, not *Fat Albert*. He gets home from his shifts in the critical-care unit, showers, and shuts himself away in his room, where he listens to sad music I can't understand. He eats rice for breakfast, the way Nay and Grandpa did, but he never ventures into the yard, let alone the mall or a nail salon. This isn't due to a lack of effort on Mom's part. She's tried. I hear their conversations in the morning before they go to work, and even though they're mostly in Tagalog, Mom's phone language that has now infiltrated our house, I can follow along. Mom tells her brother he needs to study for the driving exam, talaga na! He sits motionless, staring into a bowl of Mom's champorado. Mom says he can take his signing bonus from the hospital and put it in savings for a down payment on a house. Tito Gary pushes away from the table, his food still untouched. He grabs the bag with his stethoscope and an extra set of scrubs. He heads into the garage to wait for Mom.

His life is linear, like a Disney World monorail with only two stops: his room and the hospital.

I don't know if Tito Gary longed to come to the US or if Mom and Tita Perla convinced him he should. His motions are heavy and slow, like he's caught in a bubble of sap that surrounds only him. He moves like he doesn't want to be in our house or in his body.

Mom and Tita Perla don't have strong ties back in Manila, just a sprawling and needy family. They came to the States without husbands or children. Tito Gary is different. He has a wife and an infant daughter. He keeps a picture of them in a wood frame on the nightstand facing his bed.

Three days a week, he catches the monorail that is our Mercury Sable and rides to work with Mom, who's used her tenure to match her schedule to his.

Three days a week, they drop Amber and Arthur with Liz. Liz feeds them and drives Amber to kindergarten at my same school with her other part-time day-care kids. This means, three days a week, I have a solid hour of alone time before I have to hop on my bike and pedal to fifth grade.

I use that hour as any good ten-year-old would: to snoop.

I pick through Tito Gary's papers and rummage through his clothes, his stash of candies that taste like powdered milk, his drawer of cassette tapes with the sad music. I'm not looking for anything in particular. I'm just nosy. Sometimes I take change from his dresser. Never all of it, just enough for an extra chocolate milk at lunch or a paper cup of ice cream on Fridays. One day I pick up the photo from his end table, the one of the woman and the baby. I turn it over in my hands, the balsa-wood frame light as air. I touch the chipmunk cheeks of this little girl with pink bows pinned to her stick-straight ebony hair. I wonder if I'll meet her. Mom has told me her name is Vanity.

"Like the mirror in the peach bathroom?" I ask.

"No," Mom says.

I set the frame back on the dresser, stuff a few of his coins into my pocket, then grab my backpack and a Nutri-Grain bar to eat while I bike. I keep saying the baby's name to myself: Vanity. Vanity. Vah-nuh-tee. Three syllables like mine. Three is a lovely number.

That night, Tito Gary catches me coming out of the peach bathroom. Despite Grandpa's miniature size, his sons are tall. Tito Gary towers over Mom and Tita Perla. He has a stern and solid presence. When I look at him, here face-to-face in the narrow hallway, I see he is handsome, with big white teeth, smooth skin, and a thick head of straight black hair that he parts neatly to one side. I realize I've never seen him this close for this long. I start sweating.

Tito Gary places a rough hand on the back of my neck and leads me into his bedroom. I think he's mad about the coins I've taken. I start to apologize, the words falling fast and hot from my mouth.

"I'll pay you back, I promise, it was only seventy cents, I'm so sorry, I was going to ask Mommy, but you guys had already left and she forgot to leave money."

He bends over and places a thick brown finger over his lips.

"Shush."

He points at the picture in the frame. At the woman and the baby. Vanity. Three syllables.

"Do not ever, ever, touch that," he says, his face red, his hand trembling and hot against my neck. "Do you understand?"

I nod. My limbs are lank with shame. I feel numb, stupid, childish. I shuffle out of his room into my own and close my door softly, hoping not to alert Mom. I hear his cassette player click on. I hear the sad music. Somewhere behind it, I hear him crying. I put my Shamu doll over my face and do the same.

It takes some work, but Amber and I persuade Mom to let her ride her bike to school with me.

Thirty-some years later, the thought of a six-year-old riding 1.1 miles across a busy street with her barely ten-year-old sister seems crazy. But this was 1991. Looking back, it was probably Amber's idea. She was only in kindergarten, but she already knew herself, perhaps even better than I know myself all these years later. Amber was fiercely independent. Amber *is* fiercely independent. If I could bike to school, why couldn't she?

Mom makes Amber wear her pink helmet. She's allowed the bike ride to happen this day because she's not working, because she's taken Arthur to Liz's already, because she can walk with us to the crossing guard, because she can be sure we'll be safe.

"I have to run some errands around lunchtime, but I'll try to be back before you guys get home," she tells me over our morning eggs. "If I'm not here, your Tito Gary will be here, just use your key. Listen to me, Annabelle Marie, you better take care of your sister, do you hear me?"

I nod dutifully: Of course.

Amber wears a pink-striped skirt with built-in shorts, a pink Minnie Mouse shirt, and pink hand-me-down high-tops that have already held Liz's daughter's feet and mine. We leave early, waving to Mom as the crossing guard guides us across McGregor, seeing her get smaller and smaller. I trail behind Amber, pedaling in and out of driveways to maintain my slower speed. We get to the bike rack just in time. The bell rings as I take Amber to her classroom. I duck into mine mid–Pledge of Allegiance, pressing my hand to my heart as I tuck my backpack into my cubby: *...one nation under God, indivisible, with liberty and justice for all.*

Fifth grade has been kinder to me than fourth. The stigma of being the fatherless brown girl has worn off. Over the summer, a student and his father died in a head-on collision with a semitruck one foggy morning on State Road 80. Just last month, Rebecca Lorri's mom was diagnosed with cancer. "Stage four," the teachers whisper. "She's not long for this world." Mrs. Lorri comes for an outdoor assembly one day, and the wind blows her silk scarf off, revealing the bony plates of her bald head. It's all anyone's talked about: Rebecca's skeleton mom. My affairs are old news.

After school, I meet Amber outside Mrs. Koppel's kindergarten classroom. We walk to the bike rack, buckle Amber's helmet into place under her chin, and saddle up for our ride home. The other fifth-grade bike riders fall in love with my sister. Megan Brent and Kirsten Finch coo after her on their new mountain bikes, which have just become all the rage in the flats of Southwest Florida. They cheer her on as her little legs crank the pedals. Amber loves the attention. She tries to go faster. Instead, she hops a curb and crashes into someone's yard. Blood bubbles up from her right knee and elbow, nothing too bad, but I know Mom's not going to be happy. The bike parade stops. Megan rights Amber's bike. Kirsten straightens the seat. I try to think how we'll explain this to Mom.

"Thank you, thanks," I say, as they branch off to their respective streets and homes, where their moms are, I imagine, waiting for them with trays of cookies still warm from the oven.

Amber dusts herself off, hops back on, and starts pedaling as my mind races with worry. I get back on my bike, wondering how we can hide the cuts and bruises before Mom sees them, wondering how my little sister isn't crying.

"We won't even tell Mommy," Amber says, resolute in the face of my worry.

"I think she'll see it."

"I'll run in and put Band-Aids on then. I'll tell her I did it at school."

"But then she'll call the school and ask them about it. And if you don't clean the cuts, your arm and leg will get infected like Nay's leg and probably fall off."

I hear something over my shoulder, the low rumble of a slow-moving vehicle. A minivan is tailing us. My worry over limb amputations is replaced by a fresher, fiercer worry: *Oh, crap. We are going to be kidnapped.*

I tilt my head to the left, trying slyly to get a better look. I see a blue-gray Ford Aerostar, its hood pointy like a cake wedge. I think maybe I'm in trouble, that someone has seen Amber fall and doesn't think she should still be riding her bike. I see the passenger window roll down, and stranger-danger thoughts flood my head. I try to remember the family password—strawberry ice cream? or was it coffee?—the one Mom and I created after second-grade safety day with Officer Don.

*If they don't know the password, do not go with them,* Mom said. *If they try to grab you, hit them in their soft spots. Go for the eyes first. If it's a man, kick him in the privates, hard as you can. If it's a woman, kick her in the boobs and kick her in the privates, too.*

This is a woman *and* a man.

That's a lot of kicking.

He's in the driver's seat, she's riding shotgun. Now that I see the van up close, I realize I've seen it before. It was driving toward us earlier from the opposite direction. It must have turned around to come get us, to kidnap us and decapitate us, like Adam Walsh.

De-cap-i-ta-shun. Five horrible syllables.

I can see the bony whites of my knuckles gripping my handlebars. I refuse to look at the kidnappers, hoping they'll see my resolve and pick an easier target. Amber's still talking, still plotting how to hide her boo-boos from Mom.

"Annabelle," the woman in the van says. "Annabelle, that's you, isn't it?"

She knows my name. She's good. I wonder if I should ask for the password now or just keep pretending she's not there. We're getting closer to the crossing guard. If we can get to her, I think she'll keep us safe.

"Annabelle, it's me, Dylan's mom, Mrs. Larson."

Miss-es Lar-son. I run the four syllables in my head. Something clicks: Dylan Larson from one street over. The kid who sometimes rides his bike to school with us on days his mom knows will be sunny. This isn't exactly a stranger. I don't stop, but I do look up.

"Oh, hi," I manage.

We reach the crossing guard, and Mr. Larson pulls the Aerostar onto the grass behind us. Mrs. Larson emerges in leggings and a baggy T-shirt.

"Annabelle, what I wanted to—wait, is this your sister? Oh, my goodness, hello there, little one," Mrs. Larson says as Amber straddles her bike, as her knee trickles blood down her shin and onto her pink scrunchy socks, as my sister stares up at this woman, fearless.

"I'm, well…I'm sorry to be the one to tell you this…"

I sense fear in her voice.

"What? Is our mom OK?" I ask.

"Your mommy is just fine. But something's happened at your house."

I narrow my eyes and tilt my head the way Bo would when he heard a squirrel but couldn't figure out where it was.

*Something's happened at your house. At **our** house. What kind of something? If Mom's fine, we're fine.*

"OK, well, thank you," I say, swinging a leg back over my ten-speed.

"Well, hold on, your Mommy wanted Cathy's mom to come get you, get both of you, I guess. But Terri's car wouldn't fit your bikes, so Terri asked us."

I try to process this, this event that's required full neighborhood participation. Is our house on fire? I look north but don't see smoke in the sky.

"We're really close, Mrs. Larson," I say. "We'll be OK."

"All right. OK, then." She shuffles her feet, hesitant to leave us. "Well, Dylan will be home all afternoon. We're ordering pizza tonight. If you need to come over, you're welcome. Our door is open."

She taps Amber on her pink helmet.

"And you're welcome, too, sweetheart."

Mrs. Larson pauses, buying herself a few more seconds, still hoping I'll change my mind.

"You know what? Mr. Larson and I will follow you if that's OK. We'll park in Terri's driveway. If you need anything, that's where you'll find us."

My mind is racing. My hands are clammy and slick as I regrip the handlebars, as we wait for the crossing guard to raise her handheld stop sign, part the sea of cars on regal McGregor Boulevard, and let us pedal through. I hear the Larsons' Aerostar pull out after we cross. I hear it moving barely faster than a crawl. I hear the cars behind it honk when the van fails to break even ten m.p.h. I don't look back.

Everything I need to see is ahead of me.


I've seen police cars before, or at least their lights, spinning cones of blue and red across our yard and windows in the middle of the night, after

Mom's screams and Dad's cussing crescendoed into the neighbors' houses, forcing them to call the cops on us as I continued my charade of sleep.

I've seen ambulances at Mom's hospital, idling at the emergency entrance, medics in navy coveralls with their feet kicked up on the dash, a paper coffee cup nestled in their hands.

A fire truck once came to our school. We took turns climbing up into the driver's seat and flipping the switch overhead to make the low, booming whine of the siren start and stop. The teachers and students lined up to one side, then the firefighters turned on the hose, filling the air with water, creating our own private sun-shower.

Now I see them all lined up along our street, brushing the young mango tree we're still not allowed to climb, as they shift to let in more cars and vans, these physical obstacles of metal and glass that keep the crowds of curious onlookers at a safe distance from—from what? I still don't know.

I am no longer pedaling my bike. I am floating, like Elliott in his red hoodie with E.T. in his basket, like Dorothy in the tornado. I float above the cop cars and red fire truck, the idling ambulance and white van in our driveway. I float into the garage, and there is Mom. She looks at me. She doesn't seem to notice I have flown to her. She doesn't seem to realize my magic. She is crying. She sits on the edge of a milk crate and holds two halves of a belt in her hands. She sets them on the garage's concrete floor before she speaks.

"You're here. You're not supposed to be here."

Mom's voice is tired, like I've woken her up in the middle of the night after one of my nightmares.

"I'm sorry, Mommy. I didn't recognize Mrs. Larson's van, and I didn't think I should go with her, because I didn't know if she knew the password, and I couldn't remember the right password, and Amber scraped her knee and we need to clean it because if we don't clean it, it's going to get infected like Nay's leg."

Mom looks up at me, and I stop. Her face is puffy and red. It's a face I met thirteen months ago.

"Your Tito Gary. Your Tito Gary is dead."

I want to float again, to grab Mom's hand and fly up, up, and away like Peter Pan and Wendy, but the spell has worn off. My feet stick to the floor as if it's metal and they are magnets. I am unable to move, unable to speak.

"He hung himself in the attic." Mom's voice cracks as she keeps going, the words dribbling out slowly like the last drops of rain in a storm.

"I had to, your Mommy had to—I found him when I got home. I saw legs sticking out from the ceiling, and I thought he'd tripped and needed help. I didn't even run. I thought he was trying to find something."

She stops, and there is silence. The traffic on McGregor does not exist. The police scanners have gone quiet. I feel like someone has hit the pause button on the world.

"When I realized…what he'd done, I couldn't lift his legs. He was too heavy. I couldn't even see his head or what he hung himself with. I couldn't get to him. I had to get your daddy's freaking ladder and even then, I couldn't hold him. He was so heavy."

Mom's eyes drift overhead to the rectangle of wood in the garage ceiling that we push away after Thanksgiving to retrieve the plastic Christmas tree and the boxes of lights. Or they start to. Halfway there, she rethinks her decision and looks back to the floor.

"He is, he was, very sad, sad about leaving his family and that little baby. I knew he was sad," Mom says, her body crumpled around itself like a wad of old Kleenex. "I knew it, and I didn't even do anything."

I listen in silence. It's as if I am the silence, as if the silence I feel surrounding us is emanating from within me. But I don't understand.

I don't understand *hung* or why it makes Tito Gary dead like Dad. I don't understand why you'd choose to be hung and why Mom can't look at the ceiling. I want to grab Mom and run. I don't want to be in the garage. I don't want to stand under the attic door. I don't want more silence.

When the magnets of my feet loosen, I do none of this. I take two steps and lean into Mom. I feel her cry, the soft sways of her body, her head in her hands. I notice Amber standing beside me, silent, too. I wonder how long she's been there, if she floated in on her bike behind mine, just as magically. Amber also leans into Mom. We stand like this forever, as policemen gather under the garage door, as the white van in the driveway revs up and pulls out.

We are the eye of the storm, us and Mom. We are the calm. Life and death swirl around us.


Dylan Larson's house is bigger than ours, with a downstairs and an upstairs, where his bedroom is. Amber and I take turns playing Super Mario World on his Nintendo, clicking our Yoshis to eat Koopa shells and berries. His mom orders Domino's and lets the three of us eat our pizza slices on paper plates on his green-plaid bedspread.

When Mr. Larson drops us off, insisting we ride in the cake-wedge van instead of making the ninety-second walk, Liz is there. She's brought Arthur and stayed with Mom. A plate of her pot roast sits untouched on the dinette table.

Mom shuffles Amber and me to our bedrooms, allowing us to skip the two minutes of teeth brushing and neck scraping if we'll just go to sleep. I agree to the deal, strip down to my undies, then crouch between my desk and my door to eavesdrop. I hear details that don't make sense to me at the time. Over the years, I get more details, a clearer picture of Mom's suffering, of her failed attempts to save her brother.

"I had to cut him down," Mom tells Liz.

She couldn't get the belt from around his neck, and she couldn't lift him, so she climbed down her dead husband's wooden ladder, ran to the kitchen, grabbed a knife, climbed back up the ladder, wedged herself into the gap between her brother's limp body and the sides of the attic's opening, and sawed through his leather belt until it snapped, until all 190 pounds of Tito Gary slapped against the garage floor.

"What if the fall killed him? What if he was alive still, but then he cracked his skull and that—*that's* what killed him?"

"You can't go through all the what-ifs again," Liz says. "You know you can't."

Mom rolled Tito Gary from his side to his back. She felt for a pulse or any signs of breathing. She found none and started CPR, screaming for help through the compressions.

I don't know who heard her. Sometimes Mom thinks it was Terri. Sometimes she thinks it was Dr. Johnson from next door. But somebody heard her, eventually. And, eventually, help came.

"They tried. I'll give them that," Mom says of the paramedics. "They had the paddles out, they shocked him every time I asked them to, but there was nothing. My God, he was twenty-seven."

"Did the girls, did they see…" Liz's voice trails off.

"They came home after the body had been put in the coroner's van. I told them already what happened. I don't keep secrets from them, you know that. I told them how sad their Tito Gary was, how I should have let him go back to the Philippines like my parents did."

From my spot near the door, I still can't make sense of things. The same thought keeps rushing through my ten-year-old head: *Why would anyone want to leave America? We've got liberty and justice for all.*


Tita Perla gets in that night. She left Miami after her shift ended at Kendall Regional Medical Center. She crossed Alligator Alley in the dark, which Mom has said is a good way to die. She does not die, though. That would be too much, I think, even for us.

I don't hear her come in. I don't hear her brush her teeth or stand in my shower, her tears mixing with tap water as they flow down the drain.

I do hear her nudge my door open, slowly, carefully, her damp hair smelling of Suave. I wonder why she's not sleeping in Tito Gary's room, where she can have the bed to herself. Halfway through the thought, I realize it's a stupid one. I feel her weight push down on the far side of my bed. She pulls her legs to her chest and slips her feet under my comforter with its splotches of teal and fuchsia. She rolls to her side, facing away from me. She cries herself to sleep, the way I did thirteen months ago.

This is a good room for that, I think. Really, this is a good house for that. Our happily-ever-after home has been anything but.

CHAPTER 19

# Repetition

Tito Gary's funeral falls somewhere between Dad's and Gramma's in terms of attendance.

The Baha'ís show up, as do the nurses and even some of the neighbors, to put a period, I think, on our street's oddest chapter yet. Tita Perla's newly minted Miami friends come to show support, too. People bring more casseroles, more cheese balls, more flowers and cards. We ride in a black Buick again, with Tita Perla this go-round. She hands me and Amber strings of rosary beads, tells us they will make our prayers get to heaven even faster. I hold them in my hands and ask the Virgin Mary for a mountain bike.

At the cemetery everything looks oddly familiar. It's the same forest-green tent, the same view of royal palm trees, the same patch of prickly grass under our feet. Tito Gary's casket is simpler than Dad's, smaller and not as shiny. I feel certain the inside is less comfortable, less nap-worthy, though I have no desire this time to hop in and check it out. I'm not nearly as sad about this death. I feel detached from it, like I shouldn't be here, like the little girl in the balsa-wood frame should be and I've taken her spot. I'm more confused than sad. I spend most of the funeral ignoring the speakers and trying to figure out this weirdly familiar feeling.

In this great big cemetery, why are we in the exact same spot?

I study the ground around the hole that the gravediggers have lined with Astroturf. I see a headstone at the far edge. I can make out the first few letters of the person's name: Lou.

Mom has given Tito Gary the plot that should have one day been hers. She's buried her brother in the ground next to her husband.

"Dad didn't even know Tito Gary!" I say after the services, trailing after Mom, incensed.

"They met," Mom says, rummaging through various drawers in the kitchen and dining room for Dad's fancy Zippo lighter. "When we took you to the Philippines in 1983. They met then."

"Yeah, but they're not married," I argue. "You're supposed to be buried next to the person you marry, the love of your life."

Mom snorts and shakes her head.

"Believe me. Your daddy will never know he's there."

"What are you talking about? Of course he'll know he's there! HE'S RIGHT NEXT TO HIM."

I quickly realize arguing is futile. This makes as much sense to Mom as hoarding sporks from the hospital cafeteria or saving junk mail to use in lieu of Post-it Notes. Why waste a perfectly good grave site?

Mom pulls the silver Zippo from a spot in the still mostly empty china cabinet and wags it in my face in place of her index finger.

"They are *dead*, Annabelle Marie. You don't get to care about anything when you are dead. Go light the freaking novena candles."

I groan, still confused, but I appreciate the distraction. I am, by this point, a novena-candle-lighting pro, having overseen novena operations for what is now my third end-of-life vigil in the last thirteen months. While the candles glow, Amber and I clutch our new rosary beads as Tita Perla says a prayer that's not like our Baha'í prayers. Mom says the novena isn't a Baha'í thing. It's a Catholic thing and a Filipino thing. She says these things are part of us, just like Dad's things—spending too much money, eating too many sweets too late at night—are a part of us. I'm not sure what that means. I just like lighting and blowing out candles.

Unlike Dad's candles, which I blew out shortly after Mom lit them for fear of losing even more of him, and unlike Gramma's, which Mom quickly snuffed dark, Tito Gary's candles stay lit late into the night, long after our shows have ended and Mom's timed our teeth brushing and scraped our necks and pinched our noses. I don't know who blows out the candles, only that they're cool and waxy again by sunrise.

The candles sit in tall jars printed with holy imagery. I learn the saints on the jars by name: Saint Joseph, with the curly-haired child on his arm; Saint Christopher, with his staff and a baby lashed to his back. The guardian angel is on two candles, her wings and arms as open as her heart. But Saint Jude, with his jaunty green sash and gold medal, is my favorite. Tita Perla tells me Jude is the saint you pray to when no one else will listen, when nothing makes sense. The patron saint of lost causes. I light his candle first.


School has become a fluid thing in my fifth-grade life. Packets of work collect on my desk and the dining room table. I tear through them in sprints, plopped in front of the big screen or the TV in Mom's bedroom, multiplying fractions while laughing at the ranch hands on *Hey Dude*, reading Judy Blume while listening to *Clarissa Explains It All*.

I prefer this to going back to school. I prefer my TV pals over my classmates: fewer questions, fewer stares, more laughs. I hope the packets will last forever.

When Dad died, I became a baby bird, something tiny and fragile that had to be protected. When Gramma died, I was made of steel and covered in armor. I told no one. Grandmothers die all the time. That's their job. That's normal.

When Tito Gary dies, I become a freak. The reviews are harsh, unrelenting, and mostly fantastical lies. Not that fifth graders are known for fact-checking.

"I heard he blew his head off in their garage, blood and brains *everywhere*."—*Brian Walters, Mrs. Fern's class*

"I heard her mom killed him just like she killed her dad, but she's got some voodoo hex over the police, so they won't arrest her."—*Kevin Schneider, Mr. McCormick's class*

"No, it was a suicide. They were both suicides. Her house is haunted. It's built on, like, an Indian burial mound or something. It makes people kill themselves."—*Jenny Mitchell, Mrs. Brinker's class*

"That poor, poor little girl. Can you even imagine?"—*Every Teacher Ever*

These unsolicited assessments float by me in the halls, spoken in failed whispers, palms covering mouths to create the illusion of secrecy. Nobody asks what happened. The rumors are so much better than the truth.

"I heard Erica Hornberg telling Mark Griffin your uncle killed himself by putting his head in the oven," Cathy tells me one Saturday as we float on neon rafts in her pool, eyeing the looming puffs of rain clouds overhead.

I am quiet, processing. Middle schoolers are talking about me. Maybe that's cool?

"What did you say to her?"

"I told her to mind her fucking business, first off. And then I told her she looks prettier with her mouth shut. No one needs to see her nasty horse teeth."

I have never loved Cathy more.

* * *

Mom makes a half-hearted attempt to get me to go to this summer's Rainbow Trails grief camp, a place where I imagine parentless kids bury their sorrows in s'mores and pipe-cleaner crafts. She first mentioned it after Dad died. Both times, I never say yes or no. I just don't bring it up again, and neither does she. Instead, we get a puppy the size of a small pony. We rescue her from the pound and name her Pepper. She's a German shepherd–Lab mix with a sleek black coat and giant, fawn-colored paws. A mongrel, like us.

As I snap the ends off a stack of our backyard green beans for dinner one night, Mom says Liz has found a therapist who specializes in kids my age dealing with loss.

"Would you go with me?" I ask her.

"Oh, God, no," Mom says, scoffing. "What are they going to tell me? To feel sadder? To cry more?"

She starts to laugh, a low, rolling howl from somewhere deep in her gut.

"Yeah, right," she says, "tell me some things I don't know."

Mom takes my hand and holds it, mid–green bean snap. I look up at her, shocked by this physical affection. Her hand is rough but warm, her touch gentle. She looks me in the eyes.

"My gulay! You're snapping them too low, Annabelle Marie," she says. She waves her hand over my stack of discarded ends. "Look at all these? It's like another serving of green beans. Just like an American, so wasteful, talaga na."

She takes one of the skinny green pods in her hands and, with one long fingernail and the flick of her wrist, pops off its tippy-top. She does it to another and then another and then another, at roughly ten times my speed.

"Like that," she says. "You just have to keep doing it, until you get used to it and you don't have to think about it anymore."

*Right*, I think, *just like that.*

CHAPTER 20

# Manila

The rumors that plagued me in elementary school have worn themselves thin, their fabric threadbare from overhandling. They're too weak to make the trip to Paul Laurence Dunbar Middle School.

I am free.

I enter the sixth grade a new person. I am no longer *Annabelle-whose-dad-died-and-uncle-hanged-himself-and-who-maybe-eats-dogs*. I've become just Annabelle, or Abelle, as my homeroom teacher nicknames me when my full name doesn't quite fit into my assigned line on her ledger.

"Short and sweet," she says as I smile. "Abelle fits perfectly." So perfectly, it spreads. Mom starts calling me Abelle. Then Amber and Arthur. Tita Perla, too.

At Dunbar, a historically Black public school, I am just another gangly prepubescent sixth grader. But thanks to Tita Perla, who moved in with us after taking her brother's job at Mom's hospital, and Tammy at Supercuts, I now have a kick-ass Whitney Houston perm. And a killer tan (really just my skin tone) that allows me to float among the school's various cliques with relative ease.

It's fall 1991, and Dunbar is undergoing an experiment in reverse busing. The school is situated in the middle of one of Fort Myers's poorest, most segregated neighborhoods, and instead of sending its students of color to predominantly white schools, administrators have taken a bunch of quote, unquote "gifted" and predominantly white kids and bused them to Dunbar. The school's full-time magnet gifted program is designed to draw dorks like us from around the county, buses full of know-it-alls descending to balance the school district's racial quotas.

To keep most of the white parents happy, they've insulated us in a "gifted wing," where we bounce from algebra to biology to English II within our own smarty-pants bubble. We mingle with outside wings only during gym class and lunch.

I daresay, for the first four months of sixth grade, I am *cool*. Those four months are the pinnacle of my schooling existence. Lauren Evans and Kelly Davies are my closest friends, and they are *definitely* cool. Lauren wears bras and has four different Hypercolor T-shirts. Her dad picks us up in a BMW on the days when we stay late for group assignments. Kelly's dad raises hunting dogs out east in Alva. She has something called *acreage*, which Mom always goes on about, plus a tree house and a trampoline.

My sixth-grade life is a blend of sleepovers disguised as study sessions and after-school clubs that keep me far from home. My perm inspires Lauren to get one. Kelly, too. I teach them how to mousse their blond strands for a crunchy look and how to plump them with Infusium 23 for something softer. We call ourselves the Jhirmacks. Our tagline: *Bounce back beautiful!*

That Thanksgiving, though, Mom ruins everything.

The meal starts out promisingly enough, with a big fat turkey and all the traditional sides, plus a pot of rice and Tita Perla. She's the latest tenant of the room next to mine and by far its happiest. Before moving in, she stripped the room, cleaned it, painted its walls with a fresh coat of white and decorated them with framed photos of peach-colored flowers and prints of peach suns rising over gray beaches. Her room matches our peach bathroom. It feels fresh and new, and I like it. It's the five of us once again, the new five of us. Two adults and three kids. Almost a normal nuclear all-American family. But not quite.

"I've got a surprise for everyone," Mom says amid clinking forks and cutting knives. "We are going to take a trip."

OK, I think, ladling gravy onto my potatoes, travel is normal. It's maybe even cool. Rich people who drive BMWs travel. They take ski trips and scuba vacations. I see photos of it all the time at Cathy's, Lauren's, Kelly's.

"You know, it's been forever. I mean, Abelle, you were only three," Mom goes on.

*Only three? I don't remember skiing when I was three.*

"I love having your Tita Perla here, but I haven't seen your Nay and Grandpa since before your daddy died. And I haven't seen your Tita Cristina or Tito Vic or any of my brothers in almost a decade."

*I don't get it.*

"We are going home to Manila!"

*Is that glee in Mom's voice? I can't place it. It sounds off, like blowing into the wrong end of Dad's harmonica.*

"We'll be gone most of December and some of January, so we'll have to get your schoolwork and take as much of it with us as we can. It's going to be a long flight, but your family misses you! They haven't even met Amber or Arthur yet!"

Tita Perla claps her hands. "Pil-uh-peens! Pil-uh-peens! Pil-uh-peens!" she cheers. Amber and Arthur clap, too. Tita Perla looks to me. I stare at my mashed potatoes.

I am numb again. My face is ablaze. I feel the way I felt three years ago, when Mom told us our father painted a plastic baggie with Wite-Out and then suffocated to death in a shitty Holiday Inn on the beach.

"What about the winter dance?" I say as tears collect in the corners of my eyes, then spill into my field of view, physically blinding what little I can see outside my hot rage.

My mind races, but my mouth can't create words.

*What about Kelly's birthday sleepover? Where everyone goes and camps in her yard, and then she splits the group into second-tier friends, who sleep on the trampoline, and the serious VIPs who get to hang with her in the tree house. I have been promised a tree house spot! It's all Kelly has talked about since school started. Does nobody understand the significance?*

"Abelle, there will be plenty of dances," Mom says.

I am sobbing. Tears drip from my chin onto my plate. They leave little saline pools in my globs of gravy. They dribble down my neck to my chest and into the training bra I've started wearing.

"This is so stupid!"

It's the best I can manage.

I want to tell them how I've been saving money to buy a Hypercolor shirt and how that will finally cement my place with the Jhirmacks. I want to say how everyone thinks David Castellano is going to ask me to the dance, and how he has his left ear pierced, which is unquestionably cool.

Instead, I keep crying.

"Annabelle." It's Tita Perla's turn now. "Your mommy has worked so many extra shifts to buy plane tickets for you and your brother and sister to take this gigantic trip. She's spending a lot of money on this because she loves you."

I snort. I try to think of the last time Mom has said those words. *I love you.* They used to be part of our nighttime routine: Brush teeth for two minutes, scrape neck for dirt, pinch nose, then into bed, "Good night, I love you, sleep tight, don't let the bedbugs bite!" and lights off. Now Mom works and watches TV and cries in her bedroom when she thinks we're not looking. I can see her from my sliding door across the pool. I know when she's crying, because she holds a washcloth to her face, not wanting to waste tissues.

145

*Because she loves me? Ha, Tita Perla, you're cool and all, but you've only been here a few months. This is beyond your scope of manicures and makeup.*

"Whatever. It's just, whatever," I say.

We clear our plates, package up leftovers, and wash dishes. Amber and Arthur settle in to watch *A Charlie Brown Thanksgiving* on the big screen. I step over them on my way to my room. Moments later, there's Mom, tapping her long fingernails against my door as her way of knocking, only to push through milliseconds later.

"You are going to the Philippines," she says as I burrow deeper, face down in my bed.

She's not being mean. She's not being nice either.

"I'm sorry you will miss the dance and your friends, but this is an important trip for us. I need to see my family. I need them."

There is quiet, then the sound of Mom sniffling. She sits at the foot of my bed. I stop my burrowing and slowly flip over to look at her. She wipes her face with the front of her fuchsia floral-print housedress.

"Listen, Annabelle Marie. I know you think you're just an American. I know you want to be like Cathy and that Lauralee and whoever else with their curly hair and those hypnocolor shirts."

"Lauren and Kelly," I say. "And it's Hypercolor, Mom."

"Right. But listen to me, OK: You are Filipino. Do you hear me? You are. We are going to the Philippines, and we are spending Christmas with my family, with *our* family."

Hesitantly, I nod. I never fathomed Mom knew all this. I wonder just how obvious I've been. I see Mom's point. But I wonder if she sees mine: Being Filipino will get me nowhere in this town. She must understand that. It's why she pinches our noses, and why she's never taught us Tagalog. There's nothing normal about being Filipino if you're living in Fort Myers, Florida, USA.

My idea of normality shifts weekly, daily, hourly. When Dad and Tito

Gary died in the ways they did, I wanted to fade into the background and pretend it never happened. I hated that my mother was so open with everyone, that she couldn't just keep those skeletons in the closet, safely under wraps. With time, I've started to wonder about everything Mom does. Why does she have to mow the lawn in Dad's cowboy boots and Nay's muumuus? Doesn't she realize we live off McGregor, where everyone will see her? Why does she have to freak out when I'm one minute late? Why won't she let us use the air conditioner? Why does our house always smell like rotting fruit and fish? What's wrong with a Glade PlugIn?

I have, despite all of Mom's attempts to set me back, achieved quasi-normality in sixth grade. But now she's stripping that from me with this "vacation." I want to be mad still, but Mom looks hopeful for once. It feels like she's trying.

Mom lifts her hand to my head and pinches one of my ringlets.

"And you know what," she says, "we'll have to get you another perm before we leave. These curls aren't bouncing back like they used to."

I roll my eyes and smile at the same time, thinking maybe this trip can be salvaged, can be made *cool*. Maybe there's scuba diving in Manila?

The sky is a dusky predawn gray as Liz drives us to the airport, an eleven-year-old, a seven-year-old, an almost-three-year-old, one Mom, and twelve massive boxes and suitcases of stuff.

"Every ticket holder gets one carry-on luggage and two checked items," Mom says over and over again in the weeks leading to our departure, as she packs jars of Jif peanut butter and jumbo bags of Snickers into cardboard boxes, cushioning them with the old clothes and toys she's been so carefully saving for this moment, filling any empty space with baggies of our used crayons and markers, and with Betamax tapes of movies and shows she's recorded off TV during her sleepless nights, entire seasons painstakingly started and paused so as not to capture the commercials.

My mom was the original DVR: *Murder, She Wrote* and *Knight Rider* and *The Dukes of Hazzard* and *The Waltons*, hours and hours of American television packed into boxes to be exported overseas.

She wraps the boxes in packing tape, then silver duct tape, tying them around and around in twine so nothing will escape.

Tita Perla can't leave the same day we leave. She has only so much vacation time at her new job. She will meet us in a week or so, just before Christmas. Mom is doing this on her own. The eleven-year-old, the seven-year-old, the almost-three-year-old in a stroller; all those boxes, all our bags. Four planes, three layovers, twenty-five hours in the air, 9,195 miles to the opposite side of the planet.

At the Fort Myers airport, Mom doesn't let Liz park.

"Don't waste the money! It is a rip-off!"

Instead, we unload our freight from her station wagon and pile it along the Departures curb. Liz looks at this mountain and its three smallest inhabitants. She chuckles to herself.

"If anyone can do this," she says to me as she pulls me in for a goodbye hug, "it's your mommy."

She holds me to her bosom, then snaps up my siblings for kisses and squeezes. She bids us bon voyage, taking one look back, smiling and shaking her head before sliding back into her wood-paneled Caprice.

As Liz rolls away, waves of porters descend to try to help our family. Mom brushes them off.

"No, thank you, no, thanks, nuh-uh," she says to no one person but to the idea in general.

I look at her, brow furrowed, not understanding how this will work.

"Stand right here, don't let anyone touch anything," she says. Mom disappears inside the terminal as the sun peeks up from the horizon. We kids and this village of luggage hang out by the curb.

Mom comes back with a pushcart. She piles the biggest boxes on first, then keeps going till she has a towering yet surprisingly sturdy stack.

I have my backpack and am assigned the hard-sided blue suitcase that was Tito Gary's and a box that I am to drag along by its makeshift twine handles. Amber gets a small roller bag and her backpack. Mom slings the snack tote over one shoulder and her purse over another, locking them into place with Arthur's backpack. Mom pushes the stroller with her left hand, the towering cart with her right. Amber pulls her roller bag, I pull my box and suitcase—and off we go.

Our first flight is to Houston, and from there we go to Los Angeles, then Tokyo, then Manila. The twenty-five hours in the air are made possible by children's Dramamine and half doses of Benadryl slipped into the applesauce cups Mom pulls from the snack bag. During the layovers, we run around the terminals like wildings. We chase Arthur as his bare, chubby baby feet patter against linoleum, as Mom sets aside her fatigue and keeps an eagle's watch over us, ignoring the judgmental onlookers and the clicking tongues of the travelers we keep bumping into and cutting off.

When the final plane finally lands, the pilot greets us over the speaker, tells us in his tinny voice that it's 9:36 a.m. and 94 degrees.

"Welcome to Manila. Maligayang pagdating."

We deplane onto a blazing tarmac. Squiggles of heat blur our view of the city beyond. I wonder if we've traveled all the way around the world and back to Florida somehow. I wonder if we've time-traveled, too, to peak Florida summer when heat becomes an emotion, a feeling on your skin and in your soul.

I recognize the sticky air and relentless sun, the way it pushes down on you, shoving you into the faintest slivers of shade, the way time seems to slow down, as if it can't push through this thick air either. I feel at home, yet I am the farthest I will ever be from home.

Mom's brother Tito Vic, another handsome man with a full head of jet-black hair and a big toothy smile, meets us at the luggage carousel, which creaks and moans as its metallic gills whirl around. I've only been in four other airports in my eleven-year-old life—Tokyo, Los Angeles, Houston, Fort Myers—all in the last thirty-six hours, but this one is different. The toilets in the bathrooms are shored up by pieces of plywood. There is no toilet paper, just a red plastic bucket of water with what looks like a measuring cup inside it. A woman with cloudy eyes and no front teeth sits on a square of newspaper next to the bathroom sinks, her knees tucked up to her ears, one hand holding a cleaning bottle, the other a shallow dish into which Mom clinks her change.

"Salamat Ate," the woman says.

Ah-tay, two syllables. I wonder how she knows Mom's nickname.

Tito Vic builds another towering luggage cart, with almost the same precision as Mom. He pushes it out the exit door and down a winding ramp lined by walls of people waiting for family of their own. Mom carries Arthur in her arms. She places me and Amber between her and Tito Vic's bodies. We march in this formation, down the first ramp, around its bend, then down the next. Sweat beads at my hairline, wetting the neck of my shirt. It drips from behind my knees and into my socks, a blend of anxiety and equatorial heat. And then I hear screaming. And then Mom laughs, her voice gleeful like it was during her Thanksgiving announcement of this round-the-world trip. And then we are surrounded by jumping and shrieking and the Spanish words I now know to be Tagalog.

"Ate! Ate! Ate!"

The loudest shrieks come from a square woman with ebony hair pulled tight in a bun. Her soft cheeks and chubby chin make her look like she could be in high school. One of her front teeth is brown. She grabs my mom for dear life, holding her as she gushes a cascade of words I don't understand, pressing Arthur into a Filipino sandwich. Mom takes this woman by her arms and kisses her on the forehead. She holds her out to us.

"This is your Tita Cristina."

Our aunt laughs and curtsies, pulling up her housedress ever so slightly to reveal her thick legs and the black rubber slides on her feet. She runs to us girls with bags of candies and open arms.

The rest of Mom's brothers stand in a line behind her, their tight smiles practically solemn by comparison. On the other side of the cart, a boy who looks my age peeks from between our suitcases. His curly hair grazes the bottoms of his ears. It looks oddly like mine. I wonder if he has any Whitney Houston CDs. When he comes around the corner, it's like I'm looking in a mirror, like we're the long-lost twins in the *Parent Trap* movie, the identical cousins in *The Patty Duke Show*.

"John-John! Tumingin sa iyo!" Mom says, taking the boy by his shoulders and shoving five dollars into his hand as his smile grows from shy to bright.

"Do you remember your cousin?" Mom looks at me. "This is John-John, your Tito Vic's son. The last time here, you two were best friends. You cried so hard when you had to leave him."

My cheeks start burning. "I was three, Mom," I say with a hard eye roll, not wanting to make eye contact with this male version of myself.

John-John is unfazed by my sass. He tucks the five dollars into the pocket of his jean shorts, touches my mom's hand to his forehead for some reason, then runs ahead to our waiting vehicles, his rubber flip-flops smacking the bottoms of his feet.

Our luggage takes one van, which Tito Vic drives. John-John rides shotgun, and another of Mom's brothers, Tito Willie, sits pinched between boxes in the back. We ride with Tita Cristina. Someone Mom introduces as Tito Boy drives us. Tita Cristina sits in the passenger seat with her back to the windshield, weaving stories to Mom in English-spattered Tagalog as I try to follow along.

Our van feels as hot as the tarmac. I look for air-conditioning vents but see just one, front and center in the dashboard, a thousand miles away from me. I push open my hinged window, and a blast of smog and exhaust punches me in the face.

"You can't open the windows, Annabelle Marie," Mom says, dabbing sweat from her neck with one of Arthur's old burp cloths before reaching across me and pulling it shut again. "The air will make you sick."

I offer another hard eye roll, the force of which makes me queasy. I rest my head against the glass and watch this foreign world scroll past: streets packed with mopeds and rickshaws, women walking between them with long clusters of bananas and zip-tied snack bags balanced atop their heads, barefoot children squatting at the curbs and in any available shade. A scooter buzzes next to us. The old woman on the back flashes a toothless smile at me from beneath her umbrella. There is no rain, just blazing sun and choking smog. Overhead, jumbles of electrical wires spread like tangles of dark hair through the air.

This is not skiing.


Nay and Grandpa's house is south of the city center in the vast maze of narrow streets that make up San Andres Bukid. Tito Boy stops our van in the middle of a road that looks like all the others, clustered with motorbikes and street vendors and half-clothed kids. I wonder if we're having car trouble. This doesn't seem like a place to stop. Mom reaches over and unbuckles Arthur and Amber, who are sharing the middle seat between us.

"This is it, grab your things."

"What?"

"We're here, come on, Tito Boy has to take this car back."

Mom hops out of the van's one sliding door. She holds Arthur and tells Amber to take my hand. Before leaving Fort Myers, Mom took out our diamond-stud earrings and replaced them with tiny silver balls. She took off our gold necklaces and the gold bracelet she gave me for Christmas. She put them in the safe with Dad's death certificate. Now I understand why.

A little boy barely bigger than Arthur runs by, wearing a woman's tank top with a neck that dips down to his belly button and nothing else. Ladies in jandals tilt their umbrellas to peek at us, these aliens emerging from our rented UFO.

My fake Converse feel flashy. The JanSport backpack slung over my shoulder is filled with hair products and headbands. I feel stupid carrying it. Tita Cristina takes my other hand. We cross the road and enter an alley, the crumbling asphalt giving way to packed dirt that's the same light brown as the smog. These aren't houses. They're sections of corrugated tin, tarp, and stacked cinder blocks. The little boy in the woman's tank top pulls it up to his bare hips, then starts peeing in a nook between lean-tos.

The alley isn't big enough for us all to walk side by side, so Mom and Arthur and Tito Boy lead, with me, Amber, and Tita Cristina following. We get to a blue metal gate. I look up, and there is a wall painted pinkish beige. It's about twice my height. At its top, I see curls of barbed wire snaking through shards of broken glass.

"This is it," Mom says.

It looks more like a rickety fortress than a house, like the sandcastle towns Cathy and I build at her dad's girlfriend's beach condo on Sanibel. Most of the units we make in our sandy village are small and simple, shaped like upside-down cups. But the main building, the castle, is taller and sturdier than the rest, its top adorned with broken seashells, as this one is with broken glass. But they're all just made of sand.

Tito Boy pulls open the gate's latch and we enter a small courtyard packed with more family. The chants for Mom start again: "Ate! Ate! Ate!"

A small crowd of children greets us. The older ones come first. They run to Mom and stand before her, their heads bowed.

"Mano po," they each say. The same three syllables, one after another.

Mom passes Arthur to me. She smiles at each of the kids and gives her right hand. They take it in theirs, pressing the back of it to their foreheads as solemnly as John-John had. Mom says, "God bless you." Then she pulls crisp dollar bills from a stack in her fanny pack and hands one to each kid.

She is prepared for this. I am not. This is a version of my mother I've never met. I stand to the side in shock and awe, trying to tuck this new layer of Mom somewhere between the folds of nursing shoes and steamed rice.

This continues, mano po, mano po, the children getting younger and younger, smaller and smaller. Mom hugs some of them tight, which makes my stomach hurt with envy. When John-John comes, she scratches at his neck with her long fingernails as he laughs and bobs his head like a boxer to avoid her reach. She says something to him in Tagalog, something about giving him money already. He smiles, nods, and turns, and then Mom calls him back and hands him five more dollars. His little brothers file in next. Mom pinches their cheeks, then kisses the black hair at the tops of their heads and gives them five dollars, too.

A woman with a messy ponytail approaches, carrying a toddler in her arms. She doesn't look up, but I can see tears falling from her face. I can see her shoulders heaving with each sob. I look at Mom. She's crying, too. The toddler grabs Mom's hand and presses it to her tiny forehead. Mom grabs them both and they cry together, a rain cloud of tears that slowly dissipates. Mom takes the baby and shows her to us kids as we stand, sweaty, confused, and overwhelmed behind her.

"This is Vanity," she says. "Your cousin, your Tito Gary's daughter."

I see now the chubby cheeks and stick-straight hair, just like in the balsa-wood frame on the end table. Van-uh-tee, three fatherless syllables, just like Ann-uh-bell.

I want to take her in my arms, too. I want to tell her I know what it's like, that even though it feels like it, none of this is her fault, that it's all mine, and I am so, so sorry.

Vanity looks at me and coos.

I wonder if she knows. I wonder if it's easier to be fatherless if both of your parents are brown, if you never had a chance of passing as white. I think it must be. Vanity has all these people. She has a place where she blends in, where she's normal. I have Amber and Arthur and Pepper. All of us mongrels.

I recognize this feeling. It's how I feel at Lauren's house when her mom brings her in for a hug to commiserate over a bad grade or jerky boyfriend. It's jealousy. I feel stupid for feeling it here of all places. I have a cool backpack filled with cool headbands for my cool perm. But that doesn't make me fit in on this side of the world any more than it makes me fit in back home.

There's a hollowness in my chest. That sinking numbness that came over me when Dad died is back. Maybe this isn't jealousy. Maybe it's loneliness. Nobody's from Fort Myers, and nobody like me lives here in this sandcastle house in Manila, either.

A *kiss-kiss* sound catches my attention, the sound of someone calling over their cat, or oldest granddaughter. Nay sits on a stool in a doorway that opens into a tiny shop attached to the front of the house facing the alley. This, Mom will tell me, is the family's sari-sari, a bodega of sorts that's the size of a closet. Strings of colorful candies and instant-coffee packets dangle from its one window, which is covered in a lattice of metal with chipped blue paint that matches the gate. Inside are a few shelves lined with men's razors and canisters of Pringles and the black-ink Bic pens we packed into a long-ago balikbayan box. Grandpa wanders out from inside. I walk over and Nay hands me the same powder-milk candies Tito Gary kept in his drawers. I take them and smile.

Through the scents of smog and urine, I smell onions frying and chicken cooking. My stomach grumbles. I realize my last meal was eaten somewhere over the Pacific Ocean.

"You want eat?" Tita Cristina appears over our shoulders. Amber and I nod. I shift Arthur to my other hip, and we follow our aunt inside.

Our tape-and-twine-wrapped boxes line the small sitting area, where a TV topped with sets of foil-covered antennae and wires that creep up to the ceiling like vines is the centerpiece to a couch and two chairs covered in thick clear plastic. A narrow wooden staircase leads to somewhere above us. Through the small hallway, there is a dining area and a kitchen lined with jalousie windows that open onto the chicken coop and laundry lines out back. Nay and Grandpa's bedroom is to the right, and to the left is the bathroom.

Tita Cristina fills chipped bowls with steamy chicken stew and scoops rice from a massive cooker powered by a series of colorful extension cords that lead somewhere outside. She sits down with us at a round wooden table and nods at us to get started. She digs in with bare hands, pushing gobs of rice into the broth, then into her mouth. I try to grab my bony bits of chicken, but the broth burns my fingers. Amber and Arthur stare at their plates, no clue as to how to proceed.

"Aye, Cristina!"

Mom runs in from the courtyard. She spouts off in Tagalog. Her tone tells me Tita Cristina is in trouble.

"This is why you are fat! Ay nako, you can't even wait."

Tita Cristina says something sassy in return, a tone I know well.

"I am fat because I have three freaking kids," Mom says, pulling Arthur from the chair he's standing on and into her lap. "What's your excuse?"

Mom tends to my brother's plate first, pulling the chicken from the bone in bite-size bits. She peels tiny bananas from a bunch in the middle of the table and hands them to me and Amber to eat as our soups cool. She peels a trio of boiled eggs from another pot on the stove. Through the hallway I see the crowd of kids waiting at the front door.

"You have to eat first and then Nay will let them eat," Mom says to hurry us along.

She rummages through the drawers for a mismatched set of spoons. I realize I'm ravenous. My food disappears in a haze. I look up, and Amber has her head on her arms, asleep on the table. Arthur dozes on Mom's shoulder. She carries them into Nay and Grandpa's bedroom and switches on an oscillating fan in the corner. I follow her and slip into oblivion. I dream about my mother, the savior, handing out blessings and dollar bills to all of Manila as I melt behind her in the shadows.

My bladder wakes me. It's dark out and my siblings are still fast asleep in our grandparents' bed. I felt Mom come in earlier, scooching Arthur closer to me, and Amber closer to Arthur, so she could squeeze onto one side. She's gone now, though. I tiptoe into the kitchen. The glow of the TV catches my eye. I walk into the living area, stepping over the crates of Spam and jars of peanut butter that had been packed in our boxes. Nay and Grandpa are asleep on the couch. Tito Vic dozes in a chair next to Mom. She's awake, watching *Knight Rider* on Betamax. She pats the plastic of her chair, telling me to come sit with her.

"I need to go pee," I say.

"The bathroom is through the kitchen."

"I know, but…"

Mom hits pause on the Betamax and moves past me through the narrow hall. I follow her. The door to the bathroom is made of heavy wood with a hole where the handle should be. It creaks as Mom pushes it open to reveal a surprisingly big space covered floor to ceiling in square pink tiles. The toilet is to the right. On the far wall, a pipe juts from a ragged hole. It doesn't make sense to me as a bathroom. But that's not my current issue.

"There's no toilet paper."

"I know," Mom says. "We'll have to see if I can find any when I go shopping tomorrow."

She picks up the bucket from next to the commode and dumps it outside. She turns on the sink in the kitchen and refills it with water. She washes the cup inside it, then brings everything back.

"Pee or poop?" she asks me.

It started as the former but has since evolved. I hold up two fingers.

"OK, stay on the toilet and call me when you're done."

Mom is back a few minutes later. I try to remember the last time she wiped my butt. I can't. She puts her hand on my back and pushes me forward, folding me in half at my waist. I rest my hands on the tops of my feet. She dips the cup into the bucket of water.

I feel a rush of cold slide down my lower back. A shiver shoots up my spine. Mom pulls apart my cheeks to make sure her work is done. I feel like one of her patients in the hospital.

She grabs a towel we used for cushioning the items in our boxes. She wipes my bottom and lower back. She takes the rest of the bucket and pours it into the toilet bowl, slowly at first, then all at once, so my turds get sucked down the hole with a bubbly *glurg*.

"How'd you know how to do that?"

"I know a lot of things," Mom says, tucking the bucket next to the toilet bowl and marching back to the TV room.

I'm enchanted by this version of my mother, this woman who knows everything and draws crowds of adoring fans. Mom has so much power on this side of the planet. I can see now why my grandparents left us to come back here. Power like this must be intoxicating.

Back home, I'm happy to ignore Mom. I pretend I'm studying when she asks for help in the yard. I keep a textbook in one hand and the remote in the other as I watch MTV in bed, in case she calls me to wash dishes or iron her nursing uniforms.

Here, I start to see pieces of my mom that I admire: her poise, her self-assuredness, her ability to shame her siblings into doing her bidding with the mere tilt of her head. Mostly, though, I envy her. She, too, has a place where she is normal. A home where she belongs.


Amber and I are vampires, sleeping away our days, spending our nights watching Mom's recordings and what little grainy Filipino television we can pick up through the antenna.

We memorize the commercials for canned sardines and bottled sodas, singing along to their jingles: "Sar-dee-nez Hakone!" and, with operatic gusto, "Sarsi—angat sa iba!"

When a mouse scurries across the floor, our singing turns to howling, enough for Mom to climb down from the loft and for Grandpa to emerge from the back bedroom. Amber and I hold each other, our feet squeaking on the couch's thick plastic as they tip-tap up and down.

"Mommy," I say. "There's a mouse!"

"Where? Where did it go?" she says.

I point to a spot behind the TV. Amber keeps a firm grip around my waist.

Grandpa runs his fingers through what's left of his wispy hair. "Is mouse or *rat*?" he asks, rolling the *r* of *rat* emphatically.

I shrug and shake my head.

He holds his hands up to me, keeping them narrow and small, asking again, "Is mouse?" Then he throws his hands apart, till they're the size of a loaf of Wonder Bread. "Or is *rat*?"

I think for a second.

"A mouse, probably."

He sighs and mutters something to Mom before shuffling back down the hall.

"Is he going to catch it?" I ask.

"No," Mom says, laughing. "He says I raised two spoiled brats, and it's time for you to go to bed."

Mom is always gone when the heat of the morning creeps into our loft, pinching at my cheeks to wake me. If it's not the heat, it's the sounds of the neighborhood: sputtering mopeds, crowing roosters, fruit sellers and bakers ringing the bells of their pushcarts as they peddle their goods down the alley. Nay and Grandpa's house is the only two-story building on the street. From the slatted windows of our loft, I can see everything, including Mom as she comes back with whatever it is she's procured.

I don't know everything that Mom does when she leaves, but when she returns, it's with armloads of stuff. One day, it's bags full of toilet paper rolls and more towels. Another, it's box fans and silverware and a second mattress pad she sets up in our loft.

We have caused a shift. Tita Cristina, who usually sleeps in the loft, has moved to the plastic-covered couch. John-John, who lives with his parents in the suburban province of Laguna but who sleeps on the couch while his school is in session, has moved to a cot in our family's sari-sari. Tito Boy, who usually sleeps on the cot, has taken John-John's bed out in the suburbs.

"They need a bigger house," I tell Mom.

"I know. I'm working on that."

The first week or so, we kids rarely leave the compound. The one time we do is wonderful. We go with Mom's titas, our great-titas, on a department-store shopping spree. Amber buys a My Little Pony. Arthur gets a dump truck that's almost half his size. I buy a white pig with three pink baby pigs tucked in a Velcro pouch in her belly. I name it Ate.

But most days, we're at the house.

Tita Cristina tends to Amber and Arthur, usually watching shows, sometimes collecting eggs and chasing the chickens out back or trying to befriend Benji, the mean little dog who eats our dinner scraps and is supposed to keep rats out of the chicken coop.

I tend to myself, coming down to eat rice and eggs for breakfast, then disappearing back to my loft to read books and burn through schoolwork. One day, I see a mop of curls coming up the rickety stairs. My shirt is pulled up to my chin as I lie in front of a box fan, reading V. C. Andrews. I pull it down to hide my nonexistent breasts, then clear my throat to announce my presence. And then I hear something. *Is that singing?*

"Hellooo."

*What's happening?*

"'Is it me who you are looking for?'"

I tip my book away from my face and see my cousin-just-like-me dancing his way up the final steps.

"What are you doing? What is this?" I say, all business.

"'I can see it in your eyes!'—YOU ARE BORED!'"

I roll said eyes and try to go back to my reading.

John-John takes a half bow and waves to his invisible fans.

"Lionel Richie! Not your favorite? Come on, Abelle. You are just read all day, read, read, read," he says mockingly. "So mainip."

I don't look up.

"That means 'boring,' you know! Or are you too mainip to care?"

*Bring it, kid. I can do this all day. Sticks and stones are what I'm made of.*

"My mama can't believe Tita Josie never taught you Tagalog. You don't speak any Filipino? Nada?"

"I can follow along most of the time," I say, trying my best to sound annoyed. "Mom says it's a useless language. She says we'll never need it."

"You could use it now, hey?"

I roll my eyes again and push my book closer to my face. John-John takes the paperback out of my hands. I start to huff.

"Here," he says.

He takes some sort of Game Boy–looking thing out of his pocket and hands it to me.

"My papa says I cannot keep it while I am in my classes. He says to let you play it."

He switches the thing on, and its color screen glows in my hands. He pulls two cartridges out of his pocket: Sonic the Hedgehog and something called Columns, which looks sort of like Tetris. I can't believe he has something so undeniably cool. We play, huddled side by side in the heat of the loft, until the batteries die.

"Is this what you do in Florida? Play video games and go to Disney World every day?"

"We were supposed to go to Disney World before my dad died," I say. "I've only been once, when I was a baby."

"You are lucky. It's boring here in the Philippines, not like Florida."

"It's pretty boring in Florida, too."

"You know what's fun?" He leans his head close to the louvered windows, resting his chin on the sill. I crawl to his side, looking at the alley just beyond the shard-topped walls of our compound, at all the people passing, their umbrellas raised to block the sun, their focus on the packed dirt in front of them. He lifts his head to his elbows, takes a deep breath, then points his face sideways toward the neighbor's house and screams, "Hoy!"

His force scares me. I sink my head under the sill instinctively, where I hope no one can see me. John-John pulls me up by my arm.

"Look," he whispers.

Below us, everything has stopped. The umbrella women pause and look at the shopkeepers, who look around. Shirtless men with gray scruff on their faces step out from their stoops, hands folded behind their backs. There is a murmur, and then, slowly, life resumes.

"What does *hoy* mean?" I ask, fascinated.

"It's what you say if someone is stealing something. It's like, '*Hoy! Hey, stop!*'"

"Won't you get in trouble?"

"Not if you do it right. They never look up here."

"Can I try?"

"No, too much," he says, waving his hands in front of him. "Maybe later. You can only pause the world a little bit."

CHAPTER 21

# The Real Manila

Tita Perla's arrival eight days later is a repeat of Mom's. The cousins and uncles and wives come back to our house in San Andres Bukid. The children line up and bow to say "mano po." They press my aunt's hand to their foreheads. She hands them more crisp dollar bills.

There is another feast, this time with Mom's lumpia, a huge pot of pancit, and dessert trays heaped with hopia and creamy fruit salad and ensaymada, an eggy brioche bread topped with frilly strings of cheese. Grandpa kills the backyard rooster after it stomps a nest of chicks into the ground, one of which Arthur carried in that morning, bloodied and broken in his little hands. We eat the rooster, too.

John-John's classes are on break, and he's back with his family, so the couch becomes Tita Perla's. My cousin lets me hold on to the Sega Game Gear, tells me Merry Christmas, Maligayang Pasko, when he does.

Like Mom, Tita Perla seems restless. The first day she gets in, she's ready to go out. Her American paychecks are burning even bigger holes in her pockets on this side of the world. Mom agrees to let me go shopping with Tita Perla and Tita Cristina, my first time out of the house without her. Prior to this outing, we'd only been driven places by Tito Boy or Tito Vic. I wonder if they'll meet us at the end of the street.

"Aye, no," Tita Perla scoffs. "You don't need a car in Manila. Your mommy is too Americana!"

We walk to the street, and my aunts talk to two men leaning against a utility pole. They point in the same direction. We cross and hop on the back of a jeep-truck hybrid, its silver exterior painted in colorful scribbles, its long, covered bed lined with two benches that are almost full. People scoot in to make room for us. Tita Perla counts out three one-peso coins in her hands, roughly six cents US, then hands them to a passenger who passes them up to the driver.

"Jeepneys," she says to me, "are the best way to get around this city."

The driver honks, and another woman and her child jump in. The benches are full. Black smoke belches from somewhere overhead, and we're off. There are no seatbelts. There's not even a back door, just a gaping hole through which you can see the potholed pavement rush by.

Our jeepney squeezes through the narrow streets, ignoring curbs and what few painted road lines I can make out. As traffic thickens and our pace slows, I'm tempted to lean over and grab a bag of melon juice from the stalls and carts that the jeepney's sides seem to be scraping. I'm stunned when the woman across from me does just that, tossing a few coins to a lady under a torn umbrella as compensation.

The streets seem to be getting tighter, narrower. Our jeepney is barely moving. Tita Perla grabs one of my hands, Tita Cristina grabs the other. We hop out the back into throngs of people. My aunts push me between them, buffering me as they maneuver us along with the masses. I feel the crowds thin and the street open. I look up and wonder if we're in New York or Los Angeles.

The Glorietta mall is the most beautiful thing I've ever seen.

The place is massive, a boxy expanse of windows and beige bricks home to innumerable treasures. My aunts take my hands as we skip through one of the entrances past headless mannequins in silky dresses and cases of rainbow-colored pastries slathered in swirls of frosting.

Tita Perla buys me outfits and lip glosses and sunglasses that say Gucci, which she pays for with change from her coin purse. She buys me a coin purse, too, one that matches the pleather backpack she's also bought me, and that I now sling over both shoulders. Tita Cristina gets a matching one. I tell her we're twins as she holds my hand.

We leave the mall, wearing all our purchases. The old versions of ourselves are folded away in our shopping bags. We eat lunch on the top level of a two-story McDonald's. Tita Cristina sings, "McDo, McDo, McDo!," as she skips to the counter. I get a quarter-pounder with cheese and fries. Tita Perla opts for chicken nuggets. Tita Cristina gets a fried chicken leg and what looks like a tiny burger wrapped in white paper. She opens it, and it's a patty of steamed rice.

"What!" My voice is incredulous.

"Oh, yeah, baby," Tita Perla says, grabbing at her sister's rice patty as Tita Cristina swats at her hand with the bone of her chicken. "I told you, Annabelly, in the Pilippin-ahs, rice is life! Even Ronald McDo knows it!"

I laugh so hard, I almost choke on my burger.

On the ride home, we pile ourselves and our bags into the back of a bright pink jeepney painted with horses and the Virgin Mary. I wonder if we should hide some of these purchases so Mom doesn't see, doesn't yell at us for wasting so much freaking money.

"I should probably take the backpack off or give you the makeup," I say.

Tita Perla laughs, sucking on her paper McDonald's cup of Diet Coke as the jeepney bounces along the crumbling streets.

"Your mommy gave me this money! This was all your mommy's idea," she says. "She told me to spend it on you!"

"What?"

"She said you are stuck in the house this whole time while she is out doing her errands. This was her idea."

"Oh," I say. "That's cool."

"Your mommy can be *very cool*, Annabelly, very, very cool when she needs to be."

I straighten my shoulders a little, loosen my grip on the jeepney's bench, and lean into my titas.

The trip continues like this, with me venturing out with my aunts to go shopping and see last year's hit movies in poorly air-conditioned theaters.

We buy a Christmas tree and presents for all the cousins and titas and titos. We buy a new king-size bed for Nay and Grandpa. We buy John-John more school uniforms and, to balance them out, a pair of Nike high-tops I pick out for him myself.

Christmas is an event. Or, technically, Christmas Eve is.

When the rest of the family leave for Mass, Mom and us kids stay back to play Santa Claus. We finish wrapping the presents and stuffing the stockings and garnishing the food for the late-night Noche Buena feast.

What happens next feels like a fever dream: a parade of long-lost relatives passes through, including our great-great-grandmother. These ghosts of Christmas past bring gifts, they take gifts, they eat food, they leave food.

Wrapping paper spills into the front courtyard and out the back door, where the chickens will peck at it and nest with it come morning. We get more toys and more clothes. Mom buys an air-conditioning unit for Nay and Grandpa's room to go with their new king-size bed, and Tito Vic and Tito Boy set about installing it in the pitch dark, fueled by too many San Miguel beers. John-John shrills like an Americana girl who's seen a mouse when he opens his Nikes. His little brothers crowd around him, fighting for a look. When Mom hands them boxes of their own, they melt dramatically to the ground and bow at her feet, kissing her legs and laughing with joy.

Mom gets me a phone, a clear one where you can see the inner workings, just like the one Cathy has. Amber and Arthur obsess over little squeeze tubes of toxic-smelling plastic goo. Tita Cristina shows us how to roll the goop into balls, then insert a tiny straw and blow them into unpoppable bubbles that we bat through the air. We shower baby Vanity with the most toys and with hand-me-down clothes that have passed through me and Amber, as well as new clothes from Glorietta.

And then—we feast.

There's lechon kawali, chicken fried till it shatters, and whole fish stuffed with ginger and shallots, then steamed in verdant banana leaves. There's more pancit, more lumpia, a massive wooden bowl brimming with garlic-slicked rice, a tray heaped with nothing but fried slices of Spam that glisten fatty and pink under the harsh light of the kitchen's bare Edison bulbs.

Tita Perla and Tita Cristina mock John-John's shrills when they see the food, melting to the ground like his brothers as the house explodes with laughter. I eat mostly rice and sweets, which Nay keeps handing me every time I pass her. As midnight nears, there are fireworks. The kids pile into the second-story loft to watch them sparkle and glow.

"We don't do fireworks on Christmas in America!" I tell John-John as the sky outside the jalousie windows sizzles and pops.

"Look at Miss Americana! Loving the Pilipinas!"

He's right. I do. It's the happiest any of us has been since Dad left for the Holiday Inn. Me, Amber, Arthur, Mom, Tita Perla—all of us honestly happy.

I inch closer to the window and lean my head against its slats. I take a deep breath. I scream at the top of my lungs.

"Hoy!"

I want the world to stop. I want to bask in this joy for a moment longer.

Nobody hears me but my cousins and siblings. The room goes quiet for a second, everyone startled by my outburst. Then John-John and his brothers roll to their sides, seizing with laughter. I smile. Amber screams, "Hoy!" Arthur screams, "Hoy!" Vanity screams it, too, a "Hoy!" that's tiny but powerful.

Our Hoys! work. Our worlds pause. Not because of sadness or death or grief—because of happiness. Our joy spreads and grows and eats us up.

CHAPTER 22

# Going Home

Our final day in San Andres Bukid is spent watching Tito Boy solder lids onto makeshift cans of bagoong, a funky paste of fermented krill that Mom and our titas eat on crunchy slivers of green mango as Amber and I gag. I don't know why we need more bagoong. We have bagoong at home. Mom gets a new jar every time we drive to the tiny Asian market in the strip mall behind the Little Caesars. But Mom says *that* bagoong is not *this* bagoong. She is determined to bring as much of it with us as possible.

"They cannot confiscate canned seafoods," Mom says. She knows this as well as she knows the titrations for amoxicillin. Mom has committed the entirety of the US Customs manual to her frightening memory.

We say goodbye to our Filipino family in the same place we said hello to them, Nay and Grandpa's courtyard. There are some tears but mostly smiles; everyone seems confident we will see one another again.

This airport ride requires just one van. We leave Manila with less than we came with, at least physically. Our twelve boxes and suitcases have been trimmed to a lean seven, mostly our luggage, plus a trio of tape-and-twine-wrapped cardboard cubes holding all our new toys, all the souvenirs, and all Mom's covertly packaged foods.

She packs huge sheafs of pancit noodles between layers of our clothes. She tucks in boxes of milk candies here and crumbly polvoron shortbreads there. And then she does the one thing she knows she shouldn't: She slips baggies of tamarind and atis seeds into the middle of it all.

Mom has clear-cut ideas of right and wrong. They don't always align with US laws.

I learn this at the Los Angeles International Airport, when the cute beagle I've been eyeing howls frantically at our smallest box. A man in a starched black uniform points to it and to Mom. He tells us to follow him.

"Mommy?"

"It's fine. They cannot open my private property," Mom says.

She's wrong.

The man takes a utility knife and slices through the box's outer layers of twine and packing tape. He pulls open the flaps and, with gloved hands, sets my plush white pig with the three pink babies in her belly on the stainless-steel counter in front of him.

"Am I going to find weapons here? Or drugs of any kind?"

"Punyeta ka, what the hell do I look like?"

Mom's punyeta-mad. Amber and I instinctively take a step back.

"I have my daughters, and I'm pushing my baby in a freaking stroller. You think I have drugs? You think I am some Colombian drug horse like on *Unsolvable Mysteries*?"

*It's mule, drug mule, and it's* Unsolved Mysteries, I think but dare not say aloud.

"Are you going to strip-search me? Do you think I have cocaine taped to my body?"

Mom pulls up her shirt, flashing her soft belly and dingy Playtex bra for all of LAX to see. I turn the other way, pretend to study the ceiling, and wonder what kind of storm this will be. This is usually when Amber and I slink to our bedrooms and put pillows over our heads to mute the thunder, back when Dad was around to be Mom's sparring partner. Here, under the airport's stark fluorescent lights, there is no such reprieve.

It's like America brings out the worst version of Mom. And now that we're back, so is she. I think of the mom I met a few weeks ago, the one whose poise and self-assuredness I so admired. I wonder where she's gone. Did she get left behind in Manila? Or packed away in a balikbayan box wrapped in tape and twine? I wonder if inheriting some of my mom's traits means inheriting all of them. If having power means having all this pent-up anger, too, then no thanks, I'm good.

I wonder if this man knows what he's up against. I wonder if Mom will be arrested. My eyes slide from the ceiling to the clock on the wall. It clicks from 12:33 to 12:34 p.m.

"We're coming from Manila, sir, from *Asia*, not South America or wherever." Mom says the words slowly, like she's speaking to an imbecile or a telemarketer. "You've got it wrong. You are wasting everyone's time."

The officer is unmoved. He continues to dig through the box. He finds our candies and sets them to the right. Then he finds the jumbo can of bagoong with its hand-soldered lid.

"What's this?"

"Canned shrimp, that is admissible, canned goods and goods in vacuum-sealed jars," Mom says, as if the Border Patrol handbook is right in front of her.

"Ma'am, it's not permissible like this," the officer says, running a gloved finger along Tito Boy's squiggly handiwork.

"It is canned! I don't know how they operate the canning machines!"

The man tosses the cylinder unceremoniously into a bin. It booms when it hits bottom. He pulls out the sheafs of rice noodles, inspecting each twig, holding package after package to the light. He pulls the reading glasses dangling from a chain around his neck over the bridge of his nose for a closer look.

"Oh, ho, ho, he is looking for anything now!" Mom says, mocking the officer. "Rice noodles have never been banned! I could have carried those on the goddamn plane if I wanted to!"

"Ma'am, please."

He sets the noodles to the right in a towering stack next to the candies and cookies. As he does, a baggie filled with dark, glossy seeds falls from one of the sheafs. He holds it to the light.

"Did you declare these?"

Mom's tone and body language shift. I wonder if she'll lie, if she'll say she's never seen those seeds before in her freaking life.

Instead, she is solemn, respectful.

"No, sir. I didn't realize…"

The officer sets them to the left, once again without ceremony. He rifles through my clothes from the mall. He pulls out Arthur's dump truck and Amber's My Little Pony. When the box is empty, he turns it over and taps its bottom.

Mom smirks. "Can we go now?"

The officer takes one last look, then waves his arm over the piles of our stuff.

"Yes ma'am," he says, gesturing to a row of shelves behind us. "You'll find more packaging tape at that counter."

Mom gathers our things. She tells me to get tape and scissors and more twine. When I return, she's laughing so hard, her shoulders shake. I look at her, nervous.

"I have more atis seeds in my purse," she whispers. "He never even thought to check there."

I stand slack-jawed at her side, my arms filled with our stuffed animals and bags of sweets. My mother laughs and laughs.

CHAPTER 23

# The Promise

Pepper runs circles around the family room, up and across the couch, leaping to the chair, then to the brown carpet and back around again. Amber and I squeeze her tight, tell her how we've missed her. Liz, who we left to watch this barely one-year-old monster, says the dog's eaten half of Dad's vinyl collection and peed and pooped in all our rooms.

Seems fair. She thought we were never coming home. I'd have done the same.

Aside from Pepper, our house is eerily quiet. Tita Perla is still in Manila for a few more days. Cathy is at her family's cabin in North Carolina. Amber and I return to our vampire routine, watching *Dragnet* and *Green Acres* on Nick at Nite while our neighbors sleep, while the traffic on McGregor does, too.

I have a newfound appreciation for the little air-conditioning that Mom allows. Sleeping in my own bed feels downright luxurious. But being home means being home. It means staring at Dad's computer desk without Dad behind it. Going out to his workbench with no fear of disturbing him, hoping for ice cream and M&Ms but having Mom tell me to eat an orange from the yard instead.

"It's just as good," she insists.

Liar.

School starts, and it's not the same either. Lauren and Kelly have brought Krissy Thomas in to replace me. She has actual breasts, poofy bangs, and perfect alabaster skin. Her father is a dermatologist. She has Hypercolor shirts that go from pink to orange, purple to teal, and another with three ballerinas on the front, standing with their hands at their hips.

"That's you, that's me, and that's Kelly," she tells Lauren on the bus one morning, as my ears burn from the row behind theirs.

I try to talk about the Philippines, about the Glorietta mall and buying Gucci sunglasses for fifty cents.

"Well, they're not real Gucci, then," Krissy tells me. "Those were probably made by kids in sweatshops. That's why they were so cheap."

I start sitting at the front of the bus, where I can't hear them talk about their upcoming spring break ski trips and their holiday cruises through the Bahamas.

I find an open seat next to a girl with freckled white skin and long, frizzy auburn hair that matches our bus driver's. She always sits in the first row. I think she's the driver's daughter. She introduces herself as Artis, then looks back to the blue spiral-bound notebook she keeps on her lap, scratching long stretches of words with her push-point pencil.

I don't want to bother her. I like the silence. I peek at her notebook, and every line is packed with cramped letters. She writes until her pencil reaches the bottom-most line of the page. She flips it over, a clean slate, then keeps scribbling, face down and focused.

I don't say anything that first morning. Or the several after it. I pull out my own notebooks and check my math homework and start the next series of social studies outlines. Mom likes good grades. I can get good grades. This becomes our silent, unspoken bus routine: me getting ahead on classwork; Artis, who's maybe the bus driver's daughter, writing endless sentences in her blue notebook. Then, one morning, there's a crack.

"Hey," Artis says, her soft voice barely audible over the roar of the bus engine and the static of the driver's radio.

"Hey," I say back.

"Do you have any pencil lead?"

I reach into the front pocket of my JanSport backpack and tip a thin strand from my red-topped case. I hand it over delicately. She pinches it between thumb and forefinger, then presses it into the end of her pencil and clicks the eraser until there's just enough showing.

"Thank you," she says, looking up at me for the first time.

"Yeah, no problem." I pause. "What, what is that?"

"I'm writing a book."

"Whoa, that's cool."

"I hope so."

"What kind of book?"

"Well, there's this girl, and she's stuck in a magical forest, and she has to learn how to cast spells with crystals, but the only ones who know the crystal spells are elves who don't speak her language, so she has to befriend them or maybe kill them."

"Wow."

"It's kind of specific."

"No, that's cool."

"Thanks."

She tips the pencil my way. "Thanks for this, too."

From that shared bit of pencil lead, a slow friendship blooms. Artis is not the bus driver's daughter. She lives with her mom, a teacher, on Fort Myers Beach, a place I associate with shitty motel rooms and abnormal deaths. Artis doesn't have a father either. Hers died when their family's Piper Cub crashed in a field near their old farm in Georgia. She was on board. A long scar tracing her lower spine is her lifelong souvenir from that day, as is the rod that sometimes sets off metal detectors at airports.

When I tell her my dad died in an accident, she nods but doesn't pry for details. For that I'm grateful. Her story is so much more…inspiring? Emotional? Hard-core? Mine pales in comparison. But I love her for this commonality. For once, I don't feel so alone.

It's early summer, and despite my efforts, the house is warm. I have been incrementally inching down the thermostat since yesterday, one click at a time in hopes Mom won't notice. Each degree, a nudge toward normalcy.

I'm in a cleaning frenzy, trying to get our collective mess into something close to respectable. I scream at Amber, shoveling her markers and colored pencils into a bag and hurling it into her bedroom as she lounges in front of her television, wholly unfazed.

"Get your crap off the breakfast nook!"

Arthur is my right hand. I hand him dirty socks and Pepper's dog brush and sticky Nutri-Grain wrappers. He runs them to the laundry bin, the garage, the trash can, in exchange for my services as his stopwatch.

I hand him a set of reading glasses.

"Put these in Mom's purse."

He holds them like a track-and-field baton and awaits my start. "On your mark. Get set. GO!" His feet pound across the carpet, then over the square brown tiles of the kitchen, then back again as I count Mississippis and scrub Hi-C stains from the couch. He's back, breathing hard in a pair of faded Batman undies and nothing else.

"Six Mississippi!" I say. "A new world record!"

Arthur thrusts his arms in the air triumphantly. I hand him a pile of Mom's underwear from the stacks of laundry on the coffee table.

"New race," I say. "These need to go in the top drawer on Mom's end table."

My brother nods, takes the bras and panties, and hops into his takeoff position, one leg in front of the other. I count down this time: "Three, two, one—GO!," then turn my attention to the rack of Mom's nursing uniforms dangling from a ceiling hook next to the big-screen TV.

Our house has become a matter of function over form. Mom does our laundry in stations she's arranged around the family room: sorting and folding at the coffee table, ironing and hanging in front of the sliding door. She divides our outfits on wire hangers color-coded by person—pink for Amber, purple for me, blue for Arthur, every other random color for Mom—that we're supposed to gather and take to our closets. Instead, we use the family room as our collective dressing area.

The kitchen is a mess of its own, scattered with plastic cups filled to various levels with chocolate milk, stale Sprite, and mold-fuzzed orange juice. Mom's pots and pans live on our electric stove. She swipes them with a dish towel after cooking, then returns them to their respective burners. Tita Perla's rice cooker sits next to the stove and is always filled to some level, be it a fresh pot still steamy or the leftover clumps from yesterday, which she and Mom eat with eggs for breakfast.

Pepper's bag of Purina, lassoed shut with a hair tie, slumps next to our overflowing trash can, which sits beneath Mom's compost bowl along a counter blanketed with sprouting seeds and bunches of mini bananas given to her by a Dominican phlebotomist from the hospital.

I've got my work cut out for me. Creating order from chaos isn't easy.

Artis is coming over. She's going to spend the night. She's going to be the first outsider to see our home since Dad died. (Cathy doesn't count.) It has to look right.

As I tip the leftovers from last night's dinner plates into the garbage and send Arthur to run the compost bowl out to the mango tree—"Your old record is eighteen seconds, let's see if you can beat it!"—I come across paperwork. Or is it junk mail? The flyer says Century 21. A business card is stapled to the front of it, with a photo of a woman with poofy red shoulder pads and hair to match.

I consider throwing it away, then remember Mom freaking out when we had to dig a Publix receipt from the outside trash can so she could return a carton of cottage cheese. I take the flyer and tack it to the bulletin board next to the pantry. I memorize its place so I know where to find it if Mom asks.

You can't be too careful in this world.

When Artis comes, she takes no notice of my massive cleaning efforts. She acts like our house could be any other house. I couldn't be prouder of myself.

We stay up late, playing computer games and tallying up our scores from *Sassy* magazine's quiz "Are you a prude or a slut?" I answer seriously and am a total ice-cold prude. Artis answers hopefully; turns out she's a "fiery slut who may need to cool her jets." Who knew? We swim. We eat cold pizza for breakfast. She helps me with my yard-work chores, gathering dead palm fronds from the backyard and dragging them to McGregor.

"This is so weird, I'm so sorry, you really don't have to help," I say as we're elbow-deep in fluttery brown leaves.

"No, it's cool," she says. "I mean, it's definitely weird, but I wouldn't let you do this all by yourself."

We swim in the pool again, then fight with my siblings over the big-screen TV until Mom shoos us outside, tells us to take a walk. We head to the river, to a drainage pipe where we can throw rocks and talk about crushes: Adam McLachlan, Sean Griffin, Jacob Bradley, who told me I'd look kind of like the girl from *Wayne's World* if I'd just get a nose job, which I take to mean he loves me. As we're walking back, I see Mom in the driveway, talking to a woman with poofy red hair.

"I know that lady," I tell Artis.

"I love her heels. Is she a friend of your mom's?"

"No, I don't think so, but I've seen her somewhere."

As we approach, the redheaded woman slips into a black Lexus, the full-size version that's a couple models nicer than Tita Perla's, and purrs off down McGregor.

That evening, after Artis leaves, as the house slips back to its preferred state of chaos—a load of laundry folded on the coffee table, dirty breakfast and lunch plates stacked in the sink—I find Mom peeling potatoes over the silver compost bowl.

"Here, you do this, I have to starch my uniform for tomorrow," Mom says, handing me the peeler, then pulling the ironing board out of the bathroom closet, where I stored it.

"Why did you put all my stuff away?"

"I was cleaning, for Artis."

"What's wrong with an ironing board? Are you embarrassed that your mother irons her clothes?"

I roll my eyes and keep peeling.

"Who was that lady today?" I say.

"What lady?"

"The one in the black Lexus."

"Oh, Nancy? She's just a friend of Terri's."

My cheeks burn as I glide the peeler over the potato in my hand. I watch its brown skin slip from its white flesh and into the bowl of green bean ends and banana peels.

I cut the potatoes into cubes and start them on the stove in a pot of cold water, as Mom has taught me for fluffy mashed potatoes. I walk to the bulletin board and pull the pin from the Century 21 brochure with the business card stapled to it. I hand them to Mom.

"She's this lady. I recognized her. What was she doing here?"

Mom turns off the iron. She carefully folds her white nursing pants in half, then threads them through a hanger, adding it to the collection that's once again dangling from the ceiling hook next to the big screen. She walks to the breakfast table. She taps her hand against it, motioning for me to join her. I turn in her direction but only take a step.

I wonder if she'll call Amber and Arthur away from their movie. I wonder if this will be like the time she explained the plastic baggie and the

Wite-Out. I can feel my heart in my chest, *whump-whump-whump*. I realize Mom must have fixed the thermostat back to her preferred 80 degrees. I'm sweating.

"Mom, what's going on?"

"Listen, Annabelle Marie."

That's not a good start.

"I can't do this. I can't keep going like this," Mom says, her eyes scanning the room, her head tilting in every direction of the world. "I barely see you guys. When I am home, I am doing laundry and mowing the yard. Other than that, I am at the hospital. Your brother thinks Liz is his mommy."

I shake my head, even though everything she's said is true.

"I need help. I need more help than just Liz. I need my family."

"What about Tita Perla?"

"She's great, I love your Tita Perla, but she's seeing someone, and she's going to have her own family one day."

The burning in my cheeks spreads to my ears and scalp. My body senses fire and sends tears to quench the flames. I hate that I'm crying. I'm not sad. I'm freaking pissed.

"The reason we went home, the reason we went to the Philippines, is because I need the help of all of my family. If we live with them, I won't have to work all the time. You'd get to grow up with your cousins and your grandparents, your real family. I could send you to the best schools and then we'd work on getting you back to the US for college."

I'm not one for temper tantrums. Not when I was little and certainly not now, when I'm almost thirteen. I like to hold on to my rage and let it simmer in my marrow. I like to take it to bed with me, let it unfurl in panicky dreams where I'm riding in the back of Dad's Volkswagen with no driver and no steering wheel, careening off the side of the bridge and into the Caloosahatchee—*We don't call it the Caloosahatchee River, we're locals*, I hear Dad saying—my body seizing to consciousness just as I slam into the sun-tea waters.

In this moment, though, I can't hold on to it. I want to run at Mom and tackle her, knock her to the ground and straddle her and punch her with my left fist and then my right, over and over. It's a fleeting thought. But it's there. Instead, I stomp my feet and clench my fists at my sides like a cartoon character. I imagine the plumes of smoke rising from my comically drawn head, my face colored in shades of pink and tomato-red. I kick the ironing board, sending it clattering into the sliding door. I grab at Mom's starch-stiff uniforms hanging from the hook in the ceiling and throw them to the ground. I kick them for good measure, then stomp down the hallway to my room.

I get as far as the green bathroom, when I feel Mom's hands clamp down on my shoulders. She drags me back to the family room and shoves me into the mess I've made.

"Clean it up."

"No."

I get up to go back to my bedroom. Mom blocks my path and pushes me back into the laundry pile. I land face down in a butter-yellow nursing coat. I turn to get up, and I'm met with Mom's face inches from my own.

"CLEAN IT UP! CLEAN IT THE FUCK UP!" she screams, her right arm outstretched, ready to swing at me.

"Jesus, Mom, fine, I'll clean it up, fine!"

I pick myself up off the floor as Mom circles back to the kitchen, wiping her face with the bottom of her muumuu. I tip the ironing board back to its feet. I rummage through the nursing uniforms to match tops to bottoms and get them back onto their hangers.

"Sit down," Mom says.

I roll my eyes when her back's turned, then slump onto the couch. I tuck my legs under me and cross my arms across my chest.

"Listen to me," Mom says. "I can't go on like this. I cannot."

Mom stands in the kitchen, patting dry the sirloins she bought for dinner. We don't eat steak often. I wonder if this conversation has always been part of tonight's plan.

Her voice softens.

"Think about all the fun you had in Manila. You can buy all the clothes you want there, all the toys, all the games. You can live like freaking Cathy over there. You can be the rich girl!"

Her words are enticing. I shift one leg out from under me and place it on the floor. It kicks Arthur's dump truck, knocking its payload onto the beige-brown carpet: one plush baby pig that must've escaped from the mommy pig's belly. I think about all the other toys we got over there, more toys than I've ever seen Mom buy us in our lives. I remember the trips to the mall, the movies, the manicures, the McDonald's, the never-ending sweets.

The first of the steaks hits the big pan on the stove. Amber peeks out from her bedroom, where *An American Tail* plays for the third time in a row.

"What smells so good?" Amber says, eyes closed, nose in the air.

"We're having your favorite," Mom sings from the kitchen, "steak and mashed potatoes."

"With gravy?" Amber says.

"Of course with gravy! You can't have mashed potatoes and no gravy!"

A part of me is here, a part of me is on the pink jeepney riding back from a day of shopping with Tita Cristina and Tita Perla, trying to remember what exactly Tita Perla said. I can see her McDonald's cup filled with Diet Coke. I can feel the potholes and the smoggy heat.

*This was all your mommy's idea!*

That's what Tita Perla said.

*Your mommy can be very cool, Annabelly, very, very cool when she needs to be.*

I stomp into the kitchen, into the sizzling wisps of beef-scented smoke.

"This was all your plan," I say to Mom. "You knew we were going to move before we even went to the Philippines."

I imagine Mom gasping and clutching a string of pearls around her neck, stunned that her twelve-year-old daughter could solve such a mystery.

"Of course I knew," she says, her attention on the cooking beef. "Where do you think I went all those mornings? I was looking for a house for us. I even told you that, I told you I was trying to find some place with room for everyone."

I shake my head, remembering all the days I woke up in our loft and Mom was missing.

"Why didn't you ask me? Don't you care what I think?"

Mom pulls the steaks from the pan and sets them to rest on a cutting board. She spoons flour into the shimmery fat, whisking it into a paste with the same salad fork she used to flip the steaks.

"I've only ever cared what you think," Mom says. "That's why I didn't send you to the Rainbow Trails camp. It's why I let you come home to an empty house instead of going to Liz's. You're all I ever freaking think about, Annabelle Marie, you and your sister and brother. That's it."

"You think they want to move to the Philippines?"

"They don't get to say. Not this time."

"We can't go, Mommy. I can't live there."

"Yes, you can. You think that now, but you'll make friends, and you'll learn Tagalog, and you'll be just fine."

"I won't be fine! You said yourself that language is stupid!"

My brain is spinning. I'm living my panic dream, searching for a steering wheel where there isn't one as my car careens out of control.

And then I see it. I see it and grab it and turn it hard.

"I'll die, Mommy."

The words slither out of my mouth.

"I will die over there. I know it."

I feel icky, the same way I feel when I yell at Arthur or Amber. I know it's uncalled for, but I'm powerless to stop.

Mom is quiet, still whisking lumps out of her gravy.

"Wash your hands and set the table," she says.

My hands feel dirty. I wash them for twice as long as I usually do, scrubbing them the way Mom used to when we went on scavenger hunts for Gramma's cigarettes. I grab plates and silverware and do as I'm told.

The next morning, I hear Mom on the phone. Her tone is serious, businesslike. When I come out for breakfast, I find Nancy's Century 21 brochure atop the kitchen trash can, her poofy red hair streaked with congealed steak grease.

I'm hopeful. But not foolish enough to say anything. I pour my bowl of generic Frosted Flakes and watch whatever Amber and Arthur have on TV. Mom comes in from the yard, pours herself a travel mug of ice water, and joins me at the breakfast table, her Dollar Store sombrero blocking my view of *Saved by the Bell*.

"Listen to me," Mom says as I nod almost simultaneously. "If we're going to stay, I will need your help. Your *real* help."

I continue nodding, more forcefully.

"You can't sleep in till ten or eleven anymore, let's start there," Mom says as my nodding slows.

"I will need you to cook and clean and do yard work without me begging you every single freaking weekend. You will have to grow up, starting right now."

"And then we can stay?"

"We can stay. But you have to promise me this."

My nods become nervous, almost mechanical, as I try to think this through.

"You have to say it," Mom says. "You have to tell me you promise to help."

The cereal feels like it's coagulated into a ball in my throat. I try to cough. It comes out like a bark.

"Can you promise me?" Mom says again.

I find my airway. I breathe in and then out.

"I promise," I say.

"OK, then. We'll stay."

She takes her mug of ice water and pushes the kitchen door open. "Come outside when you're done with your cereal. I will teach you how to mow."

I nod again, even though she can't see me. I smile to myself: I've done it. The smile fades as I think about that rusty mower, how it's run over nests of rattlesnakes, how Mom wears Dad's cowboy boots to protect her shins from the flying shrapnel it shoots out behind it, how she screamed at Dad for mowing down her mango saplings.

The mower scares me. But we're not going anywhere.

# PART III

# The Trunk

CHAPTER 24

# The Eldest Mango

When you promise to step up and become a twelve-year-old co-parent to your widowed, grief-ravaged mother, there is no transition period. It would've been nice to give my childhood a month's notice, to take a few weeks to hike the Spanish Basque country and practice mindful breathing techniques.

Nope. This job started posthaste.

Mom is our captain. I am her second-in-command. To everyone's shock, this system works. Even when Tita Perla moves out to live with Uncle Peter, her new Lebanese husband who drives a black Trans Am and introduces us to the wonders of baklava. Even when Liz takes her real family on a monthlong vacation to visit relatives in Hawaii. Even as I make new friends and go on dates where I hold hands with Mike Nichols and eat hot pretzels at the Edison Mall.

I learn to pack school lunches for Amber and me the night before, to keep them in the bottom of the fridge where it's the coldest, to put frozen Hi-C boxes in the bags come morning so they'll be drinkable by lunch while also keeping our ham sandwiches from spoiling. I learn to operate the washer and dryer and how to mix forty parts gasoline to one part oil for the Weedwacker. I learn to wake up early, as Mom's leaving to take Arthur to Liz's, so I can make sure Amber's dressed and ready for the neighbor's carpool.

I learn to stop calling Mom at the hospital, to find answers myself.

One Sunday, while cutting orange slices for our sixty-third rewatching of Walt Disney's *Beauty and the Beast*, I stab a steak knife through the web of skin between my thumb and index finger, pinning my hand to our butcher-block cutting board. The pain is dull and distant. It's fear that pulses inside me.

I let go of the knife. It stands handle-up like a dart. My breathing goes from panting to quick heaving gulps that rack my torso back and forth. I hear Disney previews playing, for *Aladdin* and *The Mighty Ducks*. I look around for the portable phone. It's in the breakfast nook, well out of reach. I think of yelling for Arthur, having him bring it to me. I worry he'll freak out more than I have at the situation.

*Don't be a baby. Get it together. THINK.*

Mom once told us about a time in the emergency room in Manila, about a man who came in with a butcher's knife buried in his back. The new resident doctor wanted to pull it out, but Mom, a mere nurse, knew better. She left the knife in place and rushed the man to the operating room. Surgeons removed it and sewed the man's lung back together. And he lived—for a week, before succumbing to an infection.

"The stupid freaking doctors probably didn't sterilize properly," Mom said, "but I bought that man a week."

I steel myself to look at my injury. There is no blood. The knife must be holding it in. It doesn't look all that bad, really, just like a hand, pinned to a board, with a knife. I wiggle my thumb and forefinger. The knife wobbles. I wiggle them again, then push my left hand hard and flat against the board. I take another breath, grab the knife's handle and yank.

I wait for a spray of red. I wonder if I'll pass out, if Amber and Arthur will find me when the movie ends, face down in a slippery scarlet pool.

The knife springs free. My head half turned away, I peek sideways at the carnage. There's no blood, just a hole the size of a steak-knife's tip in the webbing of my flesh. I hold my hand in front of my face. I wiggle my thumb again. I can see muscle twitching. It looks like raw chicken. I bend my thumb back, *twitch*, and forth, *twitch*, my eyes transfixed as I move on autopilot to Mom's bathroom and the medicine cabinet where she keeps the hydrogen peroxide. I pour it over my hand and watch the bubbles burn and fizz from one side of the hole through to the other. I dab it with a clean washcloth, then wrap it in a Band-Aid. I'm back in Amber's room in time to hear the poor provincial town waking up in a chorus of song.

"Good morning, Belle!"

This is our new Tometich life, as sweet and simple as the mangoes Mom plucks from the now-towering tree in the front yard. The tree Mom planted in the months before Dad died and life as we knew it splintered and branched; the tree she guarded, watered, and fed is, after five incredibly long years, giving her fruit. Mom brought in its first ripe mango swaddled in her sweat towel like a newborn. She sliced into it carefully, offering us kids slippery slivers, reserving the pit for herself. Amber and Arthur took their bites and ran. I watched Mom wipe beads of sweat from her face as she sank her teeth into the sunny flesh. Or were they tears? Mom tucked the naked pit into an empty yogurt cup, then hurried back to the yard, smiling. Her first honest smile since we left Manila.

There is no mango feast this time. We have just the one tree, for now, and it's still new to this whole bearing-of-fruit thing. There will be no spreading of newspapers, no naked bellies slicked yellow with juice.

There's also no one to buy us bottles of Coke and ice-cream bars. No one to sing morbid songs with us as Mom picks and picks. No one to mow down the saplings that will spring from the seeds and send Mom into a tizzy.

The thunderstorm fights of our parents start to fade from memory. They are replaced, at first, by bag after bag of mangoes, by smile after smile. In fall, the tree stops fruiting and the fights resume. Minor squabbles over uneaten broccoli stalks. Tiffs over the right way to wash dishes without running up the water bill. *Who do we think we are? Richie Rich?*

Slowly, though, they build. I get a B-plus on an interim report and am forbidden to eat pretzels or hold hands with Mike Nichols at the mall. I am two minutes late coming home from Cathy's one Saturday, according to the master clock, and I'm not allowed to see her for two weeks. I throw a fit, remind Mom that *this is a free country!* She slaps me and makes it a month.

Mom is strict, sure. Heavy-handed, yes. But she says it's because she wants the best for us, and I believe her. Until The Underwire Incident of 1994.

In eighth grade, I persuade Mom to buy me a frilly underwire bra from the intimates section of J. Byrons. All of my previous bras have been of the training variety: cheap, paper-thin things that come sealed in plastic, five to a pack, in the same Walmart aisle as the Vaseline. I don't need underwire. I have very little going on up top. The padding is the bra's allure. The padding takes me from "Young man, is your mother home?" to a solid AA. The padding is my life.

I wear the bra every day to Dunbar Middle, securing it in place under my tighter training bra, so it doesn't slide up to my chin like an Elizabethan collar. I keep it on at all times, to be prepared in case boys are snapping bra straps. God forbid I miss out. I wear it through gym class, during mile-long runs and games of dodgeball. It's my companion for the after-school intramural volleyball tryouts, too, my pubescent sweat seeping into the lacy padding like a sponge.

At home, I fling it off with the rest of my clothes. Then I resurrect it from the heap the next morning to repeat its busy life cycle.

My love for this bra is matched only by Mom's hatred for it. I figure she's jealous. I am not beholden to the fickle schedules of Mother Nature for granting breasts. I am my own woman, all 30AA of me. They probably didn't have a J. Byrons intimates section in 1870s Manila, when Mom was growing up. That's not my fault. This is 1994. I can have boobs when I want to have boobs.

Here I am, thirteen, with it all figured out.

It's a weeknight. Mom's been at the hospital all day. We've eaten rice, tomatoes, and Hamburger Helper for dinner, a recipe relatively new to my burgeoning repertoire. Arthur is asleep. Amber is in the bath. Mom's folding laundry. I'm watching Steve Urkel on the big screen, my knees and bare legs tucked into Dad's old YMCA Cape Cod T-shirt.

"What happened here?" Mom says, holding my padded underwire bra up to the light of the TV.

"I dunno," I say, not looking. The words sound more like "uh-ih-uh," a quick string of grunts too lazy for consonants.

"What do you mean, 'uh-ih-uh'?" Mom says. Her voice is prickly and charged.

I straighten up in my chair, untucking my legs from Dad's shirt, thankful my show has gone to a commercial and hoping this is just a rain shower and not a storm, that we can get this settled before Steve and the Winslow family make their return.

"I mean, I don't know what happened to it," I say, looking at the lacy cups in Mom's hands. "It looks fine to me."

Mom whips the bra at my face. Its plastic front clasp catches my right temple, pinching my eye shut with a bright flicker of pain.

"Jeez, Mom."

"*Jeez, Mom!*" she mocks me. "How 'bout JEEZ, ANNABELLE MARIE! You broke the freaking thing! Did you even realize? Or do you not give a shit?"

We're studying McCarthyism in Mrs. Kyko's social studies class. *Are you now, or have you ever been a member of the Communist Party?—Did you even realize, or do you not give a shit?*

I can't remember how to answer.

"I don't…I'm not sure." Words are failing me. I still don't understand what's wrong.

"I told you you would hate underwire!" Mom screams. "What the hell did you do with it?"

Eyes watering, I feel for the bra in my lap. I hold it in my hands; one side is firm at its padded edge, the other is soft and flimsy. I inspect its inner lining. My bony chest has worn a hole near the left side of the clasp. I'd felt something poking me at school. The underwire must have come out somehow.

"I didn't do anything with it. There's a little hole here, see?" I hold the limp side up to Mom. "It must've come loose in the washing machine. I'll still wear it. I promise. It's fine."

But it's not fine. Mom has an axe to grind, and I will be her whetstone. She is frantic, yelling about how I never listen, how she pulled everything out of the washer and dryer and didn't see a piece of underwire. How, *believe me, she would have seen a piece of underwire.*

I see Amber tiptoe out of the peach bathroom in a towel, hair plastered to her head in wet strings. She scurries to her bedroom and quietly tugs the door shut, the way people do in horror movies when the monster is on the loose. I imagine Arthur pulling his teddy bear comforter over his little head.

Mom smacks us plenty. When Dad was alive, he did the spankings, as punishment. Mom just snaps sometimes, and next thing you know, your left cheek is on fire because the dog hasn't been fed or she already told you to pick up your shoes.

I know she's going to smack me over this bra. I can feel it the way you feel lightning just before it scorches the earth. But I don't expect the clothes hanger. Mom's pacing the family room when she grabs it off the ironing board. I see it in her right hand, and my eyes bulge from their sockets, allowing the tears trapped behind them to gush hot and fast down my face.

"What is that for?" I say. "*I didn't do anything!*"

"Yeah, right."

The hanger is thick white plastic, not one of my flimsy color-coded purple ones. Mom rears her arm back and it makes a sick whooshing sound as it cuts the air. The hanger flexes and whips, slashing at my upper thighs. I yelp when it lands, the way Pepper does when she wants to come in from the backyard. I try to look at Mom, to see this woman who's saved our lives so many times, but she's lost. Tears stream down her face as they stream down mine. She flings her arm back again, and again, and again. I grit my teeth. My eyes go dry. Jagged welts surface on my legs, angry red. Mom stops, sits on the couch, places the hanger in her lap, tries to catch her breath.

"Tell me what you did with it."

She doesn't want the truth. She wants an answer.

"What do you want me to say? You want me to make up some story about losing a piece of underwire? Fine! I lost it during gym."

"*I KNEW IT.*"

She raises the hanger one more time. I grab it in midair.

"Mommy, are you serious?"

"I knew it, Annabelle Marie. It didn't have to come to this. You make everything so fucking difficult."

*You make everything so fucking difficult.*

Diff-ih-cult, three syllables.

The word spins like a vortex. It opens a wormhole in my head. It takes me somewhere else, sometime else.

I am here, and I am not. I hear Steve Urkel whining on TV, but I see my childhood bed, its yellow-and-white comforter with the bonnet-topped girls and their baskets of flowers, with the polka dots in three rows of three. I hear the crashes and clangs of my parents fighting. Dad grunting as Mom charges him a second time, then a third. Mom screaming that *he makes everything so fucking difficult.*

In my head, these fights were Dad's fault. He was always the one leaving, the guilty party too ashamed to show his face and bear our breakfast-table judgment. The police arrested him. Not Mom. He's the man. In the Lifetime miniseries we watch at Liz's house, it's always the man's fault.

*It didn't have to come to this Louis/Annabelle Marie! You make every-thing so fucking difficult.*

Do we? Or does Mom?

Before The Underwire Incident of 1994, Mom's rage was almost always precipitated by something. Did the punishments fit the crimes? No. But there was always a cause.

Fighting, I am learning, is as essential to our mother as breathing. It is her cardio. Yelling and screaming are merely her warm-up. Once she finds her pace and a willing opponent, she starts pumping her arms and kicking her legs, unleashing her pent-up fury one push, slap, and thrown screwdriver at a time. Mom doesn't talk about her childhood, but I doubt this abuse is new to her. I've come to understand that these things are cyclical. They are repeating patterns that continue like dance steps: left, two, three; right, two, three; yell, two, three; punch, two, three.

Dad was an easy and willing partner. When he left, she had to find new ones.

Looking back, that wasn't the only cycle repeating. I was the oldest-sister-cum-second-mother of the house, just as Mom was in the Philippines. I boiled the rice and wiped the butts (mostly Arthur's). I dreamed of escaping, as I imagine Mom did, of creating a better life for myself somewhere far away from all of this.

A week later, I see something sticking out from beneath the dryer in the garage: a few inches of hard plastic curved like a smile without a face. I pick it up and turn it over in my hands. I hold it to my chest, cupping it under the fleshy bottom of my left not-quite breast. It's just the right size.

I bring it in and set it on the breakfast-nook table, where Mom is snapping green beans.

"What's that?" she says, her eyes going from her compost bowl of discarded ends to the *Little House on the Prairie* rerun on TV.

She shows little interest in this object. I want to be angry, call the police, seek justice. But more so, I'm tired.

"It's the underwire to my bra. It was in the garage under the dryer. I just found it."

"I thought you lost it at school," Mom says.

I stand there for a second, looking at her, the underwire, the green beans, the jeans I've worn to class every 93-degree day this week to cover the bruises on my legs. Mom never looks up. I walk to my room and close the door.

Twenty-two years later, in the courtroom with my sister, I'll remember this day. How thirteen-year-old me wished Mom could be put in jail. How the thirty-five-year-old me fears someone may have been listening.

# CHAPTER 25

# Car Rides

M om is jumping up and down, pointing at my chest and screaming, "TWENTY-DOLLAR BILL! TWENTY-DOLLAR BILL!" from the other side of the booth's plexiglass walls. The mint-green faces of George Washington and Abe Lincoln swirl around me, pushed by a fan beneath my feet. I feel like Marilyn Monroe, if she'd been a flat-chested teenager dressed in boyfriend jeans and Pumas who was thrust into a car-dealership promotion.

Happy sixteenth birthday to me.

I would, under any other circumstances, rather be dead than be in the Sam Galloway Ford money booth, grabbing for a flurry of one-dollar bills as middle-aged men in khakis and royal-blue polo shirts watch and my mother coaches me like a dance mom at her child's recital.

But I get a car at the end of this humiliation. I'm sorry, not a car, a *brand-new Ford Explorer* with leather interior and sapphire-blue paint. I will endure this money booth. I will possibly enjoy this money booth.

I swipe at my chest, where the face of Andrew Jackson is pasted to my Stüssy T-shirt. I grab him and shove him in my pocket. Mom pumps her fist in the air. From somewhere far away, I hear a man counting down:

*three...two...one.* I grab for more dollars, then watch the rest float to the floor as the buzzing in my ears ceases and my long dark hair falls back to my shoulders.

I exit the booth a new person, baptized into womanhood by cold, hard cash. The dealership's shtick—*Buy a car, get a minute in the money booth! Cash! Cash! Cash!*—is meant to lure hapless saps into the greasy clutches of car salesmen. Mom is neither hapless nor sappy. She has had her mind set on this SUV. The money booth is a fortunate coincidence. If there are such things.

Mom and I count out my haul on the hood of my new car: the twenty, a five, fourteen ones—thirty-nine dollars.

"There's your first two tanks of gas," Mom says, handing me the keys.

I take them and open her door, ushering her into the passenger seat so I can drive.

My Ford Explorer is nicer than the lavender Ford Probe that Cathy got two years earlier for her sixteenth birthday. This reversal of fortunes—my having the expensive thing, her having the cheaper one—is new for us. But in true Cathy style, it's no big deal. She's happy for me. Moreover, she's too wrapped up in a blue-eyed boy named Blake, whom she met at the Alternative Learning Center while on suspension for smoking in the bathrooms, to really care.

Cathy has veered hard from her mother's preppy cheerleader vision for her. She wears Dickies khakis and gray hooded sweatshirts with plaid Doc Martens on her feet, regardless of the weather. She listens to Rancid and the Ramones and Green Day, their CD cases cluttering the floor of her Probe. She rims her eyes in charcoal liner and keeps her long blond hair tucked into a messy bun at the nape of her neck. It's a look that says, *Don't look at me.* But her perfect cheekbones, shiny hair, and bouncing D-cup breasts give our fellow high schoolers no other option.

For my first two years at Fort Myers High, before I have a Ford of my own, this popular goth chick is my chauffeur.

The mornings and afternoons of my freshman and sophomore years are spent tucked in the back seat of Cathy's two-door coupe, pretending not to mind the blue cloud of menthol-scented smoke surrounding me. I bury my head in algebra books or the dog-eared copy of Chinua Achebe's *Things Fall Apart*, which will indeed fall apart before I've finished reading and rereading it.

Cathy's cooler friends (my word, not hers) get to ride shotgun. I make sure of it, crawling dutifully into the sardine-can back as soon as we get to Lisa Edmonton's driveway or Rien De Venecia's door. Rien is also Filipino, full-blooded, not a mongrel like me. His dad is a doctor. Rien wears a black Members Only jacket even on 98-degree days. He keeps his hair shaved on one side and long on top, so it covers his dark eyes. He sweeps it to the side with a toss of his head to light his American Spirit cigarettes. He has Cathy's swagger and my skin tone. The combination fascinates me. I never thought people who look like him, like us, could behave so boldly.

Rien says his name means "nothing," that his dad is obsessed with France and nihilism and Albert Camus. I find this ironic. This guy whose name means nothing knows exactly who he is.

When people ask Rien where his family's from, he has a short answer: the Philippines. I have a rambling soliloquy, about Manila and Massachusetts, and a grandmother from Newfoundland, Canada, and a grandfather from the old Yugoslavia, but he died when I was really young, and I'm not sure if he was Serbian or Croatian or Macedonian or Slovenian or Bosnia-Herzegovinian or Montenegrin. I'd ask my dad, but he died, too.

I once told Cathy's grandmother, Nena, that I was a mutt. She winked at me from behind her big amber-tinted glasses. "We're all nuts, ain't we, sweetheart?" I nodded and smiled. *Ain't we, though.*

Rien carries thick calculus and trig books tied together with leather lashing. He folds Steinbeck and Vonnegut paperbacks into the cargo pockets of his khakis. He says deep things like "Fuck the system, man." And he always says hi to me, even when I bury myself away in the back.

I think I may have a crush on him. If I weren't two years younger, four inches taller, and incapable of saying anything more to him than a weak "Hey," we could be something.

But I understand my place. I don't smoke, I don't know ska bands, and I don't own a single stick of eyeliner (I'm still not unconvinced those Chinese dyes won't make me go blind). I belong in the back. It's my escape hatch; the space shuttle that transports me into a universe away from Mom's rules. A place where I can cultivate and refine my nobodiness, where people won't ask about my Wite-Outed father or hanged uncle or the lady pulling weeds from our yard in a Dollar Store sombrero and cowboy boots who I sometimes claim is our maid.

Back here, those questions can't find me. Back here, I can harness the greatest power that being a nobody affords me: invisibility.

When we stop at the Sunoco on Edison Avenue so Cathy can use her grandfather's money to buy cartons of Kools for her and Blake from the Sikh man in the turban who never checks IDs, it's my job to stay in the back of the car and be the lookout.

"If you get caught, your mom will kill both of us," Cathy says on our first visit. "Stay here. If I don't come out in like ten minutes, I don't know, like, call the police or something."

I look around and see a graffitied pay phone at the far end of the building. *Do you need a quarter to dial 911?* From that day on, I keep some in my backpack, just in case.

Cathy won't let me smoke. Not that I ever ask. She and I both know the consequences. When Rien offers me one of his American Spirits, Cathy snatches the pack out of his hand and flings it at his chest.

"Her mom will hunt you down and slit your throat!"

I emerge from Cathy's car each afternoon smelling like menthol smoke and patchouli oil. She takes me to her bathroom and douses me in CK One, and then we pray to the Jo Tometich gods that Mom's blood-hound nose won't sniff us out. On especially smoky rides, I shed my stinky J. Byrons shirt and put on one of the frilly Esprit blouses that languish in the back of Cathy's closet, behind her hoodies and baggy tees. It's a symbiotic exchange. I get a new top. She is spared my mom's fury. Win-win.

I see my future husband while sitting in that back seat, not that either of us realizes it. From my vantage point, he's a tall white guy with big ears and a shorn head that grazes the fabric of the Probe's ceiling. I, of course, know who he is, even though I don't know who he'll become. Fort Myers is just big enough that way. He's the son of Mrs. Brunick, the teacher who wrapped me in her arms and kept me standing on my first days back to school after Dad died. He has a name like Bobby or Billy or Bradley—two uncomplicated, all-American syllables that I can't quite remember.

Unlike Rien, he doesn't say anything to me, just chats with Cathy in the front for the three blocks it takes to get from Fort Myers High to his front door. I don't say anything to him either. I don't say anything to most of the front-seat riders.

When Lisa thinks she's pregnant and we make an after-school stop at Eckerds so Cathy can buy her test sticks to pee on, I sit in silence, reading and rereading the same page of my book as Lisa's tears become sobs.

"Please be negative," she says to no one. "Please."

I keep my head down, my body frozen, staring at the same line from Uchendu: *But if you allow sorrow to weigh you down and kill you, they will all die in exile.*

I don't know what's taking Cathy so long. I wonder if you have to be eighteen to buy pregnancy tests, if I should fish a quarter from my backpack and call the police. My legs are asleep, and my back, pushed up against the seat, is a sheet of sweat. I shift ever so slightly. Lisa jumps like she's seen a ghost. I feel my invisibility cloak as it's yanked off me, exposing me for the back-seat oddball I am.

"Holy shit! Have you been back there this whole time?"

I shake my head to signal no while the word *yeah* comes out of my mouth.

"You scared the crap out of me," she says, twisting hard to her left to finally see me.

Awkwardly, I apologize. "I'm sorry. I'm so sorry. I was just reading, and I didn't want to bother you. It's no big deal, really. I'm just. I'm sorry, really, really sorry."

Lisa wipes tears from her eyes and tilts her head my way. I gnaw my lip, glancing side to side for any sign of Cathy, then back down at my book, which has folded shut. I'm certain Lisa's going to ask what the hell's wrong with me, who the hell just sits in silence while someone is in a full-blown crisis six inches away.

Lisa sniffs and clears her throat. "You can ride in the front sometimes, you know," she tells me, wiping her nose with the arm of her hoodie and offering a quiet smile.

I shake my head again, idly flipping through pages. "Oh, no, that's OK, I really like it back here."

I look up at her and smile back, the sort of half smile I hope will make me invisible again. Lisa turns her eyes back to the windshield. I go back to the start of the last chapter and reimmerse myself.

As I turn right out of the Sam Galloway Ford dealership, cautiously checking for pedestrians, then looking left, right, and left again for cars, I marvel at the perfect timing. Cathy left just last week for Tallahassee. She's enrolled at Florida State University, the college her parents attended. They traded her two-year-old Ford Probe for a brand-new Toyota 4Runner as her graduation gift. Now I can be my own chauffeur.

I don't know how Mom did it. The Ford Explorer, I mean. By most accounts, a single mother with three kids and a meager $10,000 payout from the one paltry life insurance policy Dad carried should be destitute.

Not Jo.

I'm not sure how much of her success is attributable to her and how much is due to the strength of the US middle class thirty-some years ago, but what Mom did still feels miraculous.

A lifetime of desperate poverty, of growing up without toys, text-books, or a guarantee of daily food, has prepared Mom for this. It has overprepared her. She hoards any and all money she can in certificates of deposit she keeps at various banks, in our college funds, her IRAs, and a 401(k) from the hospital, which she maxes out for every freely matched dollar she can get.

Any money that isn't saved goes to bare necessities: bottom-shelf cereal, Kmart clothes, what little payment Liz will accept for being our other mother. Mom grows much of her own produce in our yard, which has become more jungle than suburb. She works the extra shifts. She clips coupons, washes and reuses Ziploc bags, saves fast-food napkins, uses plastic grocery bags as her lunch boxes.

I am nine when I learn what a rain check is and how to procure it. By twelve the customer-service clerks at our Publix know me by name, know that I'm the Tometich family's Returns Person. The one who brings back cabbage that rang up at seventy-nine cents instead of the advertised fifty-five cents. The one who returns panty liners and year-old baby food and a melted tub of Neapolitan ice cream that's missing a tiny corner of its plastic safety liner.

Mom's scrimping and saving has exceptions. Travel is the big one.

Travel is one of the rare areas where my parents agreed. They format-ted their hospital schedules to get the summers off, leaving them free to road-trip up and down the eastern seaboard in Dad's VW. A two-month-long vacation to the Philippines when I was three was thanks to Mom, who saved whatever money Dad didn't fritter away on electronics and floppy-disc games. But then Amber was born and then Arthur, and then *bam-bam-bam*, funeral-funeral-funeral, dead-Dad-dead-Gramma-dead-Tito-Gary. Our vacation funds were eaten up by mortuary expenses and tombstone engravers.

"It is not cheap to die in America," Mom once told me, "especially if you're like your daddy and insist on a fancy freaking casket."

Once the deaths stopped, the travel resumed.

Our family's round-the-world trip to Manila is followed by a cross-country flight to the Grand Canyon. We become Walt Disney World regulars, visiting the parks every summer, staying in the same decrepit Econo Lodge on International Drive because it's twenty-nine dollars a night, relatively safe, and has an in-room kitchenette, where we can microwave our TV dinners and eat them in the vibrating beds while watching Showtime.

In high school, Mom takes us kids to France and Germany with my French teacher and seventy-some other people, mostly teenagers whose parents permit them to make the trip on their own. She backpacks with three kids, carrying Arthur's, Amber's, and her own stuff most days as we hike the cobbled streets of Strasbourg and up and down the steps of the Sacré-Coeur. She holes up with us in the hostels, falling asleep with earplugs in and a pillow over her face to blunt the noise of Mary Wright and Jeremy Yardis having sex on the other side of our paper-thin wall.

Mom's other money-spending soft spot: cars.

She bought her first car, a sapphire-blue Toyota Celica, brand new with all the bells and whistles. The Toyota Van we had when Dad was alive had a fully retractable sunroof and an ice maker. Though she made fun of Tita Perla's Lexus, my aunt said she spent an hour in it on her first trip to Miami running her hands over the leather and gleaming wood.

Mom still drives the Sable with its sun-battered roof and sagging headliners tacked in place with staples. This brand-new Ford Explorer is, in many ways, as much for her as it is for me.

As I merge with traffic on Colonial Boulevard, Mom reminds me of our arrangement. The car is for getting Arthur to and from Little League and YMCA games. It's for taking Amber to piano lessons and for picking her up from Dunbar Middle when she's got drama club. I can drive it to and from school and swim practice, too, but any uses beyond these require prior authorization from Mom.

"Those are the rules," she says, wagging a thick finger in my face as we sit at a stoplight. "Do not forget!"

I nod solemnly, eyes trained on the road. I am a rule follower. Especially if it means a car. Cars aren't just normal. Cars are cool. I check my mirrors and shift my hands to exactly ten and two, smiling so hard, it hurts.

CHAPTER 26

# Open Heart

The hospital's front doors glide open as I glide through them, waving hello to Betty and Marv at the front desk, where I volunteer on Sunday mornings and Tuesday nights after Key Club, pointing my way down the hall to show I know where I'm going.

They smile and wave back, wrinkled arms jiggling from the sides of their candy-striped aprons.

"How's that modelin' contract comin'?" Marv says in his thick Jersey brogue.

"I'm working on it, sir," I answer, adding a slight bounce to my step as my outlet-mall Nikes squeak against the glossy terrazzo.

"You're always working, aren't you?" Betty says, beaming. "Just like your mothah."

Their smiles are my sustenance. I absorb them like rays of sun. They feed my people-pleasing soul. I can never please my mother, but everyone else on earth is so, so easy.

Before I had a *brand-new Ford Explorer*, friends' parents would drop me off at the awning-covered entrance of Mom's hospital after Honor Society meetings or swim practice. When I get the car, I continue the routine.

I volunteer at the front desk, toting bouquets of flowers to patients' rooms and delivering VHS tapes to the scuba divers in the hyperbaric chambers. When my couple of hours of volunteer work conclude, I head to Mom's floor, to what feels like her natural environment.

Mom's nursing station is my home away from home. Her unit is up the second bank of elevators on level four.

I treasure these evenings. I get Mom to myself, her patients aside, for a few minutes while my siblings stay with Liz. Mom's coworkers give me plastic cups of apple juice with peel-off aluminum-foil tops. They save unopened pudding cups from patients' trays, and I eat them with tongue depressors that Mom scavenges from the supply closet. I like the other nurses, Dominique, Ladonya, and Linda, with her bleached bob and sassy red glasses à la Sally Jessy Raphael. When Linda asks one evening what I want to be when I grow up, I hesitate. I don't yet have a go-to answer.

I think of saying artist or writer, the things I wanted to be when I was little and didn't know better. I doubt those will earn me nods of approval, though. They won't deliver the sustenance my fragile ego so desperately needs.

"You should be a doctor," Linda says, her ruby glasses twinkling in the fluorescent light as she fills in my answer for me, "so you can live in a big house and buy your mommy a nice car."

I laugh. "Mommy hates doctors."

Linda laughs harder. "No kidding."

As we leave the hospital that night, walking past the gleaming Jaguars and Benzes in the doctors-only parking lot, the suggestion takes root. We walk one section over to the final row, where Mom's parked the gray Sable under a tree for shade. The tint on the rear window is bubbled and peeling. The paint on the hood and top has been sun-bleached to a dull grayish white that doesn't match the darker sides.

The idea of having money is intoxicating. Money equals normalcy. People with money don't know the Publix customer-service manager by name. They've never returned grapes. They've never set a Thanksgiving table with Wendy's napkins and mismatched plastic cups with dishwasher-faded logos.

When I tell people I want to be a doctor, they ooh and aah as if I've guessed their exact weight or pulled a cooing dove from my sleeve. This feeds my need to please people. It also feels wonderfully, exquisitely normal. Doctors help. They save lives. And they are well compensated for doing so. I tell anyone who'll listen about my doctoral plans.

Mom's friends pat me on the head and say it's a good thing I have her smarts. When Mom hears me, she sucks her teeth and urges me toward accounting or engineering.

"Something sensible," she says. "You do not want to become an asshole like all of them."

I'll say it again: Mom hates doctors. They overlook and underestimate her. They refuse to believe this brown bowling ball of a woman could be their intellectual equal. They refuse to get to know my mother.

Mom uses her photographic memory to catalogue dozens of formulations and titrations in her head. As the doctors flip through their reference books for the correct doxycycline dosage for a 224-pound man, Mom spits out the exact numbers. They roll their eyes and continue their calculations, licking their fingers, still trying to find the right page. They get to the formula, pull out a calculator, and do the math for themselves. When it matches, down to the decimal point, what Mom said seconds earlier, they shrug and shake their heads, like she's just gotten lucky—again.

Mom sees doctors as lazy egomaniacs happy to coast on their titles as nurses like her do the real work. They are, aside from maybe Grandpa and Nay, the only people in the world Mom must listen to and abide by. I want even more badly to become one.

The more I tell people my *I-wanna-be-a-doctor* story, the more I hone it, the more real and normal it feels. I do want this. I want a title that commands respect, to be taken seriously for nothing more than the two letters behind my name: Annabelle Tometich, MD. I want to correct people when they call me Ms. Tometich, to push back my tortoiseshell spectacles (I've never worn glasses), look up from a stack of charts, and say, "It is *Dr.* Tometich. I'm sorry, you'll have to check in with my receptionist first." I want the respect my mother still has to fight for.

That's about as much as I've thought it through, until my junior year of high school.

For Take Your Daughter to Work Day, Mom arranges for Artis and me to watch an open-heart surgery. I think she hopes this will turn me away from this path. Mom works in the Open Heart ICU, meaning she takes care of patients after coronary bypasses and pacemaker implants. Dr. Burke, a thoracic surgeon, is one of the only doctors Mom respects, and he's allowing us to shadow him. Early one school-day morning, we park the Sable and Explorer side by side in the back row, and I follow Mom into the hospital, which glows like a spaceship in the inky predawn dark.

We meet Artis at the entrance, waving to her mom as she pulls out of the drop-off area. Artis has no interest in becoming a doctor. She's just a "yeah, sure" kind of person.

> **Me** at eleven years old: "Wanna help me pick up palm fronds in the yard?"
>
> **Artis,** who'd come over to watch movies and talk about boys: "Yeah, sure."
>
> **Me** at thirty-five: "Wanna have Modelos and pupusas for lunch at this restaurant I have to review?"
>
> **Artis:** "I mean, it's Tuesday, but yeah, sure."
>
> **Me** at sixteen: "Wanna watch an open-heart surgery at Mom's hospital?"
>
> **Artis:** "Yeah, sure."

"Pay very close attention, you two," Mom tells us as we enter the surgery floor. "If you are really going to become a doctor, Annabelle Marie, Dr. Burke is the very best."

Dr. Burke is a small man, built lean like a marathon runner. He wears dusk-blue scrubs and eats a granola bar as he greets Artis and me in the surgeons' lounge.

"D'you girls eat?" he asks, peering at us through almost invisible spectacles that perch lightly atop his thin nose.

"Yes, sir, Mom sent us down to the cafeteria first thing."

"Your mom's a smart woman," he says. "Never forget that."

He tosses out his granola-bar wrapper and dusts off his hands.

"You girls might want to have some crackers, too. You're in for a long one. Quadruple bypass."

Dr. Burke raises his eyebrows and purses his lips, a face that says we have no idea what we're getting into.

"I've got to go scrub in," he says. "I suppose you do, too."

Mom takes us to a small room with lockers and gives each of us a set of scrubs. She places blue-mesh shower caps over our tied-back hair and gives us matching blue-mesh booties to pull over our shoes. She loops surgical masks around our faces, pinching the metal prongs so they hug our noses. She leads us to a trough of sinks and hands us thick bars of soap.

I've never seen Mom like this. So calm. So professional. So completely unflappable. I realize this mom is not my mom. This mom exists in a different realm. This is the mom who watches vigilantly over her patients, who fights for them and their best interests when the egomaniacal freaking doctors won't. This is the mom who took such great care of Sam Galloway that he offered her a lifetime employee discount at his Ford dealership, a discount that helped me get my dream car.

This is the mom who gets peeled off in layer after layer of scrubs plopped directly into the washing machine, the one who gets rinsed down the shower drain and who evaporates in clouds of steam so the real mom, our mom, can come home to my siblings and me.

I wish I knew more of this mom. I wish this mom could at least have visitation rights; Wednesdays and every other weekend would be fine.

Each of her motions has a purpose: unwrap the long-sleeved coats, press them onto us, tie them behind our backs. She opens packs of nitrile gloves and shows us how to grab them through the cloth of our sleeves, how to roll them onto our wrists, then wriggle our fingers into their places. She gives us safety goggles that look more like the kind I've worn in wood-shop than the kind I've worn in biology lab.

"Keep those on," Mom says as she tucks the earpieces through my hair and behind my ears, "especially when he starts the bone saw. The last thing we need is a ruptured cornea."

I think about this old man and his clogged arteries. I wonder if he sifts a yolk or two from his morning eggs the way Mom makes me do with ours, to help lower the cholesterol. I picture a bloody splinter of his sternum fly-ing through the air and lodging in my eye. The goggles stay on.

The OR feels like a Florida winter day. The locked thermostat on the wall reads 66, and the air is so dry, I keep licking my lips under my surgical mask. Mom isn't an OR nurse. "I do not have the patience," she says as she walks us to the door, introduces us to the team, then leaves to start her workday in earnest.

We arrive in time to see the final stitches go into the patient's calf as Dr. Burke's assistant harvests the saphenous vein they will move from his leg to around his heart to bypass his clogged arteries. A metal tray lined with blue paper holds the bluish-yellow tube of flesh. A wider swath of blue tissue-like cloth covers the patient's head, so we can't see his face. He has a thick tan chest that is being shaved of its gray hairs by the OR nurses. They scrub his bare skin with soap, paint it with iodine that looks like thin gravy, then drape it in a sheet of sticky film, running their gloved hands over it to smooth out any bubbles, the way you'd rub contact paper onto a cabinet shelf.

Classical music comes on over unseen speakers, and Dr. Burke appears, covered head to toe like an astronaut, ready to lead this mission. Things move quickly now. He drives his scalpel into the man's chest without hesitation. It sinks through the skin like a knife in fresh peanut butter, with even less resistance than the webbing of my thumb when I drove the steak knife through it. I hear Artis gasp, a slight almost Victorian pull of breath audible only to me. I touch my arm to hers, to make sure she's still standing. She is, just barely.

I can't look away.

The tip of Dr. Burke's scalpel disappears till his index finger drags against the man's film-covered torso. The thick layers of yellow, bubbly fat covering the man's sternum spread apart behind Dr. Burke's blade like water in the wake of a boat. Dr. Burke moves his hand slowly. A nurse's hand trails behind his with a cautery pen. It looks like the filament of a light bulb, glowing bright orange. When the scalpel gets bloody, the cautery pen swipes in, sizzling the man's flesh to stanch the bleeding, sending puffs of smoke into the air that smell of burned meat.

I'm in a trance, completely absorbed by Dr. Burke's focus, his steadiness. The bone saw comes out and I push my goggles tight to my face. There is whirring and then crackling as Dr. Burke pushes a set of forceps into the man's chest cavity and yanks his rib cage open with a sharp pop. Artis doesn't say anything. I'm still transfixed. I reach my arm out to check on her again, my eyes stuck on the lungs and fatty tissue spilling forth from the hole. My arm hits nothing. Finally I look up. Artis is sitting on a chair by a fan in the corner, holding her goggles in her hand and pulling her mask away from her face to breathe.

"You should definitely become a doctor," Artis tells me in the quiet of the surgeons' lounge somewhere around hour three of six as I wolf down peanut-butter crackers and she takes tiny sips from a cup of water.

"I don't think you've even blinked."

I take this as proof of my destiny.

My *I-wanna-be-a-doctor* speech becomes an *I'm-studying-to-be-a-cardiologist* monologue, a veritable one-woman show with acts about aging baby boomers and the horrors of the American diet. Adults love this play. They smile and applaud, and I bask in the glow of their approval. This feels not just normal but good, like this is a place where I could belong. I'm coming around to the idea that I might, maybe, one day, be Somebody. Somebody with power. Somebody in charge. The exact sort of Somebody my mother resented. The exact sort of Somebody this country never let her be.

# CHAPTER 27

# Gainesville

Gainesville is three and a half hours north of Fort Myers, a straight shot up I-75. I drive the Explorer past the industrial parks of Tampa and the interchange where I-4 forks off to Walt Disney World, through the rolling hills of central Florida and into a different swamp.

Mom follows in the new minivan, a teal Ford Windstar she bought to fill with Arthur's baseball teammates and Amber's Honor Society friends, in preparation for the forthcoming absence of the Explorer and me. My siblings are tucked in the back alongside my suitcases and boxes, which Mom insists stay in her car so that I'm not distracted on the interstate. By luggage.

I've been to the University of Florida only once before, for preview weekend, when I shared a skinny bunker of a dorm room with a girl from Clearwater with pink-streaked hair. I wanted to apply to Duke and Johns Hopkins and Vanderbilt, universities famed for their medical schools. I wanted to start my journey away from home with a bigger step than... Gainesville.

"These application fees are outrageous," Mom says as I leaf through brochures for Emory and UNC Chapel Hill. I see these places as stepping stones out of this swamp and away from my mom: 1. Get out of the state. 2. Get out of the South. 3. Never look back.

Mom, of course, doesn't see things the way I do.

"Why waste money applying to these places when you know you are not going? Americans just freaking love to throw away money."

Jo Tometich Life Lesson No. 1: *Don't freaking throw away money.*

I have a Bright Futures scholarship, after all, and a Florida Prepaid college fund fueled by Mom's scrimping and saving, a fund I helped feed with every bag of returned potatoes, every bowl of Fruit Spins instead of Froot Loops.

"It is free money, Annabelle Marie," Mom repeats, over and over, when I float this out-of-state nonsense by her yet again. "I studied my butt off to get into PLM so my family wouldn't have to go into debt for my tuition. At least you have textbooks and a freaking computer."

When I tell her Artis is going to the University of Pennsylvania, an honest-to-goodness Ivy League school that will take her out of the state *and* out of the South in one giant step, Mom laughs. "Good for her! But in this house, we do not turn down free money."

As I pull onto the Archer Road exit that leads to the south side of UF's campus, Mom following at a seven-car distance—"One car length for every ten miles of the speed limit," she's drilled into me—I realize we haven't driven this far north as a family since Dad was alive, since the pre-Arthur road trips we took to his old stamping grounds in New England. I try not to think about Dad. I bury him deep in the recesses of my mind by obsessing over everything else: the syllables of words; the time on the clock; my quizzes, tests, and essays; my carefully curated, always-approved-of, honors-baccalaureate-advanced-placement life.

Every now and then, though, the Dad thoughts sneak through.

Dad died when I was nine. I am two weeks away from my eighteenth birthday. I'll soon have been alive longer without him than I was with him. If I think about that too long, I start to cry. I don't think I miss *him* exactly.

I barely knew him. I still sometimes see him as Magnum P.I. What I miss are the opportunities he afforded us. Comfort, fun, and midnight bowls of ice cream. A person who made my big hands and bigger feet make sense. The parent who contextualized half of my existence, who made our mixed-race family make sense, who offered us a chance at Somebodiness, who made us feel like we belonged.

I wipe the tears from my eyes as I shove the thoughts back down. I check my rearview mirror to make sure Mom hasn't seen me crying. I realize if she had seen me, she'd never in a million years think I was crying over our long-lost father. Dad is not someone we talk about. And emotions aren't one of Mom's lessons.

We pull into the shadows of two soaring buildings. I arch my neck to see their tops, brick-orange against the bright blue early-morning sky. Ours are the first two cars to park in front of the Beaty Towers dorms on opening day. It's 7:52 in the morning. Mom's goal of leaving early and beating traffic has worked. Doors open at 8:00.

Jo Tometich Life Lesson No. 2: *Early is on time. On time is late. Late is grounded/slapped/lectured for two hours/all of the above.*

We tote boxes of mangoes and garbage bags of button-fly jean shorts and faded Green Wave swim team T-shirts up the creaky Beaty Towers West elevators to the thirteenth floor of my dorm. Mine is the second-to-last door on the south side of the building, room 1307.

1 + 3 + 0 doesn't equal 7. 1 x 3 x 0 doesn't work either. But there is an odd harmony to it.

"I guess the seven makes up for the thirteen," Mom says, speaking my thoughts aloud as I turn the key. I wonder if we're more alike than I've realized.

My room is in a suite. Four girls share two bedrooms, a bathroom, a kitchenette, and a small common space. I look around at the concrete-block walls speckled with screws and nail holes left by my predecessors. I wonder where they've moved on to, if they're lawyers and engineers and doctors now, if this room was their stepping stone to freedom, or if this swamp sucked them under.

My bunk bed has a view of Shands Hospital's helipad, where the tragically injured are flown in hopes of survival, and of the vast oak-laden expanse of ruralness that spreads beyond this corner of campus.

I unpack the navy-and-turquoise Bed-in-a-Bag that Mom bought at Walmart, tucking my wrinkled sheets and microfiber comforter into the top bunk as I balance on the particleboard desk we helped my roommate Emily assemble after she and her family arrived at the sensible lunchtime hour.

Emily is also from Fort Myers, a born-and-raised nobody, just like me. But a white one. We bonded sophomore year through shared stress tears in Mrs. Haugland's AP European History class and shared laps in the pool during swim practice. We also share a fear of authority and a love for reading and thorough note-taking in the form of obsessive outlines that must be color coded and properly spaced.

Our friendship is cemented by our, shall we say, *unique* mothers. Their crowning moment of unique glory happened senior year at the swim team sleepover party on Fort Myers Beach, when an unanswered phone call to our cottage led Emily's mom to my mom, and the two of them to the Lee County Sheriff's Department, which put out an APB for two missing and possibly endangered teenagers. I spent the next month grounded, not because I'd done anything wrong, but because "I thought you were lying to me and having sex with the boys!," as Mom so loudly put it upon finding us right where we'd said we'd be. "What about AIDS?"

Jo Tometich Life Lesson No. 3: *What about AIDS?*

## I. Condoms

### A. THEY ARE NOT FOOLPROOF, ANNABELLE MARIE!

### B. What if they are expired? Or he stored them in the car

and the heat has rotted them? How would you even know?

C. Ay nako, you will have AIDS for the rest of your life until it kills you. Is that what you want?

## II. Drugs

A. You don't ever take drugs, do you hear me?

B. Everyone is going to try and give you the drugs. I know this for sure. EVERYONE. Do not take them! Do not let them slip them in your drinks when you're not looking! That is what they do. With the drugs. I am telling you.

C. First you take marijuana, and then it becomes crack and heroin, and you are shooting needles into your eyeballs! I see them in the hospital. I know this. I am telling you because I know. And then guess what? You have AIDS. For the rest of your life from those needles, you have AIDS. Until it kills you. Is that what you want? Really?

As we settle into 1307, Emily, Amber, and I take turns blowing up the inflatable armchair we bought in lunar purple from the Spencer's at the Oaks Mall. Arthur and Mom blow up the hot pink ottoman I splurged on to accompany it.

Mom takes us to Olive Garden for dinner. She drops me back at the foot of Beaty Towers West with a plastic takeout bag that sags under the weight of greasy breadsticks, wilting salad, a half-eaten Tour of Italy, and a full box of lasagna Mom ordered last minute, "in case you get hungry later."

Amber hops out and gives me a side hug. Arthur wraps his arms around my waist, holding me tight till I peel him off and push him back through the Windstar's sliding door. Mom rearranges things in the hatch, then walks around to the passenger side to make sure my siblings are securely in place.

"All right," Mom says, one hand on the van's sliding door, the other on her hip. "We've got to get on the road, or we'll be home way too late. With all the drunk drivers, it's just not safe. You know that, right? You never want to be on the road too late."

Jo Tometich Life Lesson No. 4: *From 10 p.m. to 3 a.m., every driver is a drunk driver. All of them. That is suicide, you know. You want me to come scrape you off the highway? Huh? Is that what you want?*

The sadness I've tried to bury, about living most of my life without a father, about untethering myself from this unique family of mine, bubbles hot and leaden in my chest. I've been half on my own for almost half of my life. I tell myself this is my first step. I tell myself it'll be fine. *This is the freedom you've dreamed of! This is, in fact, exactly what you want.*

I nod and adjust the bag of food, trying not to roll my eyes. Worried if I do, I might start crying.

I wonder if Mom will say I love you. I wonder if I should say it. The last time I did was on my sixteenth birthday, when I went to bed with my car keys tucked beneath my pillow. I tiptoed to the family room that night. Mom was watching reruns on TBS. I stood at the end of the hall till she looked my way.

"What is it?" she said.

"I just wanted to, I dunno, just—I love you," I answered.

"Oh, that's it?" she said, turning her attention back to *Three's Company*.

"Yeah, that's it."

"OK. Get some sleep."

It wasn't what I'd hoped for. I'd rather not repeat it.

"I'll call you," I promise as Mom slides the van's door closed.

"Use the long-distance cards I gave you. Don't run up a crazy phone bill. That all gets charged to me." (*See:* Jo Tometich Life Lesson No. 1.)

I bite the inside of my lip and nod again. Mom adjusts her yellow-tinted driving glasses and rubs the bridge of her nose. A tear sneaks down her cheek. She ignores it, gets in the car, closes her door, and rolls down the front windows. I stand awkwardly by the passenger side, shifting my weight from one foot to the other, one arm still clutching the bag of pasta, the other arm clutching that arm.

Mom turns her head to get a better look at me. She sticks a hand in my direction, waves but says nothing. Finally, I break the silence.

"Love you, Mom."

The words come more easily up here, on this first step away from Mom, three and a half hours north of what was home.

"Be careful, Abelle."

Mom rolls up the window, and they're gone.

Jo Tometich Life Lesson No. 5: *Love means never having to say I love you back.*

The pulsing bass of some Spice Girls or No Doubt song reverberates through the walls and into my already pounding chest. I'm with Emily and our two new roommates, who hail from a high school in Boca Raton. We wear black flare-bottom pants and sparkly halter tops. We're standing in line at the Gruv in downtown Gainesville, our flat-ironed hair quickly frizzing in the swampy, late-August heat.

It's the weekend before classes start. I'm still a week shy of my eighteenth birthday, and knots of anxiety have joined the leftover Olive Garden lasagna in my stomach. I tell myself it's because of my ID, or lack thereof. You have to be eighteen to get into a nightclub. My roommates think my Gator One student ID card will suffice. I have doubts.

About all of this.

It's five dollars to get in. That's 5 percent of the money I have to my name until my student-aid check clears.

Should I have brought condoms?

What if someone really does offer us drugs?

I drove us here in the Explorer, but what if I can't get everyone to come home at the same time? I'd never leave Emily. But what about the new roommates?

The line marches forth. We're at the doors. One roommate goes, then another. Emily stands behind me, pushing me forward. I hold my Gator One card up to the bouncer. He glances at it, ignores the fact it has no birthdate, then draws a thick X across the back of my right hand. I exhale the breath I've been clenching in my chest and walk through the Gruv's thick black curtains. At the tender hour of ten p.m., the club is empty. We get cups of water from the bar, then stand by a wall as the song changes and Will Smith welcomes us to this new world: "Bienvenidos a Miami!"

I look around for lines of cocaine and rolled-up dollar bills, for sketchy men palming Rohypnol. I see groups of girls—women, I guess—just like us in low-rise jeans and black platform sandals, clustered in corners and around high-top tables, mostly drinking water or vodka-cranberries. It looks like a high school dance where no one knows anyone. I start to relax, to quiet the voice in my head that sounds like Mom but also like me.

*You were afraid—of this?*

My anxiety turns to boredom. Emily wants to dance, but I'd rather die. It feels like we've been standing by our wall for hours. She checks the silver Fossil watch on her wrist: It's 10:28.

"How long do we do this?" she asks me.

"I have no idea."

I go back to the bar for something stronger.

"Can I get a Coke?"

The bartender eyes the thick X on my hand and fills my water cup with a spray of soda from a push-button gun. I set a few dollar bills on the counter. I think of waiting for change, of not freaking wasting money, but something else, someone else, catches my eye.

Across the bar, I see a tall guy with a familiarly shaped head. His hair is longer, spikier. His ears look smaller, but I recognize this head. The head is with other people I know: Rich Kilfoyle, who will join Artis at UPenn next week; and Chad Torres, a kid I've not talked to since fifth grade. They are an island of familiarity in a sea of the unknown. I swim to them for dear life, motioning for Emily and our roommates to follow.

Chad sees me first.

"Annabelle motherfuckin' Tometich! Holy shit, is that you?"

I smile, happy to know someone else, if only vaguely.

I introduce Chad to my roommates. He introduces us to Rich, whom I also vaguely know, and to the tall guy with two uncomplicated syllables for a name.

Buddy.

"I know who you are," I say, cupping my soda in one hand as this familiar shape formally shakes the other. "You're Mrs. Brunick's son. Cathy used to give you rides home from school."

He nods and cocks that head of his to the side, his interest piqued.

"You had my mom as a teacher?" he says, our palms warm against each other.

"Your mom was more like my savior," I say, eyes locked to his, my words blurred by the blaring cries of Chumbawamba getting knocked down but getting up again.

"What was that?" he yells.

"I said, just, yes—yeah, I did."

He keeps hold of my hand. "You wanna dance?"

Nine minutes ago, as I sipped water by the wall, I'd rather have died. Now it seems like a marvelous idea. I squeeze his hand to say yes, and we leap into the crashing waves of the dance floor.

\* \* \*

Dancing turns into Gumby's Pizza and beer back at Chad's place, a two-bedroom apartment three minutes from campus. Chad's roommate, Jenn, is still out of town for the summer. Buddy, who shares a boxy dorm room with a guy they've nicknamed "Weird John," says we can take her bedroom. I nod, consider a beer, then nervously grab another breadstick.

Emily sees my shaking hands and pulls me into the apartment's lone bathroom. The tiny space is eighteen shades of beige: peeling linoleum in a dingy tone of apricot; an ivory sink atop a cream-painted cabinet; a khaki tub splotched with white soap scum and peach-ish mildew. Emily and I scrunch our bodies into the room, trying not to touch anything with our skin. I sit on the closed toilet seat. Emily stands in the corner behind the door, holding the keys to my Explorer. Our Boca Raton roommates are waiting outside on the front balcony, ready to go home to 1307.

"You're sure you're good?" Emily asks me. "Your mom pretty much spelled out this exact scenario, like a week ago, and this is not how it's supposed to end."

She is stone-cold sober. I'm jittery from my Cokes.

"I know," I say, fiddling with a hand towel. "She also said we'd be roofied at first chance and have cocaine thrown at us."

Emily laughs.

"So, you're good?"

"I am good."

"You promise?"

"I promise."

I look up at her, tell her to drive safely. She jingles my keys in her hand as she squeezes out the bathroom door.

"The drunk drivers!" I call after her in warning.

"THE AIDS!" she replies, looking back one more time and smiling before joining our roommates on the balcony.

I don't go home with boys. My first high-school boyfriend never saw me barefoot. I was, at the time, too ashamed of the massive, size-ten feet rooting my bamboo-pole legs to the earth. I kept them hidden in socks and shoes, safely under wraps.

My second and final high-school boyfriend got to see a bit more of me—physically speaking. With him, it was my family I kept under wraps. I never discussed Gramma or Tito Gary. I never left him alone with my mother for more than five seconds. When he asked about my dad, I kept it especially simple.

"He died when I was really young in an accident."

I don't go home with boys. I don't open up to people—until tonight.

The room's only light is from a glaring bulb dangling naked from the imbalanced ceiling fan that clicks overhead. Buddy tugs the short cord, and the room goes dark save for the glow of a streetlamp out back. He drinks a green bottle of Rolling Rock as I nurse my breadstick. Going to a club at seventeen was my big rule-breaking adventure for the night. Now I'm in a bedroom with a boy. No way I can handle underage drinking, too.

We sit on a mattress and box spring pushed into the corner of the room—talking. About him taking baths with Cathy and her sister Jenna back when his dad drove trucks for their family's Budweiser distributorship. About me meeting his older sister at Cathy's pool once. About his mom and the Minnie Mouse sweatshirt she wore on cold days at our elementary school, and how it made the morning hugs she gave me that much warmer.

"You know, my mom told me about you, about what happened to your dad," he says. I nod stiffly, holding my breath, steeling myself to give more gory details, wondering if I'm capable of it.

Buddy takes a different route.

"Your dad died right when her dad died," he says. "She seriously loved you. If I called her right now, she'd be like *You're with my Annabelle? Oh, my heavens, I LOVE THAT GIRL!*"

He slips into a Southern drawl as sweet as cane syrup, then puts his hand on the phone on the bedside table.

"We can try her if you want?"

"Oh, no, no, no," I say, laughing.

I kick his hand away from the phone with my bare foot. When I think he's not looking, I swipe tears from my cheeks, happy ones and baffled ones. What a wild idea: a mother who loves me and wouldn't be ashamed to say it.

I can see the curve of his smile around the white of his teeth through the dark. I realize I have once again stopped breathing. The conversation swirls from majors to sports to movies to music. He went to a Blues Traveler concert that summer in Live Oak.

"I've never been to a concert," I say.

He smacks my leg. "What!?"

I shake my head. "Never."

"Oh, my god," he says. "We have so much work to do."

We move on to cousins (his are mostly in Atlanta, mine are mostly in Manila) and siblings (he's got three sisters: one older, two younger). He tells me his older sister ran away from home when she was thirteen and spent her high-school years bouncing from halfway houses to boyfriends' houses to whichever parent was semi-capable of dealing with her at any given time.

"I think she just wanted their attention," he says. I nod, thinking about my 5.43 grade point average and the honor roll certificates stretching the spines of my scrapbooks.

My parents stayed married, till death did they part. His dad is on his third marriage. His mom, the woman I knew as Mrs. Brunick, started as Ms. Bailey, became Mrs. Martin, then Mrs. Brunick, and is now a Ms. Bailey again.

I think about AP Euro and how Mrs. Haugland taught us to keep track of Henry VIII's wives: *divorced, beheaded, died, divorced, beheaded, survived.* Between our various family traumas, this mnemonic device might work.

I tell him my parents were never happy. He says he thinks his parents were, at least for a bit.

I tell him my uncle hanged himself in our garage, how my mom found his body, and how I found my mom. He tells me about his aunt who had a baby out of wedlock and gave the child up for adoption without telling a soul for decades. About his youngest sister, whom he cooked dinner for every night when their mom went back to college to earn her master's degree, the sister who was recently expelled from middle school for selling Xanax.

"I wonder if I fucked her up," he says.

I nod again, more slowly this time, staring off into the dark, playing out every crappy thing I did to my siblings, every time I screamed at them to feed themselves and leave me alone. Overhead, the ceiling fan circles and clicks.

Six hours ago, this guy was an uncomplicated, two-syllable, all-American white kid to me. Now, we're neck and neck in the Dysfunctional Family Olympics. And for the first time in a long time, I don't feel so alone.

"Maybe we're all fucked up, and some of us just handle it differently," I say.

He taps my arm with his empty beer bottle. It's warm from his hands.

"You've had two breadsticks. You can't be that fucked up."

I laugh and lean closer, crossing my ankles over his.

We talk about our names, how mine came from an Edgar Allan Poe poem, how his real name is Jonathan, but his older sister started calling him Buddy one day, and it stuck.

I ask him if he watches NASCAR and eats boiled peanuts. I say it in my own Southern drawl, slack-jawed and slow: *bole'd pee-nuuuts.*

"Never at the same time," he says, "unless it's Sunday."

We talk about vacations. He says he's never been out of the country, and I gasp. When we get to food, he does the same.

"How could you grow up in the South and never eat grits?" he asks accusingly, his back against the wall where a headboard should be, his legs interlaced with my own as I lean against the wall catty-corner.

"We were more of a fish-head-stew-and-rice kind of household," I say, watching for his lips to curve into that same grin, my heart fluttering when they do.

"Oh, my god," he says. "I'm calling my mom in the morning and getting her sausage-grits casserole recipe. You can't live like this!"

"Cool, cool, I'm booking us a trip to the Philippines. Or at least England. Canada, maybe? You can't live like this, either!"

He laughs again. My heart leaps with each *ha-ha*.

The room goes quiet, save for the clicking of the ceiling fan. He leans over, till we're shoulder to shoulder in the corner. The sun peeks in, quiet and unobtrusive, filling the space with the first warm rays of daylight. I see my bare feet beyond our braided ankles, how normal mine look next to his. I take a breath, deep and unburdened. I exhale and look Buddy in his blue-green eyes.

He takes my right arm with his left and pulls me into him. He kisses my cheek and then my mouth.

I wonder who it is I've become.

CHAPTER 28

# The Jungle

I walk through the jungle of our yard and into a jungle of stuff.

It's the summer after my junior year at UF, and I'm home. Or I'm in someone's home. Yarn and spools of thread tumble across the breakfast nook. Dirty plates balance atop heaps of laundry. A mosaic of clear-plastic DVD cases shingles the coffee table. Bills and prescription-drug inserts and boxes of alcohol swabs form toppling stacks that melt from the big brown armchair across the worn carpet covering the floors.

Arthur stands in the kitchen, barefoot in a pair of basketball shorts. He pulls a pancake spatula from the overflowing sink, sending fruit flies into a shaft of sunlight that filters through the grimy slider windows.

During my high-school years, Mom jammed these windows shut with a chopped-up broom handle. She jammed all the sliders shut over time, with dowels and broken table legs and old shower curtain rods she'd salvage from the neighbors' trash cans.

"I'd cover them with bars if I could," she said as she sawed another half inch from the end of an old rake. "There are crazy people out there."

Arthur's displaced spatula rattles the sink's Jenga tower of dirty dishes. He uses his hip to push a crusty pie tin back into place, shoring up the foundation. The tower settles. He tears open a silver-foil ramen seasoning packet and pinches its contents into the pot of noodles simmering on the grease-slicked stove. He dips the spatula into the broth and stirs.

"You're back."

He doesn't look up, just keeps stirring.

"I am."

I search for a place to set down my bag. There isn't one. I switch it to the other arm, listening to my flip-flops sticking and unsticking on the brown kitchen tiles.

Arthur takes the pot off the stove and cradles it in a char-stained oven mitt printed with faded Christmas trees. He grabs a spoon from the counter, wipes it on his shorts, and walks to Amber's old bedroom, where he installed his PlayStation after she ran away to live with Tita Perla and Uncle Peter, after we sisters abandoned our baby brother, leaving him to deal with Mom all alone. He thumps me on the shoulder with the spoon as he passes.

"Welcome home."

Mom left that morning. She hopped a plane with Tita Perla to Detroit, then Seoul, then Manila.

I've spent each of my previous college summers at UF, ostensibly taking classes, staying ahead of the curve, keeping my grades up. But really, I've escaped. I've created a new life for myself, one with no screaming and minimal crying. One with friends who know the pain of family in ways similar to my own.

Take Natasha, who grew up on the not-quite-so-privileged side of white in a single-wide trailer on a strawberry field outside Plant City, whose adoptive mom died of lupus when Natasha was seventeen, who found out her adoptive dad was really her biological uncle six years after her mom's passing, who breathed a sigh of relief upon learning that her biological mom was her cool fun aunt and not the aunt who threatened the family horse with a shotgun one Christmas morning.

Take Ben, who is half Chilean and from Ocala. Ben whose born-again-Christian parents and twin brother disowned him when he refused their backyard baby-pool baptism, who balances jobs as a trainer at the student rec center and a bouncer at Café Risqué, who sells magic mushrooms in the summer to pay for his honors courses in biochemistry and organic spectroscopy.

Take Peter, the person who will go on to NYU law school and defend my mango-shooting mom in a Robert E. Lee County courtroom. His white mother wed his much-older Liberian father after taking one of his college courses at Michigan State University. Once a month, she gathers the frogs from the windowsills and gutter spouts around their Fort Myers home, traps them in a lidded bucket and, one by one, shoves them down the kitchen garbage disposal in a bloody whirr of kicking legs and fine, crunching bones.

And take Buddy. All six feet four inches of him. As beautiful as he is kind. Funny and smart, too. The sibling who's also raised his siblings. The kid who's also been thrust into adulthood far sooner than he'd have liked.

In this group of friends, I feel perfectly average and somewhat normal. I feel like I belong. The chaos of my past doesn't feel so chaotic. These friends change me for the better, and I latch on to them for dear life.

Mom is creating her own new life, too. The house she shared with her husband and three children is now just hers and Arthur's, and poor Arthur has never counted in this family. Mom no longer has to tidy up for our sleepovers and pool parties. Arthur doesn't care if Ahmed, his one friend from the end of the street, sees our house in shambles. Mom spent her whole life cleaning up after people—her siblings, her patients, her husband and children. As we left, that side of Mom did, too.

Every time I do come home, it's more and more unrecognizable. Cans of baked beans and fruit cocktail start piling up in the corners alongside pallets of Spam and the dual packs of jumbo-size Jif peanut butter Mom buys from Sam's Club. She saves it all for her balikbayan boxes. By the looks of our house, Mom is a one-woman balikbayan business.

In reality, all this stuff has sat here—with our old toys, our too-small clothes, our mismatched worn-out shoes, our chipped plates and dinged-up silverware—for years. When Mom packs and ships a box, it barely makes a dent. One balikbayan box goes out, and three more boxes' worth of stuff filters in. Till the pantry overflows into the entry hall, which overflows into the living room, then the dining room, and around to the kitchen and back to the pantry—an endless circle of stuff.

As the stuff moves in, I stay out. I live in Gainesville year-round. I take a job as a lifeguard. I work the early and late shifts and the weekends, which no one wants. I add my lifeguard paychecks to the grant and scholarship money left over from the spring and fall semesters. It's more than enough to get me through summer, which means I don't have to go home.

Until this summer. Until the day before, when Mom calls and reminds me to come back. She needs me to watch Arthur—and my other siblings, her fruiting mango trees.

"You'll be here tomorrow, right, Annabelle? I'm going to leave the picking pole in the garage. Make sure there's some yellow to them, leave them be if they're still all green."

I say yes, yes, of course, cradling the phone between my shoulder and cheek as I pull a steaming potato from the plastic door of my microwave, cut it in half, and slather it in Country Crock and a fake Kraft single.

"How long are you gone? I think I might take some classes in the summer B session. I want to get ahead on some physics stuff," I lie.

Mom's tone, always serious, intensifies.

"I am gone as long as I will be gone."

"What does that mean?" I say. "Didn't you book a return flight?"

"There is a lot to do. A lot needs to get done. Your Tita Cristina doesn't even have enough money to embalm the body."

The wadded-up plastic wrapper from my cheese falls from my hand to the chipped counter of the apartment I share with the same three room-mates from freshman year. I watch it slowly unfurl, crinkle by crinkle.

"What body?"

"Jesus, Annabelle. Your grandfather's body. He is dead. He died. He is gone. His body is probably rotting in a box in an alley behind the hospital right now."

The line goes silent. Through the quiet, I hear mom sniffling. I imagine her at her own kitchen counter, picking through papaya seeds or slivering mangoes, the portable phone tucked between her head and shoulder as she wipes her ruddy cheeks with an old dish towel.

"He…what…but you never…" I stammer. "I had no idea."

Her sniffles become screams, like a dripping spigot jammed to full throttle.

"Maybe you should answer your phone! Or freaking *call me* one time! There. Now you know. Your grandpa is dead. I will be gone as long as I am gone. Just be here tomorrow."

I want to apologize, ask what happened, ask how Tita Perla is handling it.

Then I hear the dull buzz of a dead line.


Mom's health, mental and physical, seems to have the same downward-sloping trajectory as our house.

She can no longer control through diet the type 2 diabetes she developed after Arthur was born, so she hoards insulin in the crisper drawers of the fridge. She keeps her syringes in the china cabinet alongside the still plastic-wrapped Mikasa plates she bought after Dad died, after she shattered the last of their wedding dishes in that final October fight. Mom stacks boxes of alcohol pads with empty tubs of yogurt amid Dad's old vinyl collection in the living room. She keeps glucose test strips on the shelves in front of Dad's Shirley Jackson and Stephen King books.

Diabetes and death as decor.

Mom's been diagnosed with Ménière's disease, too, an inner-ear disorder that sends her reeling with vertigo when she gets too stressed, which can happen every few hours or so on bad days. The disease is slowly eating away at her hearing. It will eventually rob her of conversation and basic social interaction, one decibel at a time.

She blows her knees out while moving a patient, her ligaments snapping and cartilage flattening like an old beach house after a hurricane. A botched knee-replacement surgery and then a second one leave her in constant pain. She gets off work, then sits in front of the big-screen TV, barely moving for days until her next shift. Her doctor prescribes her oxycodone and Vicodin. Mom doesn't like the way they make her feel, but since workmen's comp is paying, she dutifully fills each prescription, hoarding the bottles atop the TV, next to our picture-day school portraits, more test strips, and more piles (and piles) of DVDs.

The discs are another manifestation of mom's compulsions. She can no longer pinch our noses thin or scrape our necks for dirt. She can no longer scratch the plaque from our teeth with her fingernails or spend hours lecturing us on drugs, AIDS, and drunk drivers.

She must focus this need for control elsewhere.

A friend of hers gets her a machine that can burn VHS tapes onto DVDs. Mom transfers over our complete childhood collection in one sleepless week. She makes copies of her friends' collections next. Soon she learns how to burn DVD to DVD, using our Dell desktop as a conduit. Arthur makes labels for them, and she stacks them in the front of Dad's bookcases in alphabetical order by year.

1998: *The Wedding Singer, Wild Things, The X-Files, You've Got Mail*. 1999: *American Beauty, American Pie, Analyze This, Angela's Ashes, Any Given Sunday*.

Mom has no particular genre, no favorites. She does not curate. She just burns and burns. It's about amassing as thorough a collection as possible, appeasing the voice in her head that tells her to keep going, burying thoughts of her dead husband, dead brother, and, now, dead father however she can. When there is no more space on the bookshelves, Mom stores a new year's worth of titles in the dining room buffet, in old milk crates, in shoeboxes. She burns them faster than Arthur can make labels, so instead she writes the title of each with a Sharpie in her Catholic-school cursive.

When she runs out of friends' collections to pilfer, she buys a DVD recorder and starts burning shows directly off the TV, like she used to with the Betamax tapes we smuggled into the Philippines: the entire series of *Bonanza* and *Little House on the Prairie*, complete with the Turner Classic Movies logo in the corner; seasons two through five of *Highway to Heaven*, for some reason in triplicate. (Mom had a thing for Michael Landon; "God rest his soul," she'll tell you.)

At some point, she stops buying DVDs with cases and buys the discs by the spindle, one hundred to a pack. I find three spindles sitting in an old laundry basket, seemingly unused. Until I open one, flip to a random DVD in the stack (*Pick a disc! Any disc!*) and find mom's Sharpie cursive: "*Family Ties*: Season 4, ep. 11; *Matlock*: Season 8, ep. 1."

The closet in Arthur's old bedroom is reserved for the truly awful stuff: the local news recordings, forecasts from the Weather Channel, the late-night QVC hosts hawking bad jewelry and silver-rimmed collectors' plates. Mom's Sharpie labels get less specific there: "HSN 1/16/01; TWC 2/21/02." It's her own Library of Congress. No show left behind.

By the time Arthur graduates high school, when Mom's broken knees make her no longer suitable for work and her new hospital tosses her out like any other biohazard, his old closet will be filled with towers of DVD spindles: four spindles to a tower, close to a dozen towers in total, 4,800 DVDs, give or take a bad burn or two, 9,600 hours of recordings. There are, Google tells me, 8,760 hours in a year.

Back in the kitchen, back in summer 2001, Mom's hobbies still seem rather sane: crocheting bins of doilies and quilts for her Baha'í friends; state-quarter collecting—albeit by the tubful—and, of course, her yard, which has become a quarter acre of jungle, a patch of tangled wilderness that defies the neatly cut rules of suburbia.

In the quiet of Mom's absence, I hear Arthur's PlayStation queue up for another Gran Turismo race. My bag still slung over one shoulder, my flip-flops still *thwick-thwacking* on the tiles, I take in the chaos, breathe in the must.

Then it hits me: *We can clean.*

As Mom's house has devolved, I feel like I have evolved. It's like I've taken all the house's order, harmony, and normality with me to UF, leaving behind only entropy—and Arthur.

I've tried to clean in the past, to give back some of what I've taken. I've tried to get Mom to paint the smudged walls still covered in kid graffiti or let me declutter some of the toys that sit unused in my old bedroom. But I never get far. Things start fine, then Mom spies a tailless My Little Pony atop a garbage bag. She fishes it out, claims it's still functional, then digs deeper, turning the bag over, toppling its contents onto the carpet, telling me how wasteful and selfish I am.

"Don't you ever think of anyone else? Your garbage would be treasure to your cousins in the Philippines."

She orders me to stop touching things. She promises to take over, says she'll pack everything up and send it to Manila in the next balikbayan box. I come back a week, a month, a year later, and the bags are dusty and untouched.

For the next six weeks, though, Mom will be 9,195 miles away. Too far away to get in the way.

*We can clean.*

\* \* \*

I call Amber to tell her the cleaning plan. Uncle Peter answers.

"She is not here! She's never here," he says in his Lebanese accent, which always makes him sound surprised; surprised I didn't know this, surprised I'd even ask.

"I don't know where she is. If your mommy cannot control her, I *definitely* cannot control her."

Amber also got a car for her sixteenth birthday, a brand-new silver Mustang from Sam Galloway Ford that shakes the walls of the garage when it rumbles to a start. The same rules Mom applied to my Explorer apply to her Mustang. It's for getting Arthur to and from practices. It's for getting her to and from school. Any other uses must first be approved by Mom.

Unlike me, Amber doesn't give a shit about Mom's rules. She uses the car to go to parties, to her boyfriend's house, to parties at her boyfriend's house.

Two years later, on Amber's eighteenth birthday, she'll take the money she's earned busing tables at a local Mexican restaurant and buy a new car. Another silver Ford Mustang, almost identical to the first. She'll buy it from the same men in the same blue polo shirts at the same Sam Galloway Ford dealership but without the discount Mom secured by helping to mend Mr. Galloway's heart. She will drive it to the house and park it under the branches of the mango tree that now spread over the driveway. She will stare Mom in the face, drop the keys to her old Mustang in Mom's hands, then peel out onto McGregor.

She will hit Mom where it hurts. She will strip Mom of control. I will admire and fear her for it.

My sister and I have become polar opposites. Maybe we always were. We vibrate at different frequencies. Hers soars high and drops low. It moves fast, excitedly, determinedly. Mine is slower and flatter; even, steady, boring. Jam those divergent frequencies together and you get mind-splitting, brain-numbing noise. Noise that manifested in our knock-down, drag-out fights as kids. Me using my height and weight to pin my little sister to the floor when she refused to do whatever piddly thing I'd asked. Amber using her cunning to spit in my face or yank fists of hair from my head, just enough to stun me so she could make a break for it, lock herself in her bedroom, and blast Alanis Morissette.

I think we became like this to rein in our mother. I see Amber and me as lion tamers. Amber cracks the whip and screams, forcing the beast to succumb to her will. I move around it cautiously, lulling it into submission, blindfolding it when I can, to keep it at peace.

Our brother is equally outlandish in his own Arthur way. I sometimes wonder if he's alive. He moves like a zombie, from video games to Harry Potter books to the trio of televisions he keeps on in various rooms, each one tuned to a different channel. He's always doing his own Arthur thing, quietly and independently. If my sister and I are lion tamers, Arthur is the elephant in the room, looming silently off to the side, so obviously there, even though we rarely acknowledge his existence.

I resented my sister and brother and this circus of ours. The duties I took on to keep us from moving to the Philippines never fully became theirs. Amber smartly dodged them. By the time they could have become Arthur's duties—all the scrubbing, all the cooking, all the weed pulling—Mom no longer cared.

We siblings are not three points on a line. We are three far-flung points in a giant triangle. If you squish the situation just right, sometimes two of us will come together. But getting all three of us aligned has proved impossible.

When Uncle Peter doesn't know where Amber is, I leave it at that. I've got Arthur, my quiet and ever-loyal elephant. The two of us will make it work.

\* \* \*

Arthur and I start with the obvious garbage, collecting the junk mail and sun-faded newspapers. We create stacks of Mom's diabetic supplies and crates of her still-sealed pain pills. If we were more daring, we might try a few or sell them. But we fear Mom and her photographic accounting skills far more than the legal system.

Mostly, we declutter and scrub. We don't dare set foot in Mom's room or anywhere near her jewelry. We know not to touch anything that belonged to Dad or Tito Gary, to Nay or Grandpa. We toss out the expired cans and congealed sauce bottles that clog the pantry. We brave the swarms of tiny cockroaches that fill the lower kitchen cabinets, then drench them in a torrent of Raid. And then we bleach and bleach and bleach.

We don't throw away much: old pens, used notebooks, smashed Happy Meal toys that not even our superhero mother could un-break. Tupperware lids without bottoms are fair trash, but bottoms missing lids are still usable for the next day's sinigang or a side of fish sauce.

We try to think like Mom.

It takes the better part of two summer months, but Arthur and I do it. We power-wash the layers of grime from the back patio. We paint the walls with leftover white paint from one of Uncle Peter's rental properties. Tita Perla chips in and buys a new coffee table and end tables from Walmart. The house hasn't looked this good in ages. It almost feels like home. Or a home.

When we pick up Mom from the airport, we tell her we have a surprise for her birthday, which was a month earlier while she was in Manila.

"That's nice," she says from the passenger seat of my Explorer.

She looks tired but seems in a good mood.

I tap my fingers against the steering wheel in tune with the radio. Arthur bounces in the back seat, drumming his hands on the armrest and the window's glass. This isn't our thing, surprising Mom with such a thoughtful gift. Surprises in our house are never the good kind. They are the kind that involve police cars and coroners' vans. This feels downright all-American. I have created a new, quasi-normal life for myself, and I am using that life to make my old one better.

We pull into the driveway. Arthur leaps out the second I shift into park.

"My suitcases! You need to get my suitcases!" Mom yells.

"Just come inside for a sec," I say. "We're really excited to show you your present."

Arthur drags open the iron gate and unlocks the front door. We swing our arms in a dramatic *ta-da!*, motioning for Mom to enter.

"What on earth is it?"

She hesitates, peering her head around the door slowly, shyly, like maybe we've gotten her a pony or a US Customs agent. She sees the cleaned-up entry hall, no longer piled with tins of meat and jugs of canola oil. She drops her carry-on backpack. It crunches in the pebbles outside the metal gate.

Mom walks through the freshly painted living room and entry hall in silence. She gets to the kitchen and puts her hands on her hips, her eyes shooting from the cleaned-off counters to the empty sink to the new table-cloth on the empty breakfast nook table. I have one foot in the house and one outside it. I shift my weight back and forth and back again. I look at Arthur nervously. He's still smiling.

Mom calls me in with a low "Annabelle Marie." She asks about the hampers she keeps next to the TV so she can watch her shows while she folds her socks and underwear. I tell her the laundry's all done and put away, that the hampers are in the bathrooms, where they belong.

I look back. Arthur is still in the doorway, his smile faded.

"Where are my hangers? I keep the hangers next to the TV so I can hang my uniforms right away when they come out of the dryer. Why would you move them? *Why would you even touch them?*"

Her voice goes mean and off-kilter. Instinct tells me to take a step back.

"If you ever did laundry in this house, you would understand. But no one helps me with a goddamn thing around here!" Mom screams, kicking the new coffee table.

"And what the hell is this? Who paid for this? You are always asking me for money, how did you find money for this? What is wrong with my old coffee table? Why would you waste your money, my money, on something I do not freaking need?

"Jesus Christ, you really are a freaking American."

Her face turns red. Purple-green veins pop from her temples. She grabs her hair in two large fistfuls, pulling it away from her head.

I am crying again; twenty years old and sobbing, thanks to my mom.

"Tita Perla and Peter bought it," I say. "They helped us. Peter gave us the paint."

Mom storms through each room, asking about missing moth-eaten comforters and the bleach-stained hand towels she kept in the olive-green bathroom. She sighs in relief when she sees we haven't gone into her bedroom. But the reprieve is short. She spots two garbage bags we set near the door to the garage. She flies to them, tears them open, and dumps them across the brown tiles of the kitchen.

"Why would you throw out these pens?" she screams, tearing through clumps of Pepper's dog hair and sticky yogurt cups to grab a blue Bic pen missing its cap. She scratches the tip against an old receipt. It creates a faint scrawl. She hurls it at me. It hits me in the chest, leaving a single blue dot on my T-shirt.

I point to a jar of pens we've saved atop the television. Mom scoffs.

"You have no business touching my pens."

She asks if there are more garbage bags and what else of hers we've trashed. Arthur mumbles about bags in the trash cans out front. Mom bolts out the door and throws off their lids, an addict desperate for a fix.

I look at Arthur, and he at me. From outside the front door, we hear

Mom screaming curse words in Tagalog: more punyetas, a few pakshets, a "demonyo ka na!" shrieked at earsplitting volume. These are my sign to leave, they've always been my sign to leave. I tell my brother I'm going to Buddy's mom's house, my home away from home here in Fort Myers. I offer to take him with me, tell him he can sleep on the couch. He shakes his head, goes to his room, closes the door, and clicks the lock.

CHAPTER 29

# Square One

I roll down the Explorer's windows as I pull out of our triplex's small parking lot, trying to flush the soggy morning heat from the car's interior. It's a fifteen-minute ride from my place to Mom's house. I wonder if I'll still be sweating when I get there. If I'll ever stop sweating. I crank the air-conditioning to full blast.

Buddy and I live in an eight-hundred-square-foot triplex unit on the edge of Cape Coral and North Fort Myers, not far from the house where Amber was born, and near Gramma's old condo with its overflowing candy dishes. My UF stepping stone hasn't led me out of this state; it's funneled me deeper into it, all the way back to my starting point. Sometimes I feel ashamed about this. I tell people it's temporary, that I'll be moving on to bigger, better things soon. But quietly I'm happy. I'm happy to have a person who loves me and accepts my family and all its messiness. I'm happy to not have student loans weighing me down—maybe Mom's lessons aren't all outlandish?—to start my adult life fresh and unencumbered.

Our three-room apartment feels like a rebirth, like me starting over in this nobody city on my own terms.

Now I have to explain those terms to my mother.

It's been almost a year since I graduated with a degree in psychology, a year since I took the MCAT and filed my right-at-average score into a shoebox as my way of ignoring it. I told Mom I'd be taking time off before applying to medical school, and I have. What I didn't mention was that I had no plans of actually going to medical school, that I'd been drawn to a different line of work.

I see the air rifle the moment I walk through the kitchen door. It leans against the bookcase, the one where Mom's burned DVDs have overtaken Dad's paperbacks. Considering the news I'm here to share, the presence of a firearm is concerning.

The BB gun is something new. In this house, there's always something new.

The pool has become a swampy shade of green. Speckles of duckweed blanket the water's surface, crowding out the space where we kids used to flip and cannonball. They look like verdant scales, tiny green shingles protecting whatever new creatures frolic in its murky depths.

There are the floors. Mom tore out the trampled and stained carpeting after Pepper died. She's gotten quotes from various flooring companies to replace it with tile or hardwood, but "Those people are freaking insane! They must think I'm made of money!" So the floors are pieced-together boxes of laminate that Mom bought from Sam's Club and installed herself with Arthur's help. They pop hollowly underfoot with each step. They end at the hallway leading to our bedrooms, trailing off in Tetris-like strips to bare concrete.

The mess Arthur and I cleared out those few summers ago has trickled back in and multiplied. The broken-down big-screen TV, our father's 1988 pride and joy, now serves as a TV stand for a smaller TV. Mom has replaced the overstuffed armchair with an exercise bike she claims helps keep her surgically replaced knees shipshape. Even though she constantly complains about her pain. Even though she's gained more weight. Even though the bike is smothered in clothes and boxes of diabetic supplies, like everything else.

My head feels like Mom's house most days, murky and discombobulated. I've poured myself into school for most of my life, always graduating with honors, always at the top of my class, always basking in the glowing approval of others. Never stopping to consider what I want.

I didn't have premed friends at UF. I had premed study partners and premed mentors and premed workout buddies who'd invite me to kickboxing after hours spent cramming organic chemistry formulas into our brains.

My friends, the people I went out with on Saturday nights, the people who spring-breaked with me and held my hair back when I drank two piña coladas too many in Cozumel—they majored in economics, history, education, public relations, and journalism.

My premed acquaintances talked about the best research projects to apply for and the best MCAT prep courses money could buy. My friends talked about ninety-nine-cent Blizzards from Dairy Queen and nickel-beer night at Calico Jack's. They talked about their own fucked-up families and "unique" parents. They made me realize the fallacy of normality. That abnormal *is* the norm, and it's something to be treasured. Our abnormalities don't have to define us, but they do shape us. They rough up our edges and give us texture. They make us less vanilla and, in my case, more tangy green mango dipped in bagoong.

There is no such thing as normal. Not when you're half Black or half Asian or 100 percent white. We created a family of our own, one that cared nothing about my ambition or my ability to explain hydrogenation—one that cared about me. One that loved me and had no trouble saying it.

This family, I begin to realize, is what I've really wanted. I far prefer it to four more years of seeking the approval of others in medical school. I find myself yearning for this sense of belonging as we drift our separate ways after graduation. I find myself clinging to what pieces of it I have left—though I've managed to snag a big one.

Through magic, tragedies, time spent apart and reunited, Buddy and I are together. One plus one equaling this new family. He's taken a job with a friend's fledgling computer company in Cape Coral. I've taken a job waiting tables and making salsa at the same Mexican restaurant where I worked as a hostess in high school, the same one where Amber bused tables to save for her own Mustang before leaving for UCF in Orlando.

I've tried to spark some kind of passion for medicine. I've interned with our local emergency medical services. I've volunteered with doctors at clinics for the poor and underserved. I've hoped and hoped these places would inspire me. They haven't.

That restaurant salsa, though, that salsa is a different story.

During this yearlong sabbatical, the passion I discovered is food. I ate my way through Europe using the small inheritance Gramma left me once I graduated college. I ate my way through Hawaii, too, with Mom and Arthur and Buddy for Mom's fiftieth birthday, with poke and poi and Spam musubi. With locals who called me "hapa," who gave me a word for my multiracial complexities and made me feel, yet again, like I belonged.

I cherished every bite.

I'm here at Mom's house to tell her I won't be going to medical school. That I'm considering culinary school, and in the meantime I'm going to be a prep cook, making taco salads by the mall. Standing in Mom's kitchen, reality hits me: I'm telling my Filipina mother that I am going to be a cook and not a cardiologist.

There's no way we both survive this.

Outside the family room's sliding glass door, I see Mom in the backyard, clomping through rows of spiky pineapple plants and willowy banana trees. Dad's cowboy boots, cracked and faded, peek out from beneath her floral muumuu. The same Dollar Store sombrero Mom saved from my elementary school project on Mexican musical traditions perches atop her head. She is the opposite of murky and discombobulated. She is happy.

I watch her, steeling myself to go outside, have the talk, break the news. *No medical school for me, Mom! OK, cool, good talking to you, see you later, bye.* But then I see the rifle and think again. Mom's not the *OK, cool* kind. Flaring rage and fits of screaming are her normal.

Who would give this woman an air rifle?

"She's a really good shot, you know."

I jump, a shudder shivering my spine, making me wonder how long I've been standing there, how long my little brother has been behind me.

"Holy shit, where'd you come from?"

"I was reading in your old bedroom," he says. "It's got the best light this time of day."

His voice has gotten low and man-like. Whiskers sprout from his chin. He's taller than I am.

"Who's a good shot? Mom?"

"Yeah, like, *really* good. It's pretty wild."

I'm still at the slider, watching Mom shoo a cattle egret from the side of the pool-swamp. Arthur disappears into the kitchen. I hear him dig around in the fridge for a snack. A *whoosh* sound comes from the freezer as it clicks open and then shut. He hands me a bag.

"What's this?" I ask. "Sausage?"

"Uh-uh. Look closer."

I examine the icy layers of double-bagged plastic, the kind Mom makes us wash, dry, and reuse. The contents are stiff and brown, oddly light for their size. I see a spot of red on one side, deep and inky like wine. And then I see fur—fluffy, adorable fur.

"What the fuck? Is that a squirrel?"

I launch the bag back at Arthur. He catches it with one hand, juggling a half-eaten chicken leg in the other. He tucks the frozen rodent under his arm like a football, going back to work on the chicken.

"Yup. She shoots the ones that eat her mangoes," he says between bites. "This is like her fourth or fifth. And Tito Robert only gave her the BB gun, like, two weeks ago."

Tito Robert. Of course.

Tito Robert isn't our uncle, he's Mom's cousin. Mom got him to the US by setting him up with a friend of hers from the hospital, by a different kind of health-care pipeline. Tito Robert and Aunt Ann fell in love when she visited him at construction sites he worked in Dubai and Tokyo. They got married when I was in high school, then built a house in Lehigh Acres, a rural town east of Fort Myers known for big-wheel trucks and camouflage worn unironically. Tito Robert fit right in.

Mom's cousin is tall and wiry with a glossy slick of jet-black hair that bounces atop his head when he walks. If you need a tire replaced, a bathroom renovated, a feral hog field-dressed, scalded, scraped, and steam-roasted in an underground pit lined with Mom's banana leaves, Tito Robert's your man.

To this day I understand only every third to fifth word he says. He speaks English as he learned it in Saudi Arabia, where he built palaces and hotels from the ground up. We've never spent much time alone together. On one of the rare occasions we did, as I helped him onto Mom's roof to clear a gutter clogged with mango leaves, he told me about stabbing a man who tried to jump him in a construction elevator in Riyadh. I remain in awe and slight fear of him.

Tito Robert is an earthy, independent Filipino redneck. He's the kind of person you call when you have a squirrel issue. And he's the kind of person who teaches you how to deal with the issue yourself so he won't have to be called again.

"Seriously," Arthur goes on, tapping the plastic bag with the end of his chicken bone, "she shot this thing off the very top of the mango tree. What is that, thirty or forty feet high? She shot it from the side yard by the fence.

She was at least fifty yards away, and she freaking knocked it. First shot, right through its head. Insane."

I am simultaneously nodding and shaking my head, my brow furrowed by a mix of disgust and disbelief.

"So, what? Is the freezer full of all her squirrel kills now? Does she just save them in there till it's garbage day or something?"

"Nah, she gives them to Tito Robert."

"*What!*"

"Yeah, I think he makes stew with them, maybe he barbecues them, I dunno. He eats them, though."

Arthur tugs the last shreds of meat from his chicken bone, then flips it into the trash can. As he turns to put the squirrel back in the freezer, Mom opens the door, scraping dirt from Dad's boots before coming in to refill her big gray travel mug with more ice and Diet Coke.

"What are you doing with my squirrel?" she says, her voice high-pitched and happy.

"He was just showing me."

I answer defensively, worried Arthur might be in trouble, my muscle memory telling me to jump in front of the oncoming train as I tried to when we were little, my reflexes unable to recognize that the train is currently idle.

"I've got to get that one to your Tito Robert," Mom says, unfazed by my defenses, "make sure it doesn't go bad."

Arthur tosses the squirrel-cicle back into its frozen tomb. Mom sings to herself, Stevie Wonder, as she pulls a two-liter of diet soda from the fridge. I blink, wondering if this is real. I think my teeth may fall out or I'll look down and see I'm naked or flying.

Mom is happy. There are squirrels in the freezer. This is such a weird dream.

"What're you here for?" Mom says, as the ice dispenser shoots cubes shaped like crescent moons or Cheshire Cat smiles into her cup.

I remember what I'm here for, to break the medical-school news to mom. To tell her I may start cooking, like Anthony Bourdain and the pretty women with the toothy smiles on the Food Network.

But now's not the time. This is too good a dream to ruin it with my reality.

CHAPTER 30

# The C-Team

After sending out the final chicken wrap from our new *Light Juans* menu—"eighty-six bacon, ranch on the side"—to a table of ladies-who-lunch, I realize I'm ravenous. I slap together a bean burrito, take it to an overturned bucket near the dumpsters out back, and flip open my cell phone as a blip of sour cream splats against the asphalt by my clog-covered feet.

A giant truck peels out of the parking lot, spewing thick smoke from its tailpipe. I wave my burrito in front of my face to clear the air. I look at my cell. There's a voice mail from Mom. I press 1 and lift the phone to my ear.

"Your Tita Cristina is here now! You need to come say hi!"

*Click.* End of message.

*Huh?*

The door to the kitchen creaks open behind me. I hear the metallic pop of a Red Bull pull tab. Sergio, our kitchen manager, goes in for a fist bump, sees my hands are full, and instead claps me on the back.

"You good? You want to stay for dinner service? Randy is being a little bitch."

I shake my head. "I can't. I've got something going on at my mom's."

Sergio drinks his Red Bull in two fast gulps, burps, then chucks the can into the dumpster. He's a man of few words. That's what I admire most about him.

"Your mom good?" he asks as he heads back to the kitchen.

"I dunno."

I'm still staring at my phone when the door creaks shut.


My nails are stained with cilantro, their beds tingling with the lingering heat of raw jalapeños. I've been cooking for a few months now, and I love it. My young-adult life to this point has been purely cerebral: thinking about this, analyzing that. Cooking is doing. It's about precision and consistency; making the exact same thing the exact same way time and time again. It's thinking about everything and nothing simultaneously; considering heat, time, movement, momentum, but focusing only on the dish in your hands and the tickets in your window.

When I found the courage to tell my mother, it wasn't a storm she unleashed but an explosion: The Great Burrito Bombshell of 2003. At least two knives were thrown, which, in a way, seems poetic. At least one slap was dodged. At least I sobbed for only a few minutes before stomping out of Mom's house and vowing never to return.

And yet, here I am. Drawn by that cryptic voice mail. Wondering what the hell it could mean.

I should've showered or at least put on deodorant. I wipe my hands on the inside of my neon T-shirt, then tuck it back into my khakis before punching Mom's garage-door code into the keypad: my birthday, then Arthur's. Mom changed it after Amber bought the second Mustang.

I smell like onions and fryer oil, a smell that melds nicely with Mom's house as I open the kitchen door, its walls infused with fish sauce and the earthy scent of decomposing fruit peels.

Mom is in the kitchen, standing over a bowl of ampalaya that she's plucked from the vines along the backyard's chain-link fence. She's soaking them in salted water. She's midway through her own prep work, her own mindless escape. Instead of saying hello or offering basic pleasantries, she points her paring knife down the hall.

"They're in your bedroom."

"Who's *they*? How long have *they* been here? How long are *they* staying? What's going on?"

"Jesus Christ, Annabelle Marie," Mom says, wiping either sweat or tears on her sleeve as she chops more bitter melon into the salted water.

"Your Tita Cristina is living here now. They got in last week. Her and her four children."

I slump into a seat at the breakfast nook, trying to wrap my head around this sandbag of information.

Mom says she started the process seven years ago, petitioning the powers that be to sponsor a green card for Tita Cristina. She filled out the paperwork, signed the affidavits, pledged her financial support. As Tita Cristina had kids, Mom sponsored them, too, marching dutifully to the immigration office downtown with each birth announcement, starting another petition, sending off another batch of forms.

Here I am, thinking Mom's hobbies are limited to yardwork and DVD burning.

I shake my head, trying to sift these granules of information into place among the pink folds of my brain. I'm impressed by Mom's work. And only mildly shocked that she's just now telling me all this. I don't question her further. I mean, I probably should have freaking called more. I probably should have thought to ask.

*Hey, Mom, I know you've never breathed a word of any sort of family news to me, ever, but any chance five of our relatives will be coming to live with you in the near future?*

*Why, yes, cherished oldest daughter. Remember your Tita Cristina, whom you last saw thirteen years ago? She's coming to live with me! She's an adult now! With four kids! They're all coming! How are you, by the way? It's so great conversing. I love you!*

It's an easy fantasy to dismiss.

"You need to talk to them," Real Mom says, back in the real world of her fish-sauce-scented kitchen. "I don't know what to do. I thought it was jet lag, but the kids never leave your bedroom. And your Tita Cristina is... just—I do not know what to do with her."

Mom wipes her face on her sleeve again. Not sweat, tears. It's so hard to tell in Southwest Florida.

I pace the long hallway to my old bedroom at the end. The door is closed. I hear my TV playing. I lean in and hear "Who lives in a pineapple under the sea?" and four giggly voices: "SpongeBob SquarePants!"

I tap my knuckles lightly against the door. The room goes quiet. I hear the TV click off. I hear little feet echoing hollowly across Mom's poorly (but finally fully) installed laminate floors. I hear my bed creak. Then, silence.

I knock properly, three quick raps—and then a fourth; one per cousin, balance.

Still, nothing.

I figure I should introduce myself. I can't figure out how.

1.  Hi, I'm your cousin. I'm Annabelle. You never met me, but your mom took me to McDonald's once, a really big one in Manila! We have those here, too!
2.  Hey-oh! I also like SpongeBob!
3.  Open this goddamn door, you ungrateful little bitch! (Wait, that was Mom's line.)

I try the handle. It's unlocked.

I find my cousins piled on my old bed, a tangle of brown limbs and black hair. A plastic bag of Mom's dried mangoes sits amid them, the sweet honey scent mingling with what smells like a wet diaper. Amber's old underwear covers the two girls' bony bottoms. Arthur's old T-ball shirts hang loosely from the two boys' slim chests. The girls dart under the covers. The boys roll over, burrowing their faces into the old pillows I left behind.

"Hi! I mean, hey," I say, modulating my voice, trying to make it sound friendly and nonthreatening.

I go with option B: "You guys like SpongeBob? Me, too."

The room stays silent. Nobody budges.

I feel someone behind me, their energy sharp and severe. I stifle a scream, almost joining the jumble of kids in the safety of my bed.

"Ay nako, see? They barely know English, and your Tita Cristina won't let me teach them."

It's Mom, still clutching her paring knife. She points it at me when she talks, not meaning to be threatening, just meaning to be Mom. The cousins burrow deeper.

"Cristina won't leave your sister's room."

She points the knife at the door next to mine, Gramma's room and Tito Gary's room, the room most recently inhabited by Amber before she escaped to Tita Perla's house and then the University of Central Florida.

"And the children won't leave your stupid room unless Cristina comes out. I don't know what to do, Annabelle Marie. I think Cristian is peeing in the freaking corner."

That explains the smell.

Mom tells me their names are Cristine, Cristal, Cristian, and Cristopher.

They are the C-team, and we are the A-team. I wonder if that's a Filipino thing or a Mom's-family thing, naming all your kids with the same initial. I wonder the same about the crying and the sad music, both of which I can hear coming from the room next to mine. Or does the room itself induce sadness?

Mom whacks the heel of her paring knife against the door, her way of knocking. She then jams at the handle, which doesn't budge.

"Punyeta ka! Buksan mo ang pintuan!"

I don't know much Tagalog. But I know what Mom's saying. I feel it in the memories of my muscles. She's chosen option C: *Open this goddamn door, you ungrateful bitch!*

It's always worked on me. It's not doing the same to Tita Cristina.

We listen as feet stomp at the room's far end, as the CD player blares louder, all those sad songs I listened to through my wall years ago spinning back to life.

The music. The distinctive heat of Mom's house, where the thermostat never dips below 80. The faintly fishy smell oozing from the drywall. I'm in a time machine, slipping down through a wormhole and into fifth grade.

I am the kids in the bed, doing whatever I can to ignore the pool of sadness seeping from the room next door. I am Mom, trying to coax the sad person out, hoping they can find some meaning on this side of the world, something to keep them going until the rest of their family can join them, so they can be saved from the rising waters.

Here in the wormhole, suspended between then and now, the sad person is Tito Gary and is Tita Cristina. It's an Humberto Machado illusion: sad Tito if you tilt one way, sad Tita if you tilt the other. It's Schrödinger's sibling, alive and dead at the same time.

I sit with Mom back at the breakfast nook, still in my neon, onion-smelling T-shirt. We draft a plan: Mom will find (illegally burn) *Sesame Street* DVDs, and I will search for playmates for Tita Cristina's kids. Buddy's mom, still an elementary-school teacher, knows kids their age. She can help get them into school. I can look up English-learning techniques. I can create outlines and index cards. Index cards were practically my college major.

They're going to love it here. It's only a matter of time. This is America! With liberty and justice for all!

\* \* \*

Two days later, I call Mom to tell her I've found an English-language teacher fluent in Tagalog.

"Her dad was military. She grew up on the naval base in Subic Bay," I tell Mom, gushing with excitement.

The line is quiet for too many seconds.

"Well," Mom says in a tone the opposite of mine, dull and unusually nonchalant. "Your Tita Cristina is going home."

"What?"

More silence.

"What do you mean?" I say. "What about the kids?"

"They're going with her. She is not happy, and your Tita Perla said to let them go. I cannot do this again. We cannot do this again."

There's more quiet. I'm worried Mom's going to hang up on me. Cut me off. End of story.

I choose my words carefully, hoping she'll open up, maybe just a little, and not implode into another black hole.

"I'm sorry, Mommy."

I should be thinking of her feelings. Of the stress this has put on my aunt and my cousins. But all I can think about is money. The money Mom paid for five one-way plane tickets. The money she paid for five more. The clothes and suitcases she bought. The hoops through which she jumped to make this happen. To try to save, in the only way she knows, her youngest sister and the four nieces and nephews she'd never met.

Mom only spends money on things she loves. Cars. Travel. Family.

"I'm so sorry, Mommy," I say again, still fearful the line will go dead at any moment. "We can throw a going-away dinner, maybe? I can cook. We can take the kids to swim in Buddy's mom's pool before they go. Maybe that will change their minds?"

"Cristina won't leave the house unless it's to get in a car and go to the airport," Mom says. "She is a stubborn goddamn idiot just like me."

Mom cries, but she keeps going. Words stream from her mouth as tears stream from her eyes, garbling her sentences: "Cristina misses her husband. I've done more for her than anyone on this planet has, but she misses him somehow. Cristina dropped out of school after I left. Nobody showed her how life could be more than that freaking slum. She was too young when I left. I didn't mother her the way she should have been mothered. It's all my fault."

Her words make me think of Buddy's words and my own worries. As a kid raising kids, is it your fault if they fuck up? How much of Amber's anger and Arthur's ambivalence is due to me? How do you stop these cycles from repeating?

Mom left her home in Manila to help her family. I left my home, too. I didn't go far, but I wasn't trying to help anyone other than myself. Maybe I am just a selfish freaking American. Maybe I avoid Mom because my greatest fear is becoming her, taking on her rage and anxiety, her all-consuming need to control everything and everyone around her. She raised her siblings, I've raised mine. She obsesses over us. I obsess over numbers and menu items and slicing onions to precisely the same width.

But I'm happier and more easygoing, aren't I? I have a *much* longer fuse. I take care of myself. I wear makeup, get pedicures, go to the gym to stay in shape. This means I'm not her, right?

"It is your Tito Gary all over again," Mom says. "I'm not cutting another freaking body from my attic. I'm not."

My mother and I cry together, each for our own reasons. We listen to each other's tears, neither of us hanging up.

A few days later Tita Cristina and her kids are gone.

\* \* \*

Tita Cristina died in 2016. She developed type 2 diabetes and spent the money Mom sent her for insulin on things she loved more: Jollibee Chickenjoy and halo-halo. Her blood turned to acid and poisoned her organs.

Six weeks later, her son Cristopher died, too. He drowned. Possibly from sadness. Physically from inhaling water after falling from a boat and disappearing into the murky waves of Manila Bay.

I don't learn this until years later, while writing this book, when I text Mom to ask how Tita Cristina is doing.

**YOUR TITA CRISTINA IS DEAD,** she writes, possibly screaming, possibly just stuck in caps-lock as she so often is. **DIDN'T YOU SEE FB???**

**I don't ever check Facebook,** I text back. My head races. *I've talked to Mom. A lot lately. I've freaking called. I've freaking texted. She's never freaking mentioned this.*

**YES SHE IS DEAD.**

**I'm so sorry,** I write. **What happened?**

I look for the three little dots to flash, to see she's typing a reply. When my phone goes dark, I keep it close, listening for its telltale ping. When it remains silent, I realize what's happened.

Mom's hung up.

CHAPTER 31

# The Paper

I walk into *The News-Press* carrying trays of spinach salad and rolls stuffed with grilled chicken and Swiss. The box of plastic forks tucked under my arm clinks with each rubbery step of my clogs. I smell like toasted almonds and poppy-seed dressing. Heads turn as I walk through the newsroom's rows of desks with a pink, pansy-printed apron knotted at my waist. I'm trying to convey *chicly professional*, just like my new catering company.

Reporters glance up at me from their screens, corded phones pinned between shoulders and ears. They crane their necks to see what I'm carrying. Their eyes follow me as I duck into conference room 2. I smile as I pass them, wondering who's writing about what, wondering where *Monsieur Jean Le Boeuf*, the pseudonymous food critic my father introduced me to all those years ago, sits, and if he might pen a piece on this breakout new catering company from Fort Myers's own rising culinary star.

It's 2005. Anything's possible.

Southwest Florida is filthy with real-estate money. My infant catering business hopes for just a taste of it. My partner and I offer a simple breakfast-lunch menu perfect for mortgage brokers, title companies, and every hair salon/dentist's office/dog groomer/*name-any-business-it's-2005* with money to spare.

This is my second time walking into *The News-Press*, Lee County's newspaper of record since 1884. The first was a week ago, when I sat with the sports editors in a too-warm conference room, discussing the ins and outs of a part-time night job as a clerk.

"You'll need to take a typing test and pass a basic copyediting exam," the senior sports editor says. "If those go well, we'll go from there."

I'm not sure I'll get the job. But the interview lands me this catering gig: forty people's worth of salad, mini-sandwiches, and my partner's signature cookies.

After working as a prep and line cook at the Tex-Mex restaurant, I moved on to a full-service catering company and café. I parboiled shrimp for massive wedding receptions and grilled bacon-wrapped chicken skewers for baby showers. Then I switched to the café side, which handled the daytime catering operations, churning out massive sandwich trays, huge fruit platters, and pasta salad by the bucketful.

I loved the café's hours. I was in at eight and out by three. I got to see my friends again. I got to spend daylight hours with Buddy.

He's still with the computer place, which now calls itself a technology company and is booming like every other industry in the area. His half-decent salary offsets mine, which is almost but not quite minimum wage. And yet we buy a house—because it's 2005. It's a cute ranch home in Fort Myers proper, less than ten minutes from Mom's. It has a one-car garage, three bedrooms, and two baths, like taking Mom's house and slicing it in half. There's no pool and less of a yard, but it's mine, ours. It even has a mango tree in the backyard, a massive one that reaches high into the sky.

The first summer after we move in, a loud explosion jerks us out of bed. It's raining and windy outside, nothing unusual for July. Then comes a second bang and a third, both equally deafening. It's the mango tree dropping fruits onto the tin roof of our back porch, each one exploding like a bombshell.

I pick some and cut into them. They're stringy and tough, almost all seed. I take a bite and spit it out. It tastes like resin.

"Those are the Cuban's mangoes," Mom tells me the next day when I bring her a bagful to glean her mango expertise. She makes it sound like she knows this Cuban and she can't believe he dared plant such fruits. "They are not like my mangoes."

Still, she insists I save them so she can send them to her Filipino friends in New York and California. "They'll take any mangoes they can get!"

I'm not much of a planner. I take after Dad in that way. I tend to let life happen to me, as opposed to trying to compulsively control it, as Mom still fights to do.

I never wanted to live in Fort Myers. I'd hoped to be many steps away by now. But here I am in this house with its own mango tree, and with this guy who still makes my heart flutter, doing this job I chose, this job I love.

It's 2005. Anything's possible.

My time at the catering company and café inspires me to branch out on my own, which is how I end up carrying trays of food through the halls of *The News-Press*. But my catering company is deep in the red. I need a night job that will pay me actual money, not checks to be put toward credit-card balances.

I pass the typing test and ace the copyediting exam. The sports editors offer me twenty hours a week as an agate clerk, a job that no longer exists and never will again. I come into the newsroom around seven p.m., after wrapping up the day's catering gigs. I leave around midnight, when the building is dark and mostly quiet, save for the last few designers and the folks working the press. I take calls from the trailer-park shuffleboard leagues near Gramma's old condo in North Fort Myers and from golf pros at the country clubs where the wealthier retirees while away their hours. I fold this data into teeny-tiny boxes that I scrunch into teeny-tiny columns in 5½-point type. I squeeze it in amid the night's NFL roundups and MLB stats that I pull from the wire.

If one of our sports reporters writes too long a story, one of our designers, Dave K. or maybe Robyn, will approach my teeny-tiny desk crammed into a nook facing the wall. They'll be twitchy and nervous, as I'll learn to be when deadline looms. They'll say things like "I need four inches. Dorsey blew through his space. Ed cut as much as he could," as they drum their fingers across the worn-out legs of their jeans. Then they'll leave to smoke or to pace, further wearing out the threadbare carpet squares lining this section of the newsroom, while they wait for me to do what I love: make things add up.

Agate clerking and my obsession with numbers and order are a match made in journalism heaven.

The agate page, back when newspapers had such a thing, was meant for gambling addicts and fantasy-team fanatics. It was espn.com pre–espn .com: every stat from every game/match/race that mattered. And I got to pick what mattered and then wiggle it into place.

If Robyn or Dave needed four inches, that meant, So long shuffleboard scores. I'd lop them from the page, then save them in a file for another night. I could crunch some sections down to 5-point type, but if I went smaller, the editors would get angry calls from Benny and Carl at the club, complaining they had to *get a frickin' microscope out just to see how their ponies did at Gulfstream! Why, I oughta…!*

Instead, I'd take the greyhound track results down from five places per race to three, which seemed to bother no one. I could leave out Formula 1 results, too, so long as it wasn't August, when all the Europeans come to visit.

As Robyn paced or Dave smoked, I'd rush over, thrumming my hands on my hips, ten minutes till first edition.

"We're good," I'd say. "I got you at least four inches, probably closer to five."

They'd bow in thanks, and I'd bow back, happy to be able to make anything possible.

A few months into agate clerking, I become a part-time sportswriter, too. I cover high school and youth events. I sit between our boating writer and our fishing writer, across from our golf writer.

My earliest articles are smoldering garbage. The first is about a youth softball team moving into a new facility across the river in Cape Coral. My closing line, "Now they truly have a league of their own," makes bile gurgle in the back of my throat when I read it now.

I have given up my cooking dream to pursue journalism. To put it another way: The catering company never made money, and *The News-Press* is willing to pay me, even hire me full-time. I am, like Dad, along for the ride, happy to go wherever life takes me.

As more assignments filter my way, things start to click. Writing and reporting aren't all that different from agate clerking: Just make it add up.

The editors give me a topic and a finite amount of space. They give me a keyboard and a phone and time to explore said topic, and then they give me a deadline. I have to connect the dots, make 1 + 2 = 3.

Once the dots start aligning, I learn there are prettier ways to connect them, ways that keep readers reading and honor the stories I get to tell. I don't care much for sports. I learn the rules of soccer, volleyball, and high school football while huddled in booths next to team statisticians, copying their notes. I google "what is PAT" on my clunky laptop, praying to catch a wisp of Wi-Fi. When that fails, I swallow my pride and ask one of the guys sitting next to me. I listen to them sigh, hear the thoughts in their head—*When did they let Chinese girls into the stats booth?*—then scribble down whatever answer they give me, tucking it into a folder in my brain, *point after touchdown,* in the P section between *pancit* and *punyeta.*

But sports writing is rarely about sports. It's about the people who play the sports and their stories. It's about layering together the pieces in a way that makes readers care. And then moving on to the next story. In a restaurant kitchen, there's always another dish. At a paper, there's always another story.

To everyone's shock, none greater than my own, I win awards for my sports writing. I get the attention of other editors. I get a chance to write about things I do care about.

The words float across the newsroom like twinkling fairy dust: *One of the old Jean Le Boeufs is leaving. Who, oh, who could take their place?*

I feel them caress the backs of my ears and lift me from my squeaky roller chair at the far end of the sports desk. I feel them carry me to my editor's office, the way delicious smells carry Mickey Mouse to warm-from-the-oven pies. In my head, I say something like *OH, SWEET BABY JESUS, PICK ME!* In reality, it's probably more like *OH, SWEET BABY JESUS, **PLEASE** PICK ME!*

I have manners.

As I find my bearings in sports and get a feel for the newsroom, I start pitching the occasional food story: on the booming growth of Asian grocery stores (in the mid-2000s, Fort Myers went from one—to two!); on the celebratory power of pancit; on lumpia as a love language. Some (Asian markets) are snapped up. Others are politely ignored.

When the opportunity to be the iconic Jean Le Boeuf arises in 2006, to dine out on *The News-Press's* dime and pass judgment on restaurants while disguised by a Frenchman's pseudonym, I refuse to be ignored.

This is the dream I never thought to dream, a life so patently unimaginable, as a fatherless, mixed-race kid growing up with a manic-depressive

Filipina mother in Robert E. Lee County, that the mere possibility of it makes my head tingle.

All I wanted as a child was to be normal, to hide my weird family, their weird deaths and weird antics, behind a big GPA and a spot as captain of the swim team. As an adult, I still strive for this ideal, knowing full well the impossibility of it. I have a normal and tidy house with a normal and tidy yard that we mow each week like good, normal citizens. I have normal friends who talk to me about normal things over normal after-work drinks. I have a normal husband, too, one whom I've never punched in the face, one whose mother has never called me a Chink bitch, although she did say "Bless your heart" once, which is close in the South.

But if I could be Jean Le Boeuf, it would be like winning the *Price Is Right* Showcase Showdown of normality. The boat, the car, the dining room table and chairs, all wrapped up in one French-sounding pen name.

It would be the ultimate hiding place. It had to be too good to be true. I grew up reading Jean Le Boeuf. I worked in restaurants reviewed by Jean Le Boeuf. I loved and worshipped Jean Le Boeuf.

Me—*as* Jean Le Boeuf? No way.

I ready myself for a fight. I figure the line to be the Notorious JLB will stretch out the door and down Dr. Martin Luther King Jr. Boulevard. I freshen my résumé, gather my best clips, dust off my catering apron, and prepare to make my case. I plan a menu of pesto and roast-turkey sliders with cranberry aioli. I figure if my writing doesn't win them over, my skills in the kitchen just might. I wait to hear a date, to learn who I'll be up against. One afternoon, the features editor catches me in the breakroom.

"You still interested in the JLB thing?" she asks as we watch her Lean Cuisine twirl in the microwave.

"Yeah, of course, for sure," I say.

"Great. If you're free next week, I'll have James get you started."

"Like started-started, like start-reviewing-places started?" I say, glancing up from her bubbling tray of Alfredo pasta with chicken and broccoli to study her face.

"Yeah, you were the only one interested. It's all yours."

If she says anything more, I don't remember. The fairy dust sweeps me away. I am walking on air.

I'm at the new Pollo Tropical in Cape Coral, staring at sunny-yellow trays of grilled chicken, ropa vieja, rices, beans, tostones, and soups; one of everything, just about, from this fast-food menu. An old man with a big belly and flip-flops walks by our overflowing table, looks at me and my mentor, our notebooks situated surreptitiously in our laps.

"Damn. Y'all hungry?" he says, cackling with laughter as his shoes *thwick-thwack* past.

I'm near the shores of Captiva, listening to the shimmery melodies of a steel-drum player while sipping a Key lime martini, trying to figure out if the swaying fronds overhead are coconut palm or royal palm, picking gingerly at my Key lime grouper, trying to save room for the Key lime bread pudding and Key lime cheesecake we'll be ordering for dessert.

I'm eating and getting paid for it. I'm pinching myself, wondering when I'll wake up.

At these restaurants, I'm not Annabelle Tometich. I'm the legendary Jean Le Boeuf.

And, holy shit, it feels good.

But hold on. "Who is Jean Le Boeuf?"

I'll write this story with this exact headline in various iterations through the years.

"Good question," I write by way of answering in 2018.

"'Jean Le Boeuf' isn't a person. It's a nom de plume (if you want to get fancy), a pseudonym (if you'd rather get scientific), or, simply, a fake name. This fake name has been used by *The News-Press*'s restaurant critics since…1979."

I have an affinity for parentheses. One day an editor will ask me what I'm trying to hide in all my parentheses (what? nothing!), if I'm using them to mask thoughts I don't want to take ownership of (*pfft!*). I'll think about his words every time I use them thereafter.

I learn to be Jean Le Boeuf from another Jean Le Boeuf. He shows me the ropes at fast-food grilled-chicken places and tourist-trappy island places and Fort Myers staples not far from the rental house where I was born.

This other Jean Le Boeuf is from Wisconsin. He's like everyone in the newsroom, all these other Somebodies from real cities and real towns, here in Fort Myers on extended vacation. Our features editor is from Indiana. The sports editors are from Boston and Upstate New York. Robyn's from Rhode Island. Dave K. is from Illinois.

Nobody's from Fort Myers. Except me.

I like being a nobody, fitting in, living that quote, unquote "normal" life of my teenage dreams. But as Jean Le Boeuf, I get to be a Somebody. Better yet: I get to be a Somebody *Else*.

Being Jean Le Boeuf is the best of all worlds. It's everything I've ever longed for—respect, invisibility, a place to hide my messy past—wrapped in a fancy French cloak.

My anonymity allows me to take jabs at chefs and rail against their rubbery deviled eggs without fear of repercussions. But that's just the surface. The real power comes in envelopes addressed to *Mr. Jean Le Boeuf – The News-Press*. And in emails that start: *Dear sir* and *Cher monsieur*.

When the first Jean Le Boeuf, a white guy, created the name in 1979, it was simply a veil. Jean was meant to be gender neutral and purposely pretentious. It was meant to add authority to the paper's reviews but also levity, to poke fun at the highfalutin big-city food critics of the day.

John The Beef. It's funny.

Jean could be a man or a woman. Jean could be *anybody*. But many people, my long-dead father and my younger self included, assumed Jean to be a white French guy. When I took over the role, a changing of the guard that went unannounced, as all Jean Le Boeuf switch-ups had, those assumptions continued.

There is power in anonymity. There is infinitely more power in being a white dude.

Who's going to trust a half-Filipino former Tex-Mex-line-cook girl about the redolent qualities of a perfect bouillabaisse? Maybe Buddy.

Who's going to trust the legendary Jean Le Boeuf? Definitely Buddy. Probably Arthur. And also everyone else in Fort Myers.

When I write as Jean Le Boeuf, I write with the authority of the most privileged. I get on my soapbox, rallying against imported seafood and frozen mozzarella sticks (*how dare they!*). When people listen, when they flood the JLB inbox with so many messages that I devote one day a week to answering them, I realize what I have.

A voice. Or, rather: (a voice).

The parentheses, I've come to understand, were hiding me. The real me. They were hiding my broad nose and dark skin and the fact that I'm a woman in an industry where the gender wage gap is still massive. They hid the fact that I felt like an impostor, that I've always felt like an impostor, whether I'm among white people or Filipino people or even other mixed-race people.

I didn't go to culinary school or journalism school. In my head, I have no right to be doing what I'm doing. But when I'm Jean Le Boeuf, none of that matters. The real me and her anxious, ever-racing mind goes au revoir. I throw off my Clark Kent glasses and rip off my reporter's clothes to reveal my shiny JLB cape. When I'm in this cape, people disagree with me respectfully, due to the content of my reviews and not the color of my skin or the gender on my birth certificate. They listen to me. They follow my advice. And then they write to thank me: *Dear Mr. Le Boeuf, You were so right about Taqueria San Julian! We ordered the tacos al pastor just like you said! We loved them!!*

As JLB, I'm anybody and everybody. I wear this cape proudly. I cling to it for fifteen pseudonymous years.

## CHAPTER 32

# Shit

The warm water buffers the pain of my contractions. Or it's supposed to.

As the blinding agony seizing my lower back and distended abdomen eases, from a 49/10 to a mere 20/10, I wonder if the water's doing anything. I wonder if it's too late for drugs (it is) and if I'm going to shit myself (I am). I realize I hate Ricki Lake. Her *Business of Being Born* documentary, which led me to this godforsaken shit-tub, is a work of hate propaganda.

My anxieties swirl: an eddy of pain, foolish hope for medicinal relief, hostilities toward a nineties talk-show host, and fears that I'm going to fill this birth center's jacuzzi with my own feces before hurling a baby into it.

*WHY AM I JUST THINKING ABOUT THIS NOW?*

As these thoughts rage through my mind, my body is the picture of calm. I grab the edge of the bathtub with one hand and Buddy's near-broken forearm with the other. I have a freakishly strong grip. I want him to feel this pain as I feel it. I want him to suffer for what he's done to me. He's No. 2 on my shit list. That's the worst spot.

I breathe and squeeze, my fingers digging deep grooves into his flesh, my mind racing, my body still. I am my mother's daughter: perfectly capable of holding fantastical portions of pain.

Amid my shitty thoughts and unfounded fury, I see Mom sitting at the edge of the bed next to the tub, humming as she crochets another powder-blue baby bib.

Mom is at her best at moments like this, when lives are hanging in the balance. It's what made her a great intensive-care nurse. It's what held her together after Dad died, and then his mom, and then Tito Gary. In those moments of death, she had other lives to consider, three of them, all with names that start with A.

Now her As are gone.

Arthur is in college at the University of Florida, my old stomping grounds. Amber has her own husband and her own house/yard/fruit trees across town. I'm here in this soon-to-be-shit-speckled whirlpool, about to give birth to Mom's first grandchild.

My mother is an empty nester. She's moved on to plan B: banana trees, burning more DVDs, *Bonanza* reruns at three a.m. The house that used to be ours is now all hers. It too is turning to shit.

I become a mother on June 21, 2010. The summer solstice. The longest day of the year. My son enters the murky waters of my bathtub at 3:48 p.m. It doesn't add up, $3 + 4 \neq 8$, and yet it feels exactly right.

Buddy dutifully scoops any stray poops with one of those little green nets you use to corral goldfish at pet stores. It helps that he worked in a pet store through high school and college, six years slinging dog food and collecting squirmy bettas to pay his way through UF. The experience makes him, makes us, marvelously adept at this task: filtering my shit from our new family's waters, helping us keep our kid, and three years later, our two kids, clear of it.

Perhaps the beauty of this mixed-up, abnormally all-American childhood I've had is the keen hindsight it's helped me develop. Every obsessive thought, every hashing and rehashing and re-rehashing of the fights and deaths and frustrations, every attempt to make it add up has, in its own way, prepared me for parenthood. Inasmuch as anyone can be prepared for this wilderness.

I know my mom—no, that's not true. I know the parts of my mom I do not want to become, the layers of her I hate most: her temper, her rage, her furious need for control. I still see her as the strange lady who works in our yard, the person I tell my middle-school busmates is our maid, the woman who must be kept at arm's length lest she rub off on me, the person I'm happy to reduce to her absolute worst moments to justify going weeks and months without contacting her. And yet she's the person I come back to in times of need.

Three months after Lincoln's birth, when Buddy and I are back at work, Mom takes on the task of watching the baby—of feeding him and burping him and changing the diapers he fills with stinkless, pea-colored poops.

"Don't tell me you're going to waste all your money so some strangers can let him choke to death on hot dogs?" Mom says by way of proposing and accepting the job. "Don't be freaking stupid."

Were I a smarter, less sleep-deprived, not quite so nipple-chafed person, I would think this offer through. But I am the mother of a three-month-old. I am desperate for help. Even if that help is Mom.

She fills her already jam-packed family room with play mats and toys and a walker she buys from a neighborhood garage sale. Once she has one of everything a baby could need, she keeps going. She scoops up a second stroller from a friend, "still in the box!" She gets another high chair and a third tummy-time play mat, this one jungle themed, to complement the airplane-themed one and the one plastered with farm animals. An infant needs choices.

When there is no more room in the house, she stores her backups in the garage, amid her bags of fertilizer and manure—useful shit—by her lawn mower and Weedwacker and the long, hand-rigged poles she uses to snag mangoes from the tippy-tops of her trees.

Mom's children have left her. Her fruit trees have not.

The yard looks much like the house: chaotic with Mom's treasures.

The avocado tree she planted when I was in middle school is now a good forty feet tall, teetering near the edge of the street, casting Cathy's old yard in shade come afternoon. Mom's ripped out the ornamental shrubs that once surrounded the house and replaced them with droopy clusters of banana trees and prickly pineapple plants.

Outside Arthur's old window, a lone tamarind tree with wispy fernlike leaves and fingery pods stands in the shade of the property's original citrus trees. It's grown tall and spindly in the shadows of its older siblings. Its trunk shoots high in the air, quietly vying for oxygen.

The left side of the yard is home to Mom's atis and star-apple trees, which she planted when Amber ran away to live with Tita Perla. This complex patch of land is where Mom's green thumb struggles. Sand-wiched between the house and Dr. Johnson's estate, it doesn't get much sun. There's a grapefruit tree on that side. A chico tree, too, a fruit better known to Cubans and Puerto Ricans as sapodilla. There's a small guava tree and several attempts at papaya trees that, to Mom's chagrin, rarely grow beyond sapling stage. The bushy longan tree against the fence is easy to overlook. Its juicy, candy-sweet fruits remind me of fat grapes inside shells: hard on the outside, soft and complex within. They grow in heavy clusters during the hottest months of summer—June, July, August—when everything else feels dead.

Mom still has trellises of green beans and tomatoes lining the once-pebble-filled portion of the patio near the pool-swamp. The far side of the pool houses pots of okra, sweet potatoes, and sometimes bell pep-pers, if the mood strikes during Mom's early-fall planting sessions.

The chain-link fence separating Mom's yard from the neatly trimmed lawns of her rear neighbors serves as a trellis for her sitaw plants, also known as yardlong or snake beans. It's where the vines of Grandpa's ampalaya still cling, sending out curlicue shoots and then shiny-green gourds come rainy season.

It's where the rear neighbor will eventually erect a tall and impenetrable fence, a wall that allows them to pretend this muumuu-wearing, cowboy-booted, sombrero-topped woman with a pond for a pool doesn't exist. Mom uses the fence to grow more sitaw.

The front yard houses mom's prized calamansi tree. It bears little citrus fruits the size of Key limes with a sweet-tart flavor that's a perfect finish for mom's pancit. That's where her star fruits are rooted, her soursop and jackfruit, too.

There's a small mango tree in the backyard, a tiny one as compared to her others. It yields honey mangoes, or what mom calls Thai mangoes, thin fruits as yellow as sunshine. There's a larger mango tree in the front right yard. It droops with small, sugar-sweet Hadens in summer.

In the front left yard, at its dead center, is the mango tree that started it all. The once-fragile trunk we were forbidden to touch is now as thick as a dining room table, its roots reaching deep into the earth, its leafy tops towering some seventy feet in the air—high above the house and the neighbor's royal palms. The yard beneath it is bare dirt, all its sun eaten up by the mango tree's limbs, all its rain falling secondhand, leftovers from the tree's leaves and flowers and fruits.

Mom never wanted lots of kids. She still calls Arthur a happy accident. Mom had lots of kids, her younger siblings in Manila, and she left them in San Andres Bukid to chase happiness. She's tried to get them to come back to her. Like the seeds she's scattered across the yard, she's scattered I-130 forms and green-card applications across the chaotic lawn that is US Immigration Services. Some took root: Tita Perla, Tito Robert. Others didn't.

A big yard of fruit trees, though, that has always been Mom's dream.

The one dream her racist mother-in-law, dead husband, hanged brother, and wildly Americanized children couldn't quash.

Turns out, she didn't need acreage to achieve it, just a postage-stamp suburban lawn, some ironclad will, and the ability not to give a shit about societal norms.

Lincoln calls Mom "Lola," which is what we should have called her mom, our maternal grandmother, way back when instead of "Nay," had anyone corrected us. When he learns to talk, he comes home from Lola's house rambling on about the adventures they've had, picking fruits, catching lizards, and "pow-powing the squirrs."

"The squirrs? What do you do to the squirrs?" I ask, wrist-deep in mango guts as I peel and prep a batch for the freezer.

"Squirrs bad!" he says from his high chair, wagging a chubby little finger dyed yellow by his after-dinner snack. "Squirrs eat mango! My mango!"

Buddy looks at me with the sideways glance of a concerned parent. I roll my eyes and sigh, realizing this shit is mine to clean up.

When Mom comes to pick up Lincoln the next morning, I try to be casual about it. I mention how his vocabulary is exploding, how he's talking nonstop.

"Of course he is! I talk to that boy all day long," she says. "I tell him all my stories, and he loves them! Don't you, my Lincy Lou?"

My son runs to his grandmother, wrapping his sausage arms around her thick legs.

I smile, take a deep breath.

"Well, he told me about how you guys pow-pow the squirrels together, too."

"POW! POW!" Lincoln yells, with the perfect timing of a toddler, turning his pudgy hands into tiny six-shooters, leaning against his lola's calves for surety.

"That's right," Mom coos as she musses up his hair. "We pow-pow those nasty squirrels, don't we!"

"Mom."

"What? He loves it! I'm showing him how to solve problems," she says. "It's just a BB gun."

I want to lay down the law. I want to tell her it's wildly inappropriate to be shooting things, BB gun or not, with a two-year-old. I think of how to start, how to stand up to this woman who's owned me for so long. Then my phone buzzes in my hand. It's my morning assignment, wondering if we can meet thirty minutes early.

I let Mom go.


My mother makes a point of picking Linc up and dropping him off. She says she doesn't want to inconvenience me, that I can pay her for gas if it really bothers me, that she *dreamed* of having such help when she was a new mom.

I don't question her intent. It's twenty fewer minutes for me to spend in the car. Pick him up all you want, Lola.

I'm a full-time food writer now, having happily given up my sports gig when the other Jean Le Boeuf left for a job in academia. Happily hoarding the white-sounding pseudonym and its many privileges for myself, I have a more 9-ish-to-5-ish schedule most days.

Today I get off work early. I have a restaurant to review tonight. I leave our downtown office after lunch. I drive to get Lincoln so we can hang out before I ship him off to Buddy's mom for the evening. I call my mom to tell her I'm en route. She doesn't answer. I let myself in using the garage keypad.

I walk into the familiar chaos but amplified: TV blaring, pots simmering on the stove, dishes stacked in the sink, seedlings sprouting along the counters, the floor littered with toys and books, junk mail, boxes of alcohol pads and insulin syringes.

The room smells like shit. Not proverbial shit. Human shit. Not baby shit. Lola shit—musky and intense.

I see Lincoln, sitting amid the mess, playing with a canister of BB pellets.

I sprint across the room to grab the tin from his fat toddler hands. In my rush, I knock a stack of clothes from the handles of Mom's exercise bike, triggering a disastrous series of dominoes. The clothes topple the towers of medicine bottles on the breakfast nook's bench, which knock over Mom's giant travel mug of coffee, left out from this morning or maybe a morning last week. She rarely drinks coffee. "It makes me poop too much!" she always says, which tells me it probably is from this morning, which also explains the smell emanating from the olive-green bathroom.

The coffee mug knocks over a pyramid of old pain patches from her last knee surgery that have been sitting at the far, unused end of the breakfast table since perhaps the dawn of time by the yellowed looks of them. The boxes of patches tumble to the floor and erupt, unleashing a plague of tiny and not-so-tiny cockroaches, a tsunami of little brown creatures that go skittering across the cheap bamboo laminate in search of new places to nest.

I swat them from my feet and legs, stomping as many as I can as I shriek and dance in quick, coffee-splashed circles. Lincoln finds this hilarious. He laughs those deep baby giggles that, normally, would have me laughing, too. He drops the canister of BB pellets, scattering them across the floor, a counterattack to our roach invasion. They let off a metallic whine as they roll across the laminate, over old electric bills, sticky candy wrappers, and bags of unopened pills from the Publix pharmacy.

The floor is alive. Everything is moving, whether roach or rolling pellet.

"What the hell? Is that you, Abelle?"

Mom's voice echoes from the near end of the hall. I scoop up Lincoln and walk him to the bathroom's wide-open door, that musky smell smacking me in the face. I peer in and Mom is sitting on the toilet, muumuu hiked to her armpits, elbows on knees.

"When did you get here?"

"I got off work early," I say, Lincoln in one arm, the other pushed against my nose, to blot out the stench and also my tears. "Mom. The house is bad. This is really bad."

I can't bring myself to look at my mother's face. I don't want to see if she's angry or shocked or maybe in agreement with me. I no longer care. She's in no position to fight. She doesn't even try. Not that I stay around long enough to let her.

"I'm taking him home," I say. "I think it's time to sign him up for day care. He can't stay here."

I duck away from the bathroom door before Mom can see my tears. They're tears of frustration, at the situation and at myself. Standing there, amid all mom's shit, I realize this has always been the logical conclusion. This house will always return to chaos without us there to stop it. I should have seen it. I should have made it add up. But I chose not to.

CHAPTER 33

# The Shot

My phone rings early in the evening. Its screen shows a number I don't know. I silence it and go back to the dishes filling my sink, vowing to get them cleaned and put away before bedtime, ignoring my aching feet and my rose-colored Fitbit when it buzzes to congratulate me for hitting 20,000 steps, all walked through our ticky-tacky house and its postage-stamp yard.

The sky outside the front window glows orange-pink at the horizon. The day's been brutally sunny. Hot and humid as late June always is, the kind of weather that turns mangoes from thin, green, and chalky to fat, yellow-red, and bursting with juice, sending them tumbling from their branches to rot in yards like my own, so often ignored.

My phone rings again, same number. I send it to voice mail.

I grab a garbage bag and take a lap, collecting empty juice boxes, half-filled Solo cups, cupcake wrappers, and Popsicle sticks; the remnants of a five-year-old's birthday party. Buddy is in the front yard, swatting mosquitoes from his legs, with Peter. Peter who officiated at our wedding eight years ago. Peter with the frog-hating mother. Peter who graduated from NYU law school only to get sucked back into this swamp to take care of his ailing father. Peter who now works as a defense attorney and lives two streets over from us.

I pull an empty seltzer bottle from a bush of Mexican petunias, its purple flowers closed against the still lingering heat of evening. I check on the last few kids left. Their screams have faded, from earsplitting shrieks to the ignorable patter of tired but content children. They move up the ladder of the giant, rented inflatable waterslide like zombies: not fully alive, not able to stop themselves. They slide down its slippery slope like they've done so a thousand times, because they have.

I plop the garbage bag into the big green trash can at the side of the house. I go back to the kitchen, wash my hands, and stare down the tower of dirty dishes. I should dig in, get cracking, avoid the impending fruit-fly infestation, make sure the entropy that's consumed my mother's house doesn't infect my own. Instead, I check on Penelope, the daughter I birthed in the same center's same bathtub eighteen months earlier (some people never learn). Her room is silent, save for the *whoosh* of the white-noise machine and the soft click of her lips as she sucks her thumb. I linger in her doorway, soaking in the calm after a day of happy chaos.

Today feels like a good omen for the trip we're planning. Mom left the thickly packed hermit shell of her house for the first time in a long time. She cooked her pancit and lumpia, and interacted with humans for about forty-five minutes, until the candles had been blown out and she could sneak back to her lair.

She and I are supposed to go to the Philippines this year for the first time since 2009. It's why we've started talking again. She's renewed her passport and reached out to her siblings and cousins and titas. I've been tracking flight prices and am hoping to book tickets for after the holidays, when the weather in Manila is cooler and dryer.

Mom asks if I want to take Buddy and the kids. I answer with a quick no. I tell her we can't afford it, which is part of the truth. The rest is complicated. I don't think I'm built to take a five-year-old and a two-year-old halfway around the world. I don't think these even more all-Americanized children of mine would survive with no hot water, no Wi-Fi, no *Bob the Builder* on demand.

Lincoln calls lumpia "egg rolls" and pancit "noodles." He thinks adobo is "too spicy!" He and Penelope have never even tried sinigang or sisig or kare-kare. I've never offered it to them. I like to think this is because I am lazy and unwilling to risk making a meal that won't be eaten. But maybe there's more to it, maybe it's because I still struggle with my Filipino-ness, maybe I worry that embracing this side of my roots will make me more like Mom. It feels like a slope as slippery as the waterslide. One day you're making your kids chicken tinola, the next you're mowing the lawn in a muumuu. I'm thirty-five years old, yet this still feels plausible.

Another seemingly good omen today: Amber and Arthur came to the party, too.

Their visits were intentionally staggered, orchestrated through text messages to make sure the wrong people, Mom and Amber, weren't together at the same time for too long. Amber has also become a mother, to a three-year-old son and an infant daughter. Not that that's changed her attitude toward our mom. If anything, it's made her more self-assured, more stubborn. More like Mom.

My mother and sister still fight like rhinos, bashing their heads together, upending everything around them. With my kids, Amber's kids, Arthur, and Mom, that's an octet of humans with Josefina Tometich's blood in their veins, all under one roof in the same twelve-hour span. And no one's been hurt. After rarely seeing Mom for the better part of three years, I see this as progress.

My phone chimes from the kitchen counter, reminding me I have a voice mail. I leave the bliss of my daughter's doorway. I raise the phone to my ear, waiting to hear a robot tell me my car's warranty needs to be renewed, ready to hang up and hit delete. Instead, I hear a man with a northern accent; Chicago, maybe Pittsburgh. He says he's looking for mom. He says it just like that. "I'm looking for your mother."

*How does he have my number? How does he know who my mother is?*

The man identifies himself as a detective from the Lee County Sheriff's Office. He says he's been to Mom's house and she's not answering the door, even though her car is in the driveway.

"If you can help us ascertain your mother's whereabouts, that would be a tremendous help," the detective says before wishing my voice mail a good night.

Worry seeps into my bones as my mind and heart race. I picture Mom comatose on the couch, overdosed with insulin and unable to reach one of her candy stashes. I see her splayed across the peach tiles of the bathroom, having slipped coming out of the shower, her skull bashed in, lying prone in a slurry of blood and cerebrospinal fluid.

I have a certain way of worrying. I get it from my mother.

The phone buzzes again. Mom's face takes up the screen, a photo of her holding toddler Lincoln and baby Penelope, a rare smile spread across her cheeks: crooked teeth and crinkled eyes, the real deal. I tap the green circle and jerk the phone to my ear as my heart lunges from my throat to my stomach and back up again.

"Are you OK some detective called you weren't answering the door but your car was there," I say in a gushy tangle of words.

"I am fine." She sighs. "I just could not hear them."

Mom sounds tired. Her usual screaming phone voice has dulled to something almost conversational.

"Why was a detective there?"

"The neighbors must have seen me fighting with *that man*," she says, spitting out the last two words like mucus. "It is fine. I am fine. Tell my Lincy happy birthday again."

Mom hangs up. I look out the front window as I try to process this. Twilight has brought clouds of gnats to join the mosquitoes. Lincoln refuses to stop sliding until absolute exhaustion drives him into the ground. He's blown out his candles and opened his presents. We've eaten Mom's pancit splashed with calamansi juice from the tree by her front window. We've piled her lumpia onto our plates by the fistful.

I baked my son's favorite cupcakes that morning, pulling them from the hot pan with my flameproof fingers, their tips tempered by years of heat in restaurant kitchens. The night before, I made mango ice pops, using juicy Kents from Mom's big tree in the front yard. I sliced, pitted, and peeled them, scraping flesh from the skin with a spoon, staining my nail beds yellow-orange; the same mango manicure I've worn each summer for as long as I can remember.

As I stow the dregs of pancit noodles, preparing to finally tackle the tower of dishes, Mom's unscreaming voice echoes in my mind. She didn't sound right. But I'm too tired to make much of it. I save my energy for the last bit of cleaning, then fall into bed.


Our bedroom is the hottest room in our little house. One wall is lined with windows, the other is filled by a poorly insulated, 1970s sliding glass door that leads to a small patio shaded by our Cuban's mango tree.

When my phone rings at 7:30 a.m., I'm already sweating. When the robo-voice on the other end tells me I have a collect call from an inmate at the Lee County Jail, I sweat harder.

Mom's voice is faint but strong, like someone screaming from inside a vault. Her words crackle with static.

"Hello, Annabelle! Annabelle! Are you there?"

She sounds like she could be calling from the Philippines, from the little phone on my grandparents' counter that only works if it isn't raining. I try to say hi, to ask what the hell is going on. Mom won't let me.

"OK, listen to me, Annabelle Marie. Call your friend Peter. Tell him I am in here for defending my property. Tell him they have no right holding me. That man was stealing my goddamn mangoes, and they won't give me my insulin! Tell him that! And the woman says you need to tell him my first appearance is later today. I need him to be there, OK? I cannot talk very long. Do you understand? I don't have my hearing aids, so I hope you understand! OK!"

"Yes, Mom," I say, readying the list of questions that have been flooding my mind.

*What man? Defending how? When? Where? Huh?*

"I can't hear anything, Annabelle? Did you hear me or not?"

"YES," I repeat, louder.

"OK, OK, then. I have to go. They are charging you for this phone call! I have to go."

"But, Mom—" I say, as the line clicks dead.


I am early to the courthouse, as Mom's taught me to be. I meet Peter in an alcove. He's holding paperwork and talking to a man in thick spectacles, a friend of his who clerks for our judge.

"You're lucky they didn't classify it as a firearm," the man tells him, "then she'd be looking at Ten-Twenty-Life mandatory minimums. That's twenty years at least."

I piece together that "it" must be Mom's BB gun, the one she uses to snipe squirrels, the only weapon she's ever owned beyond the occasional hurled vase or wedding china or launched screwdriver.

I let his words sprout in my mind. Twenty years from now I'll be fifty-five, old enough to captain a shuffleboard league and send my scores into *The News-Press*. Penelope will be old enough to buy alcohol. Lincoln will be able to rent a car. I picture us toasting Mom's release over shuffleboard pucks in a rented Lexus. I squeeze my eyes shut and shake my head, trying to snap back to the present.

I blink and steady myself against the cool marble of the wall. When the clerk leaves, I look at Peter. I am the picture of calm. I am designed to conceal my pain.

"You cut your hair," I say.

He runs his free hand over his freshly shorn head.

"I didn't think the afro would bring us much luck today," he says, "and we're going to need some luck."

Mom has confessed to everything. When the detectives interrogated her, she sang like a Catholic choir girl.

*Yes, I shot at this man. He was stealing my mangoes. What was I supposed to do?*

"Ma'am, why did you wait till he was leaving?" *Not on purpose, I couldn't get the freaking safety unlocked.*

"Why'd you shoot at him as he drove away? When he no longer posed a threat?" *I meant to shoot his tire out so I could call the police myself and have them arrest this man as a thief. My aim must have been off, even though it is **never** off. I shot out his rear window by accident. I meant to hit the tire. That man is the one who should be in custody!*

"She handed them their case," Peter says. "Wrapped it up tight."

He says Mom's lucky to have gotten the charge she got: "firing a missile into an occupied dwelling, vehicle, building, or aircraft." This means she'll avoid a twenty-year sentence in the Homestead women's prison on the edge of the Everglades. But a five- or ten-year sentence is still very much on the table.

"We have to show the judge your mom is an upstanding citizen," Peter says. "She's a first-time offender with a loving family who's spent her life in service to others as a nurse."

He asks if Arthur and Amber are coming. He says defendants with loving families are often shown leniency or at least cheaper bail. I raise an eyebrow when he says "loving," hoping my outward appearance camouflages my inner fears. I've tried so hard to distance myself from my mother and her sombrero-wearing pool-swamp ways, if not geographically, then physically, emotionally. Today I must accept her as one of my own.

I text my siblings as Peter's talking, to make sure they're on their way. Arthur can't get off work. Amber is looking for a parking spot.

I duck into a bathroom to reapply my lip gloss, check my hair, and adjust my ivory cardigan. Amber shows up in a dress and heels. She knows how to play this role almost as well as I do. We are loving daughters. We are visions of calm and order. Totally normal.

My newspaper's headline reads "Mango Leads to Fort Myers' Woman's Arrest." Mom's mug shot is plastered beneath it. She doesn't look sad. There's no hint of remorse. She has puffy bags under her eyes, and her mouth is pursed shut between the bulldog folds of her cheeks. She looks tired and slightly pissed off, like when Amber broke curfew or the time Arthur hid in her closet instead of taking a math test at school.

The foolish optimist in me hopes the story might get lost in the shuffle. Surely there will be an actual shooting, maybe a horrifying car crash, like the one I still tell people killed our dad—something more than a manic-depressive Filipina woman avenging her mangoes with a BB rifle.

My paper is fairly kind. The TV stations are not. Their cameras catch my sister as she brings Mom lunch after bailing her out of jail, as Amber jokes about hanging more no-trespassing signs around the yard while pushing her way through a small crowd of reporters to the iron bars of Mom's front door. The TV stations introduce the clip with "a family member of the mango shooter had this statement," followed by Amber in dark sunglasses, holding a bag from Panera.

A coworker of mine tweets how this is a case for stricter gun laws. Facebook commenters chime in with calls to "send her back," saying, "She don't belong here!" But Mom has been a tax-paying citizen for more than thirty years. Nothing in the news coverage says otherwise, just the color of her skin and that big, broad Filipino nose of ours. The one no amount of pinching and prodding could contain.

Mom takes to Facebook to make her own case, posting how this man was in her yard taking her things, how she had every right to defend her property. We send Arthur to the house to delete the post and lock down Mom's account. We try to explain how such things can and will be used against her in a court of law.

"But people support me!" she says. "They agree. I did nothing wrong."

Mom's court hearings are a nightmare. With all the media attention, the prosecuting attorneys seem to hope this will be the case that pushes them up the ladder. They throw the book at Mom, threatening prison time if Mom doesn't plead guilty and accept the "deal": five years of probation, reparations, and spending the rest of her life as a convicted felon, which at the time means no more voting, no leaving the state or country while on probation, and no more owning firearms. Not even squirrel-sniping BB guns.

I knew my mother would face consequences. I knew she was guilty. But this? A felony conviction and possible jail time for a sixty-four-year-old grandma who spent her life mending broken hearts as an ICU nurse? For a woman whose only prior was a speeding ticket on Alligator Alley in 1991 when I got sick from a gas-station empanada?

The little kid in me remembers a time when we wished for this, when Mom's rage was our second parent, and we hoped for it to be handcuffed and locked away. But the adult me knows this doesn't add up. BB gun + shattered rear window = jail? In Florida?

I thought all the work I'd done to normalize myself and our family would mean something. This veneer of invisibility I'd so meticulously crafted: the good grades, the shiny hair, the house with the neatly manicured lawn. I thought it would shield us from things like jail. I did all the things to belong. Yet in this courtroom, they mean nothing.

I realize the court is treating Mom just as harshly and unforgivingly as I have. The justice system does not see her as a whole person worthy of leniency and redemption. And up until this point, neither did I.

When I was pregnant with my daughter, a family friend told me she knew I was having a girl because daughters steal their mothers' beauty. I gritted my teeth, stifled a laugh, and managed to walk away without injuring anyone. I dismissed it as internalized misogyny, an old wives' tale that had somehow survived in this woman's family well into the year of our lord 2013.

Now, however, I wonder.

Maybe it's not that we steal their beauty; maybe it's that we as daughters, as children, tend to flatten our parents, compressing them into the characters we need them to be. We reduce them to the sidekicks, the villains, the kooky court jesters of our life stories. In some cases, we do this because we have to. Because parents are capable of serious soul-crushing harm, and we must minimize that to survive. But in doing so, we forget they have life stories of their own. They have reasons for their actions. Not always justifiable ones, but ones that should at least be considered.

As Peter runs through our options once more over beers at my dining room table, scratching at his head as his fade tries to bloom back into an afro, I see that this normality I sought was really me trying to prove my whiteness. If I could find those white threads in the brown fabric of my DNA and tease them to the surface, surely people would see that I am white, too. If I could write as a Frenchman and get away with it, surely that validated me as white-adjacent. People address me as "sir" and "monsieur." They go to restaurants because I tell them to. They believe me. They trust me. They respect me.

Or do they?

This respect is finite. It ends. The moment I stop typing and close my laptop, it no longer matters, just as my carefully curated facade of normality does not matter in this Robert E. Lee County courtroom. I'm not white, and Mom's definitely not white. Not even close.

I look at my mother, a Filipino immigrant who's done everything she was supposed to. A single mom who pulled herself up by her dead husband's cowboy boots, worked her ass off, raised three kids, took them all around the world, bought them cars, sent them to college—on her own.

A brown woman who used her pellet gun to shoot at a truck carrying a white man and his white girlfriend, who waited a hair too long to pull the trigger, who could have shot them with a real gun with little fear of repercussion if they'd been a few feet closer, trespassing on her property and not in the road, driving away. This is Florida, birthplace of the Stand Your Ground law. Mom would have been within her rights as a tax-paying Sunshine State citizen. But Mom didn't time it properly, and now she has to plead guilty or face a jury of her so-called peers who could send her to prison for fifteen years. That's not much of a choice.

As attention spreads, I do what I always do when Mom gets out of hand. I slink away. I pretend she's someone else's problem. Tita Perla's or Amber's or Arthur's. Not mine. I stop planning for our trip and stop inviting Mom to Lincoln's soccer games. She stops asking about Penelope's milestones and swim lessons. We branch out: me to my growing family, she to the crowded comforts of her house.

Her sentencing hearing, six months after the shooting, is the next time I see her. It's another shit show, this one more figurative than literal. The girlfriend of the mango-craving victim shows up under a crown of curly blond hair with neon-pink lipstick. She makes a teary-eyed plea to the court about her near-death experience at the hands of my mother.

I'm tempted to stand, to tell the judge about the knives and screwdrivers Mom's thrown at me in her fits of rage. *She never means to kill anyone. Just scare them.* I realize my words will not have my desired effect. Not that I could squeeze them in over Mom's growling and the stream of profanities she continues to mutter. Peter attempts to hide her words with well-timed coughs and constant throat clearing.

Still, some break free.

"That woman should be going to jail!"

*Cough, cough.*

"Ask her where they put all my freaking mangoes they stole!"

*Ahem, I'm sorry, Your Honor. My throat is parched.*

"Bullshit. That's what this is. Freaking bullshit."

The judge asks Peter if he needs water. Peter declines. The judge tells him to control his client.

"I am trying, Your Honor."

After the prosecutors make their case, hoping to wring sympathy with their emotionally scarred victim, the judge asks if Mom understands the plea: what it means to be a convicted felon, what it means to say she's guilty.

Mom growls again.

"Mizz Toe-meh-tick," the judge says. "I need to know you understand."

"Oh, I freaking get it. I understand I will die in jail! I will not get my insulin. They'll just let me freaking die. I understand that one hundred percent. You're trying to kill me! I will die in there!"

I peer around the courtroom, making sure no reporters have come in, from my newspaper or any other outlet. Peter has done the best he could with this unwinnable case. He's tamped down the media attention. If only he could tamp down my mother. If only any of us could.

This version of Mom is no stranger to me. I met her at LAX when I was eleven and she flashed the US Customs agent her dingy Playtex bra, unrequested, to show she wasn't hiding drugs (just atis seeds). I met her when a policeman pulled her over for rolling through a stop sign while Amber, Arthur, and I started World War III in the Mercury Sable's back seat, when Mom screamed at the cop that she had three hungry, tired children to get home and he wasn't freaking helping. The officer shooed us along that evening, and we kids were stunned into a silent truce.

Perhaps the US brings out the worst in my mom because that's the only way she knows how to be taken seriously in this country. Here in the courtroom, Mom's digging into her old playbook. She knows this system isn't designed for people like her; brown folks who *become* "American" don't get to live by the same rules, regardless of their 401(k)s. So, she's resorting to muscle memory: She's fighting.

I can't bring myself to look at Mom, so instead I focus on the victim's girlfriend and her blond curls. I can see only the back of the woman's head, but I imagine she's laughing. I imagine her attorney is, too. Laughing at this frantic and out-of-control Filipina woman. Laughing at the mess that is our family. Laughing the way kids laughed at me in elementary school as they made up stories about our haunted house. Only this story isn't made-up. It's all too real.

The judge slams his gavel against the mahogany of his desk, *one two three four* times, then an exasperated fifth, trying to pummel my mother into order. The judge corrects Mom, tells her she would have access to insulin and any other medications she may need in jail, should it come to that, should she forgo the plea deal and take her chances with a jury.

"If you are pleading guilty and accepting this deal, Mizz Toe-meh-tick," the judge says, "it has to be because you understand the ramifications of your plea, not because you feel coerced by falsehoods. I need you to tell me you understand that, and then you may enter a plea of guilty."

I hold my breath and finally look at my mother. I see her fists clench around either side of the podium. I watch her lean in.

"GUILTY!" Mom screams as the microphone at her podium whines with feedback. "GUILTY! GUILTY! GUILTY!"

## CHAPTER 34

# A Legend Is Born

Each winter, as the tourists fly down and the snowbirds feather their seasonal nests, the mango shooting fades from our family's collective memory. And then the summer storms roll in, and the air turns hot, soggy, and emotional. The mango tree's branches droop with thick fruits, and we kids droop with worry.

The police strip mom of her two BB rifles, which she's been surprisingly OK with, maybe because she never has been a fan of firearms.

"If I had a gun back then, I probably would have killed your Gramma," she says, "and my God, probably your father, too, who am I kidding?"

She laughs, not because she's joking.

Amber, Arthur, and I talk about building a fence, but Mom won't hear of it. It would take up too much of her precious postage-stamp plot. So, true to what my sister told the crowd of TV reporters that day, we put up more no-trespassing signs. We nail them to the palm trees and citrus trees at the edges of her property. We post them on all sides of the thick trunk of the original mango tree in the center of the yard and collectively hope for the best.

\* \* \*

The books on this stranger's shelf are arranged in rainbow order, from the deep red of *The Scarlet Letter* to the brilliant indigo of *The Color Purple*. I run my fingers across the spines as I sip an old-fashioned, admiring the detail, jealous of this person's eye for organization.

Buddy floats over from across the room, laughing as he trails away from whatever new group of friends he's made in the twenty minutes since we've been at this neighborhood dinner party.

"Warren works for the Economic Development Council. He knows Matt and Molly. He wants me to sit on the board of the regional technology partnership," Buddy says, motioning to a man in silver glasses near the buffet.

I nod, trying to grasp how he gained such knowledge in the time it took me to pour a drink and find a quiet corner. I look him in his blue-green eyes, which rest seven inches above my own, then slug down another gulp of bourbon in hopes of mustering half his self-assuredness.

"I know you hate these things," Buddy says, "but it's probably good to at least get to know other families from Linc's school."

He clinks his pint glass against my rocks glass, then grabs my hand, stares at me with a clownish smile on his face, and drags me over to introduce me to his new pals.

The event is a progressive dinner party. It starts with cocktails and tapas at the house with the rainbow-coded bookcases, moves to a 1920s carriage home hidden under sprawling oak trees dripping with Spanish moss for a paella feast, and ends at a mid-century ranch for dessert and more drinks along Manuel's Branch, a winding tributary of the Caloosahatchee.

Many of these people are also from Fort Myers. Like me. But not at all like me. Their forefathers owned cattle ranches and orange groves. They are landed and moneyed. They have fair skin and names that end in roman numerals.

A few drinks in, I find a fraction of my husband's confidence. I wander group to group, listening from the outskirts to bits and pieces of conversation: parents swapping stories about their kids, the best and worst teachers, the drama over such-and-such, and the divorce of so-and-so.

I pop into the kitchen, looking for a refill, more confidence. I find something else.

"Did Mitch tell you? I woke up the other morning and some guy had a ladder out and was picking my oranges," a woman says to a man who's cutting into a wheel of Parmigiano-Reggiano with fishing line.

She's wearing a black-and-white-striped blouse and crisp white jeans, her lips stained a candy-apple red that would fit nicely on the left side of the first house's bookcase.

"He brought a ladder! And was just helping himself to *my* oranges at, like, seven o'clock on a Sunday morning. Can you believe that? I called the police."

I fumble open a bottle of pinot noir, listening intently as I start pouring.

Someone else chimes in about her mango tree and how she lets her lawn guys pick it clean each summer.

"I don't even like mangoes," she says, "and if I don't let them take them, strangers will, just like your guy with the ladder! You find these people just waltzing through your property, acting like they own the place."

I press the cork back into the pinot, swirl my glass, and take a long sip.

That's the thing with mangoes in Fort Myers. The trees thrive here, but most of the people who live here don't care for them. The people who can afford big houses with bountiful fruit trees come from Ohio and Michigan, places I once saw as meaningful. They'd rather eat apples and Skyline Chili. Even the so-called locals grew up eating oranges, maybe, at least for a couple of months of winter, then it's Chilean grapes and Canadian cherries from the Publix produce aisles.

Mangoes? Ew.

The Mexican lawn guys, though, they get it. The Haitian housekeepers and the Guatemalan dishwashers do, too. Mangoes taste like home to them—to us. When we see them rotting on some neatly manicured lawn with a six-figure SUV in the driveway, we can't always help ourselves. Nor could my mom's victim, who was just some white dude from the wrong side of the railroad tracks who underestimated his target. Mom's victim thought this was just another McGregor house, just another well-to-do transplant who lets their mangoes rot in the street. He gazed over the wilds of Mom's yard, the peeling paint of her walls, the wrought-iron bars on her windows. He didn't realize what he was up against. He didn't see that this Fort Myers mango tree was anything but normal.

Mom is actually quite generous with her mangoes—if you can get her attention and have the decency to ask. She's happy to give them away, to find them loving, squirrel-free homes.

I once saw a woman with a Jamaican-flag head wrap piling Mom's mangoes and avocados into a box while I was on a morning run. I got nervous and started jogging in that direction. Then I saw Mom coming out of the garage with plastic Publix bags to help her.

"Abelle! What are you doing here?" Mom said, her tone disturbingly joyful.

"I was just out running. Do you...does she need help?"

"This is Angelia," Mom told me. "She stopped me while I was weeding this morning and asked if she could have some mangoes. Don't worry. I told her I save the best ones for my grandchildren, but I've got so many this year! And you and Amber never eat my avocados! I didn't think you'd mind."

"I don't mind at all," I said. "I just wanted to help."

I plucked sticky mangoes and deep green avocados from the sagging, overloaded box and placed them into the plastic bags. We carried them to the woman's car, a sun-bleached Ford Taurus that looked a lot like our old Sable. The woman grabbed Mom's hands and held them high in the air.

"Thank you, Miss Jo," she said.

Mom smiled. The way she smiled in San Andres Bukid as our cousins lined up for her blessings and dollar bills. The way she smiled when we met Tita Perla at the Miami MetroZoo. Crooked teeth and crinkled eyes. The real deal.

Back at the dinner party, the woman with the candy-apple lips says if her husband had been home, she'd have sent him out there with his Smith & Wesson.

"Just to scare the guy off, you know? You can't shoot someone over an orange."

"Sure you can."

I'm deep into my pinot refill when those three words grab my attention. I worry that I've said them, that they've escaped from my bourbon-laced thoughts and into reality. But my mouth is full of wine. It couldn't have been me. I look up to see the room filling up. A late-night rain shower has driven people inside.

"The woman on McGregor shot that man who was stealing her mangoes," the sure-you-can man continues. "And she had every right to. He was on her property."

Heads nod. People have heard the story. The mango thief had it coming. The McGregor mango shooter, a person I think they assume to be like them—affluent, gun-owning, probably white—did the same thing they'd do. Where do these trespassers get off, anyway?

"The problem is she waited too long," another man says.

No, *the problem is she's brown*, I think, filling my mouth with more wine.

"She shot him when he was off her property," he says. "She should have shot him sooner, then she wouldn't be in jail. She'd have gotten off scot-free."

I feel my husband's eyes on me. I don't look up. I am studying the legs of my wine as they melt down the sides of my glass. I feel like a fifth grader again, listening to my family's rumors float all around me. I shake my head just barely, my signal to Buddy that I won't be entering this fray.

A woman across the counter chimes in: "But, wait, she shot him? Like, shot him dead?"

Something inside me shifts. I can't help myself. I'm overconfident, my voice empowered the old-fashioned way. The words pour reflexively from my mouth: "Nobody died. She missed. She's just serving probation. It was a BB gun."

The room goes quiet. Slowly, smaller conversations sprout, about gun ownership, the Second Amendment.

I swig the last of my wine and give Buddy the wrap-it-up-time-to-go look, which is just me arching both eyebrows to the ceiling and looking with panic from him to the door and back again. The crowd is still murmuring. I think they're putting it together: my defensiveness, my intimate knowledge of the case. *Did she bring that delicious mango salsa? She did!* I wait for them to finger me as the mango shooter's daughter, to raise their pitchforks and drive me out of this nice normal kitchen in this nice normal house.

This is what I've always feared—being found out. I'm a nobody who comes from nothing, whose family does weird things and dies in weird ways. I've spent my life trying to conceal that. I've shoved it down and packed it tight, like gunpowder in an old rifle. And it keeps exploding, jerking me back. Is hiding all these parts of myself worth this constant worry?

I've been so afraid of becoming my mother, I've failed to recognize her many strengths. I've forgotten the superpowers I so admired in her as a child: her fireproof fingers, her photographic memory, her ability to (almost) reshape our noses with her superhuman hands.

I realize now, she did that in an attempt to make my life easier, to help me fit in as I've long tried to. Her nose pinches were my first signals to hold my Americanness close and my whiteness closer, the way you do with friends and enemies, I suppose. Even if she didn't want me to waste money like a freaking American, she wanted me to have the easy life of an American. She knew my brown skin wouldn't help. She hoped a thin nose might.

It dawns on me just how long a game she's chosen to play by migrating to the United States. I wonder how quickly she realized that the privileges of being an American would never fully be hers. Was it when her mother-in-law called her a Chink bitch? When her colleagues ignored her? When her husband did, too?

Maybe she knew all along. Maybe she never wanted the American dream, just an anything-but-the-Philippines dream. She'd watched her country be ruined by colonizers; if you can't beat 'em, join 'em.

I've been so afraid of becoming my mother, I've been blind to what she's built. With no parents or older sister to guide her, she left her Somebodiness behind and made her way in this far-off land. She staked a place for herself and her family in a country that refused to make that easy. Uncle Sam wanted her as a tool, an IV pole that could insert catheters and clean bedpans, not as a human. In this exotic, inhospitable terrain, my mother made a home for us, one she planted and grew on her own.

This home has granted me privileges it never gave her. I have the privilege of hindsight and context; of seeing how hard she worked to offer us a semblance of stability where she had none. And I have that staked place, a backstop that has been there and will be there to catch me (and maybe slap me) should I fall, a firmly rooted foundation on which I can build better, stronger, and far more easily.

I've been so afraid of becoming my mother, I've refused to see how her superpowers have evolved over time. Mom stands up for herself and her family. She doesn't give a shit about people's judgments. She doesn't need to be a Somebody. She is who she is.

The room gets louder as I meet Buddy at the door. Before leaving, I hesitate. What if—*I confessed?* What if I took a page from Mom's playbook and was my whole, unabashed self, warts and all.

I pause long enough to hear the woman with the candy-apple lips speak to what's left of the kitchen crowd.

"I think that's genius," she says, reaching for my bottle of wine. "I need to get a BB gun."

Perhaps now's not the time for confessions.

# THE BRANCHES

I collect Mom's blood as she's taught me to do over the last few years. I swab the ringless ring finger on her left hand with an alcohol pad, then press the pen and its fresh needle into the side of the fleshy tip. I click the pen's button, snapping the sharpened steel into Mom's skin, puncturing her superhero suit of armor with yet another teeny-tiny hole. I squeeze her finger and watch the blood bubble ink-red to the surface, a library of information trapped in the glossy confines of this droplet.

I catch the blood with the tip of a test strip. It flows upward against the force of gravity, sucked into place through capillary action. The glucometer, no larger than a mango pit, beeps as it tears through this library at lightning speed, rushing to the only section it knows how to read, blurting out a quick summation of Mom's morning sweetness: 122.

I give her a thumbs-up. On the little dry-erase board we brought to compensate for my mother's deafness and her stubborn refusal to wear hearing aids (*They hurt my freaking ears!*), I write that Tita Fe made champorado, and that she can eat some after we do her Levemir and NovoLog injections. I remind her about the buffet tonight and tell her we'll head down after Ate Josa and I take the kids to Glorietta.

It's November 2022, and I'm spending Thanksgiving in a high-rise hotel in Metro Manila with Mom, Lincoln, and Penelope. Buddy stayed back to work. We will FaceTime him tonight over plates of carved turkey, heads-on prawns, and garlic rice slick with butter.

This is the trip we were supposed to take in 2015. Before Mom's rage got the better of her. Before everything everywhere changed and changed and changed again. Before I shed my Jean Le Boeuf pseudonym in early 2021 to write reviews as my half-Filipina self, a move I thought would be met with anger from readers who loved the Le Boeuf secrecy and legacy, but was instead met with cheers and congratulations for finally, *finally*, being me. Before Trump, Hurricane Irma, the pandemic, and, just a few weeks ago, Hurricane Ian.

The first *I*-named storm took out Mom's original mango tree, snapping it in half at its thick-as-a-dining-room-table base. The tree wasn't uprooted or upended. It was stricken down, splintered, shattered.

That tree was our fourth sibling, another child that kept Mom busy long enough for us other kids to create lives of our own, to go on dates and get into whatever bits of trouble we could before Mom turned her need for control back on us. It gave her an outlet for her obsessions and compulsions that was not flesh and blood but root and bark. And it repaid her for her efforts, sending juicy-sweet thank-yous by the bushel every summer like clockwork, while its human siblings couldn't even freaking call.

When a person has lost so much, what's a tree? When a person has lost so much, how can they lose anything more?

The next *I*-named storm ripped apart Mom's second-largest mango tree, which gave its life to protect her house from the lumbering trunk of a falling royal palm.

I think back to the biology classes I took on my misguided doctoral path. How trees take in carbon dioxide and store it in their branches, stems, leaves. How, when a tree is cut down, all that carbon escapes back into the world. If other trees aren't there to absorb it, it goes into the atmosphere; temperatures rise, ice caps melt, sea levels surge, and we end up underwater. Or in Mom's case, under more unopened boxes of pain patches and pallets of canned foods.

At Glorietta, the same mall where my titas indoctrinated me into Filipino life with knockoff Gucci sunglasses and Jolly Spaghetti, my cousin's wife and I do the same for my children. John-John, my onetime doppelgänger, who showed me how to pause the world, married Ate Josa. She and I take the kids to eat every kind of lumpia we can find, chasing each with halo-halo after halo-halo. We go to McDo's for burgers and rice, then hit the crowded streets of Binondo for fried siaopao and bamboo steam trays heavy with siomai. We ride in a trisikad to ice-skate at the Mall of Asia, then shop till we drop, the kids' eyes widening in amazement every time they do the 55:1 conversion of Philippine pesos to US dollars.

I watch my children create connections with this far-off land, and it gives me hope. It cracks open the part of me that never felt like enough—not American enough, not Filipino enough, not "normal" enough—and it fills those hollow spaces with laughter and fish balls and Just Dance 2015. My kids love it here. They ask to stay longer. They beg to come back soon, even though we haven't left yet. It dawns on me that I should have trusted them to feel this attachment, like a belly button that forever reminds you that your life is not wholly your own. Of course they'd fall in love with this place. I did, too, thirty years ago, on that Christmas Eve night watching fireworks with my cousins from the louvered windows of my grandparents' loft.

I would have liked to come back to Manila sooner. When Mom could still hear and walk without help. The US legal system wouldn't allow it. Mom passed all the drug tests during her probation. She went to all her court-mandated check-ins. Yet she still had to serve every single day of her five-year sentence. For early termination, she would have had to show remorse. Every time we brought this up, her answer was the same.

"I am not sorry! Why should *I* be sorry? That man is the one who should be sorry!"

And so I waited. I waited for 2020, when Mom's probation came to an end, but 2020 had other plans. I waited for vaccines to be developed, quarantines to ease, and the Philippines to reopen, and now, finally, here we are.

Maybe we don't always get to choose the timing. Maybe the timing chooses us. Maybe it needs to make a point, a nice circular point. One with no beginning and no end.

I'm forty-two. My son's twelve. My daughter's eight. Back in 1991, on the only trip we took to the Philippines as a family after Dad died, my mom was forty, I was eleven, my sister was seven, and my brother was almost three. I don't have an almost three-year-old, but I do have my prone-to-tantrums, needs-help-walking, can't-always-control-her-bladder mother. Close.

I could have, in theory, come without Mom. But I need her for this. I need her as my conduit and my credentials, as a flesh-and-blood reminder that I have a place here. That I belong here, too.

On day three, we visit her titas and cousins at the same Tambunting row house where they've lived since World War II. I watch Auntie Lina and Auntie Crising, the older sisters of my late grandmother, both in their nineties, help my seventy-one-year-old mom up a small step and through their front door. Tita Anita, Mom's cousin, bounces from one side of her to the other like a sprite, holding my mom upright, keeping her from falling. Tita Anita is seventy-two.

"I cannot believe this is my Josie!" she says to me. "I couldn't keep up with your mommy when we were young, and look at her now."

Over paper-towel-lined plates of lumpia and bowls of pork menudo, Tita Anita tells me and the kids stories about their lola. How Mom would climb to the tops of trees to hide from their grandmother's switch. How she was the star of the basketball, volleyball, and track-and-field teams. How at the end of their senior year of high school, the mayor came to hand out awards to the best students in each subject area and sport.

"Your mommy won everything," Tita Anita says, sweeping her short hair to one side and pushing her black-rimmed eyeglasses tight to her nose. "The mayor kept calling her name—best athlete, best in calculus, best in history—until finally he looked through the rest of the certificates and asked if anyone else even goes to this school."

I wait for her to laugh, but she just smiles, lost in the memory. I look at my mother, with her cane for walking, her dry-erase board for communicating, a glucose monitor tacked to her belly to tell me how sweet her blood is. I add this award-winning data point to the Mom algorithm, and it brings me slightly closer to an answer that adds up. I think of the path that took her from that to this and all the branches along it; some broken, some dead, some sitting on the floor in front of me in awe of their lola.

When it's time to go back to Florida, I pack our things into backpacks, suitcases, and a giant balikbayan box that I will end up dragging through the Atlanta airport when the final leg of our thirty-some-hour journey is delayed. After hugs and farewells, selfies and more selfies, Tito Vic stacks our belongings onto a luggage cart and sends us into the Ninoy Aquino International Airport. He looks at me, at Mom in a wheelchair, at the twelve-year-old and the eight-year-old, at this towering cart of stuff. He asks if I'll be OK. I nod and thank him, blinking back tears.

I tell him we'll be fine, that I know the way home. If anyone can do this, it's me.

# ACKNOWLEDGMENTS

I'd first like to acknowledge the diligent readers of acknowledgments. Perhaps you've come to the end and aren't quite ready to go: *I acknowledge you!* Perhaps you're tangled up in *The Mango Tree*'s middle, curious who the marvelous team was that helped bring this luscious book to your hands: *I acknowledge you, too!* Perhaps you've hit a sticking point and are here for a palate cleanser: *I see you. I am you. I ACKNOWLEDGE YOU.*

As for that marvelous team, thank you kindly and wholeheartedly to Vivian Lee. You were my dream editor. You are my dream editor. Who knew reality would be even sweeter?

Thank you Morgan Wu for your keen eyes and prompt emails, and Lucy Kim for your juicy design skills. Elizabeth Garriga, Anna Brill, Sabrina Callahan, Sarah Maymi, Gianella Rojas, and Darcy Glastonbury thank you for being such an extraordinary marketing and publicity team and for making the scariest part of this process so genuinely fun. To my copyeditors and proofreaders, Michael Noon, Jayne Yaffe Kemp, and Pamela Marshall, thank you for doing the lord's work, for making my 10s into tens, and for lending me your Oxford commas.

To everyone at Little, Brown: thank you. Vivian is my dream editor. Y'all are my dream team.

Speaking of dreams, Kayla Lightner, thank you for believing in me and this story. Thank you for your checklists and spreadsheets, for your patience and phone calls and willingness to fight/clarify/push/pull as needed. Thank you for your *woo-woo*, too. A little has gotten us so very far. Thank you, as well, to Katrina Mercado and the whole team at Ayesha Pande Literary for being so beautifully collaborative, for refusing to gate-keep, and for all you do to champion diverse voices.

Thank you to my earliest of readers and earliest of believers: Grace Talusan, Minda Honey, Artis Henderson, Robyn George Holmes, Sarah Chaves, Asmaa Elgamal. I called this thing a mess of words. You called it a book. (OK, you were right.) And thanks to Seth and Shannon, the last of The Assassins, for keeping me going with your sharp insights.

Cinelle Barnes, Leigh Stein, Courtney Maum, Natalie Lima, and Kiese Laymon, thank you so, so much for your guidance and for the type of abundant generosity that transcends DMs, emails, and Zooms.

Thank you to Jen Balderama of the *Washington Post*, and to Matt Ortile and Cinelle (again!) of *Catapult*, for your Fil-Am editorial brilliance on the essays that helped make this book real.

Margaret Lee, Hyeseung Song, and Talia Tucker, thanks for the endless texts and equally endless support. I am honored to debut with y'all.

Molly Grubbs, Kinfay Moroti, and Amanda Inscore, thank you for making me look good and for your decades of friendship, too.

To everyone at *The News-Press* and *Naples Daily News* who, over the course of eighteen years, allowed me to be a horribly messy writer, then a messy writer, then a writer—thank you. Find more at news-press.com :)

Thanks to all the folks at Key West Literary Seminar, The Porch, GrubStreet, Hedgebrook, Tin House, and HippoCamp. Your workshops and retreats made this book possible, made me-as-an-author possible. And a special thank you to the incredibly exclusive Jello & Skittles Writing Residency for opening your doors to me in fall 2020 when I needed a quiet, kitty-filled space for revision.

Beth, Brooke, Emily, Natasha, y'all are my soul and my sanity, my genies-in-bottles, my Nachos BellGrandes on the bathroom floor of life. Peter, you are Peter, and that is enough. To Lorie, Katie, Caitie, Angela, Andy, and everyone who picked up a kid, dropped off a kid, or watched a kid so I could write* (*scroll TikTok), thank you!

Nene, thank you for the tissues and hugs all those years ago and for the hugs that warm a new generation of this chaotically beautiful family. Meghan, Sarah, and Ansley, thank you for making Buddy Buddy. His kind heart is your handiwork (/knife-chasing-work).

To Amber and Arthur, thank you for letting me share these stories and for enduring/surviving my oldest-sister-who's-also-a-Virgo ways. Tita Perla, Uncle Peter, Tito Robert, and Aunt Ann, thank you for your balance. Van, Kuya Jong, Ate Jo, Tito Vic, Tito Boy, Tita Fe, Tita Anita, and all our family in the Pilipinas and beyond, thank you. Maraming salamat po!

Mom-of-then, you are the reason for everything. Mom-of-now, you are the reason I've learned to love wine. Thank you. I will text this to you later so you can see it in larger font, and then again when you forget, and then again when you forget.

Lincoln and Penelope, you are my heart. Buddy, you are our pericardium, surrounding us and reducing the friction of each heartbeat. One day, maybe, you'll read this book without crying, or probably you won't. That's why I love you.

# ABOUT THE AUTHOR

**Annabelle Tometich** went from medical school reject to line cook to journalist to author. She spent eighteen years as a food writer, editor, and restaurant critic for *The News-Press* in her hometown of Fort Myers, Florida. Her writing has appeared in the *Washington Post, USA Today, Catapult*, the *Tampa Bay Times*, and many other publications. Tometich has won more than a dozen awards for her stories, including first place for Food & Travel Writing at the 2022 Sunshine State Awards. She (still) lives in Fort Myers with her husband, two children, and ever-fiery Filipina mother. You can find her online at annabelleTM.com.